A Nick Hern Book

Elyot: Four Plays first published in Great Britain as a paperback original in 2004 by Nick Hern Books Limited, The Glasshouse, 49a Goldhawk Road, London W12 8QP

Reprinted in 2015

Coming Clean first published in 1984 by Faber and Faber Ltd, London. The other three plays were first published by Nick Hern Books Ltd. All four plays have been revised by the author for this collection.

Cover photograph of author: © David Whyte

Extracts of the song 'To Love Somebody' by Barry and Robin Gibb, reprinted with permission in *The Day I Stood Still*

Typeset by Country Setting, Kingsdown, Kent CT14 8ES
Printed and bound in Great Britain by Mimeo Ltd, Huntingdon, Cambridgeshire PE29 6XX

A CIP catalogue record for this book is available from the British Library

ISBN 978 1 85459 830 1

C000173095

KEVIN ELYOT

Born in Birmingham in 1951, and educated there at King Edward's School and then at Bristol University, Kevin Elyot was an actor before becoming a writer.

He won the Samuel Beckett Award for his first play, *Coming Clean* (1982), staged by the Bush Theatre, London. Subsequent stage work includes a version of Ostrovsky's *Artists and Admirers* (RSC, 1992); *My Night with Reg* (Royal Court Theatre, 1994), which was hailed as 'a play of genius' by the *Daily Mail*, won the Evening Standard and Laurence Olivier Awards for Best Comedy and ran for almost a year in the West End; *The Day I Stood Still* (National Theatre, 1998); *Mouth to Mouth* (Royal Court, 2001), which also transferred to the West End; and *Forty Winks* (Royal Court, 2004).

Kevin's screenplays include *Killing Time* (BBC, 1990), which won the Writers' Guild Award for Best TV Play or Film; an adaptation of *The Moonstone* (BBC, 1996); the film version of *My Night with Reg* (BBC, 1997); *No Night is Too Long* (2002), adapted from the novel by Barbara Vine (the pseudonym of Ruth Rendell) for BBC Films/Alliance. He adapted six of Agatha Christie's *Marple* novels as well as three of her *Poirot* novels for television, including the series' final episode *Curtain*. Other screenplays include *Twenty Thousand Streets Under the Sky* (BBC, 2005), adapted from the novel by Patrick Hamilton; *Riot at the Rite* (BBC, 2005); *Clapham Junction* (2007), a film for Darlow Smithson and Channel 4, starring Rupert Graves, Paul Nicholls and Luke Treadaway; and *Christopher and His Kind* (Mammoth Screen/BBC, 2011), based on Christopher Isherwood's novel, starring Matt Smith, Lindsay Duncan, Imogen Poots and Toby Jones.

Kevin died in June 2014, shortly before the Donmar Warehouse revival of *My Night with Reg*. The production transferred to the Apollo Theatre, the play's second West End appearance, in 2015.

Kevin Elyot

FOUR PLAYS

Coming Clean

My Night with Reg

The Day I Stood Still

Mouth to Mouth

With a Foreword by the Author

NICK HERN BOOKS
London
www.nickhernbooks.co.uk

Contents

Foreword	ix
COMING CLEAN	1
MY NIGHT WITH REG	73
THE DAY I STOOD STILL	159
MOUTH TO MOUTH	249

Therefore: appear, shine, and, as it were, die.

Jean Genet, *Letters to Roger Blin*,
translated by Richard Seaver

Foreword

The choir of St Peter's in Handsworth, the Birmingham suburb where I spent my early years, consisted of a handful of grown-ups and myself. On certain Sundays we'd process through the streets with the vicar, carrying a cross, swinging incense and singing hymns. I was quite short at the time. Janet, one of the women, was fairly large. She had a childlike face, curly hair, a kind heart and a simple disposition. She'd regularly plonk herself down next to me in the vestry, both of us in cassock and surplus, and say, 'Every picture tells a story.' Then she'd laugh, and I'd smile, but I didn't have a clue what she was talking about.

My parents often took my sister and me to the theatre: variety bills at the Hippodrome, where the number of the act would be displayed at the side of the stage, and pantomimes and plays at the Rep and the Alexandra. We had a family outing to Stratford when I was about ten to see a matinée of *Richard the Third* with Christopher Plummer and Eric Porter. That was the start of my love affair with the place: I'd do the hour's journey on top of the 150 from Birmingham, queue for standing tickets and see shows two or three times. I was addicted, but it was St Peter's that gave me my first fix.

*

For the briefest time I was taken into the confidence of Peggy Ramsay, the revered literary agent. In her office in Goodwin's Court I perched on the sofa, where I fondly hoped Joe Orton had sat, and listened to the gossip and her occasional barbed opinions, sometimes of her own clients.

She'd taken me on after reading *Coming Clean*, my first foray into professional writing. From 1976 to 1984 I'd acted in several productions at the Bush Theatre, and Simon Stokes, one of the artistic directors, had casually suggested I try my hand at a play. I presented them with a script entitled *Cosy*, which was passed on to their literary manager Sebastian Born. He responded favourably and, largely through his support, it finally opened on 3 November 1982 under the title *Coming Clean*. *Cosy* had fallen out of favour – a pity, as I'd always liked the pun on the opera which plays such an important part. I came up with the present title as a necessary compromise after what had proved to be quite a bumpy ride from acceptance to premiere.

The Bush was the perfect space for David Hayman's intensely intimate production, as Tony tried in vain to come to terms with his 'open' relationship with Greg. These were hedonistic times, when the worse that might happen, health-wise, was usually sorted by a trip to the clinic, where you'd pretend not to recognise each other, alarmingly aged in the cruel light of day, and when AIDS was a barely credible rumour filtering from across the Atlantic. The play's final scene has an elegiac quality – in retrospect, almost a sense of foreboding. When Peggy saw it, she was in tears. 'That's the saddest thing I've ever seen,' she said, disgorging the contents of her handbag on the floor. From then on, it was downhill.

'If you don't write your next play soon, you'll never write again,' she warned. Alarmed, I forced out a piece called *A Quick One*. 'Rather than write stuff like this,' she said, 'you should take up a hobby, like squash.' Then I thought I'd try my hand at a radio play, *According to Plan*, which she insisted she wouldn't be able to sell. I asked Sebastian Born, by now a literary agent with James Sharkey Associates, if he thought he might be able to sell it, which he did. It was transmitted in 1987 on Radio 4, directed by Pat Trueman, with Sheila Reid, Jean Anderson and Tom Wilkinson. Sebastian became my agent and the manuscript of *A Quick One* disappeared without trace.

I've yet to try my hand at squash.

A year after its London premiere there was a production of *Coming Clean* at the Palace Theatre, Westcliff. From the *Leigh Times*:

*Let me say immediately that I did not enjoy this evening. In
fact, it made me feel ill.*   J. T. (theatre critic)

*The play itself was a nasty, horrid little piece . . . Whatever
happens to actors who have to perform such scenes night after
night? . . . Do they spoil their own souls in order to divert us?*
                        Councillor Joan Carlile, Southend

*My family have attended the Palace Theatre . . . for thirty
years, but not any more if this is the kind of beastly filth they
are going to present us with . . . I consider* Coming Clean *to be
a perverted horror.*   David Price (letter to the editor)

*

One evening in the summer of 1993, alone in a house outside
Todi, I thought, 'So this is how it ends.'

The malaise had begun during what proved to be my last
acting job – ironically, a tour of Molière's *The Hypochondriac.*
The gloom of fetching up in wintry, wet Worthing, or Swindon,
or Poole, week after week in a fairly dismal show, was
compounded by private fear as I obsessively weighed myself,
wondering why the pounds were slowly shedding. By the
summer, still refusing medical advice, I insisted on holidaying
with friends in Umbria, where I spent most of the time in bed,
high on fever and a diet of paracetamol. I even took some old
antibiotics I'd come across, which brought me out in a fearful
rash. My friends took me to a dermatologist, who, when he
saw it, muttered, 'Bestiale,' and told me to take a blood test at
the hospital in Todi. This I did with no intention of finding out
the result.

The evening in question, I noticed a storm threatening on the
horizon. It reached the house, cutting off the electricity, so I
went outside to the fuse box, a pointless exercise even if I
hadn't had a fever. Back inside, huddled up on the sofa in the
dark, I thought, for the first time in my life, that this was it. It
wasn't, but things would never be quite the same again.

Within days of getting home I was hospitalised with
pneumonia. The love of family and friends, and the exceptional
skill of Margaret Johnson and her team at the Royal Free,

pulled me back from the brink – also, quietly but insistently, *My Night with Reg,* already scheduled for production the following year. Though I learnt later how close I was to snuffing it, I never once, after diagnosis, believed that I wouldn't pull through. Since then I've clung to projects almost like fetishes to keep together body and soul.

My Night with Reg had been a long time coming. I thought of the title in 1983, but didn't write it until nearly ten years later. In the meantime it started to emerge: a David Bowie concert I'd been to at Bristol's Colston Hall in 1973; listening to 'Every Breath You Take' on the roof of an apartment block overlooking Central Park; the death of a dear friend and the funeral of another – gradually the pieces began to fall into place.

In 1991 it was commissioned by Hampstead Theatre. In 1993 they passed on it and Sebastian submitted it to the Royal Court. He got a swift response, and Stephen Daldry, in the process of taking the reins from Max Stafford-Clark, scheduled it for Easter 1994 in the Theatre Upstairs. He suggested Roger Michell should direct it, and our first meeting took place while I was still in the Royal Free. And so it moved forward, and I was determined to see it through. What seemed at times to be so nearly an ending proved, in fact, a beginning.

*

During the run of *The Day I Stood Still* at the National I got a card from someone I'd known at school, moved and disturbed to see parts of our story reconfigured on stage – but this was not the whole story. One summer's afternoon, around the time of the death of Rolling Stone Brian Jones, I was enjoying an unlikely friendship with one of the school's star sportsmen. He suddenly asked if I'd ever read James Baldwin, and for some reason I didn't pursue his line of enquiry, a decision I regret to this day. Thirty years on, this tickled my imagination, and these and other little histories amalgamated in a fiction to the point where the play hardly accords with any actual fact. The past stalks the characters at every turn, so deftly achieved in Ian Rickson's production that the ghosts onstage seemed at times to drift across the footlights. On a couple of occasions people told me they'd been convinced they'd seen their first lovers sitting in the audience.

Ideas can come from unexpected quarters. A visit with a friend one Sunday morning in August 1997 to Seville's Hospital de la Caridad, where we saw Valdes Leal's 'Fin de la Gloria del Mundo', then going back to the hotel and catching a news bulletin announcing Princess Diana's death, somehow transmogrified a few years later into *Mouth to Mouth,* which is not about Seville, Valdes Leal or Diana. *Mouth to Mouth* was the second time I'd worked with Ian Rickson, and the first time I'd written a part for a particular actor: Lindsay Duncan. Old friends from Birmingham, it was, in a way, a testament to teenage aspirations.

After the purdah of writing, it's always something of a treat to work again with actors, but any bonding is usually tempered with reserve, like being let back into the playground, but not back into the gang. Their commitment never ceases to amaze, none more so than the cast of *Mouth to Mouth,* led by Lindsay and Michael Maloney, at both the Royal Court and the Albery.

Once it had opened in the West End, a transfer plagued with difficulties, I went to Rome where I came across Magritte's 'L'Empire des lumières' at a Surrealist exhibition, which set me thinking about a new play.

Another picture, another story, and a faint echo down the years of Janet in the vestry . . .

At the time of writing, Forty Winks *is due to start rehearsals at the Royal Court, directed by Katie Mitchell.*

Kevin Elyot
August 2004

COMING CLEAN

For

Jack Babuscio
(1937-1990)

Coming Clean was first performed at the Bush Theatre,
London, on 3 November 1982. The cast was as follows:

TONY	Eamon Boland
WILLIAM	C. J. Allen
GREG	Philip Donaghy
ROBERT	Ian McCurrach
JÜRGEN	Clive Mantle

Director David Hayman
Designer Saul Radomsky
Lighting Designers Bart Cossee and Simon Stokes

4

Characters

TONY, *thirty-three*

WILLIAM, *thirty-six*

GREG, *thirty-eight*

ROBERT, *twenty-five*

JÜRGEN, *thirty-eight*

Setting

The living room of a first-floor flat in Kentish Town. The essentials are as follows: two doors – one leading to the hallway, bedrooms, bathroom, and front door; and one leading to the kitchen; hi-fi equipment and record shelves; a window looking down on to the street; a dining area; a drinks table; a side table; a sofa and various chairs. The atmosphere is sparse: it has the potential of being tasteful, but lacks the necessary care. It isn't homely, and also not very clean or tidy.

The action takes place from April to October 1982.

SCENE ONE

*The Adagio of Samuel Barber's String Quartet begins playing.
The house lights fade. As the stage lights come up on* TONY
and WILLIAM, *the music fades.* TONY *is in a dressing gown,
pulling on a pair of socks.* WILLIAM *(from Bradford) is rolling
a cigarette. On a chair, in a pile, are a pair of jeans and a shirt.
A bag of doughnuts stands on the side table. Late morning.*

TONY. Was it fun?

WILLIAM. No.

TONY. I'm surprised. He looked quite promising.

WILLIAM. I know.

TONY. Big, hairy, brutal, verging on the psychopathic. Just
your type.

WILLIAM. That's what I thought. But he wasn't.

TONY. He looked like he ate babies for breakfast.

WILLIAM. He eats rusks for breakfast. Don't let me hold you
up.

TONY. I won't. (*He starts to pull on his jeans under his robe.*)

WILLIAM. The lights in that disco'd put cosmetic surgeons
out of business. I thought he was a virile forty, but in fact
he's a rather limp fifty. (*He lights the cigarette.*) And all
those monosyllabic grunts he breathed down my ear in the
club soon disappeared when we were sat in that taxi.
Crystal-clear enunciation – Oxford English, a hundred per
cent proof. And he wouldn't shut up. He went on and on
about some opera or other. I mean, I'd expected him to talk
about lorry-driving, or hod-carrying, or oil rigs. But no – it
was all legatos and top Cs! It's not fair, is it? I thought I'd
tricked with Steve McQueen, but I ended up with a leather-
clad Richard Baker.

TONY. Steve McQueen's dead.

WILLIAM. He'd still have been more fun.

> TONY *goes into the kitchen.*

> Honestly, Tony, I reckon some of these guys are contravening the Trade Descriptions Act.

TONY (*off*). What's he do?

WILLIAM. Something in chemicals. He did explain it all to me, but it went in one ear and out the other. Like the rest of the rubbish he came out with.

> *He wanders over to the kitchen door to speak to* TONY.

> Mind you, he's obviously well-off. More money than taste. His flat's horrendous. An emetic combination of Salvador Dali and the Ideal Home Exhibition. Gallons of dark-blue paint everywhere, with hundreds of mirrors, and glass-topped tables, and concealed lighting. He was so proud of his dimmer-switch. Kept readjusting it to get the mood just right. I nearly said, the only thing that'd improve this room'd be a power cut.

> TONY *enters with two mugs of coffee and a jug of milk.*

TONY. I quite like the idea of dimmer-switches. (*He puts the coffee and milk on the side table.*)

WILLIAM. And you couldn't move for all these statuettes of Michelangelo's *David.* Everywhere you looked. There was an epidemic of them. And endless plants of every description leaping out at you from all directions. Like a Triffid attack. And the bedroom! I tell you, I was frightened of falling asleep in there in case I woke up embalmed.

TONY. I knew I shouldn't have gone. I spent a fortune: ninety p for a pint of lager!

WILLIAM. No one was twisting your arm to drink six.

TONY. I felt so uncomfortable. It's such an effort holding your stomach in for four hours. Black?

WILLIAM. Yes. With a drop of milk.

TONY. It's a beautiful day. You ought to go for a walk. Get some fresh air.

WILLIAM. My lungs'd collapse from shock.

TONY. God, those windows . . . (*He takes off his dressing-gown and puts on his shirt.*)

WILLIAM. We didn't get to bed till five – he wouldn't stop talking – and when we did, it was the same old story: he rolled over as soon as we hit the sheets. Talking of which, I think he must have lost the instructions to his Hoovermatic, cos I'm here to tell you, they hadn't seen the inside of it for weeks.

TONY. You fucked him?

WILLIAM. If only to shut him up, but it didn't. He liked talking dirty. Well, that turns me on. Sometimes. But not when he sounds like a Radio Three announcer.

TONY. Did you enjoy it?

WILLIAM. Not at all. It was like slopping around in a bowl of custard. Loose? I expected to find half of London up there. Do you want a jammy doughnut?

TONY. No thank you . . . (*He checks himself in a mirror.*)

WILLIAM. It's so disillusioning! All these men who give the impression of being such studs, when in fact they're just big nellies who want to get poked. Anyway, I made up for it this morning. I met his lover.

TONY. He has a lover?

WILLIAM. Yes. He'd been out all night, whoring, and he came back while my number was in the shower. So I introduced myself.

TONY. How civilised.

WILLIAM. Yes – I blew him off. Very nice it was too, until we were interrupted. From the state of the sheets, I should have realised – that guy was going to take a quick shower!

TONY. Did he mind?

WILLIAM. He minded. God knows why. They both screw around, but when it's under their noses – well! So fucking hypocritical! I don't know why they put themselves about. They'd obviously be happier living together in a Wendy house, watching the roses grow round the door. So, while they were going at it cat and dog, I thought it prudent to make myself scarce, which I did, and I left without so much as a cup of instant.

TONY (*looking at his watch*). Christ, he'll be here in a minute. (*He starts tidying up: cushions, books, papers, ashtrays.*)

WILLIAM. That's what you're paying him for!

TONY. We haven't even met. I've got to make a reasonable impression.

WILLIAM. Cleaning up for a cleaner! It's like wrapping up rubbish before chucking it in the bin.

TONY. He hasn't definitely said yes. I don't want to put him off.

WILLIAM. Well . . . So what happened to you after I'd gone?

TONY. Nothing.

WILLIAM. I might have guessed. You were on the brink of a sulk when I left.

TONY. Well, it developed into a major depression.

WILLIAM *attacks a doughnut.*

WILLIAM. What about the guy in the construction helmet?

TONY. He deigned to look at me once during the whole evening, and his expression made me feel about as attractive as an anthrax spore.

WILLIAM. There were others.

TONY. He was the only one I fancied. Anyway, you know what I'm like. When it comes to the crunch, I get facial paralysis. I can't even smile, let alone speak. I'm not exactly the greatest cruiser in the world.

WILLIAM. Rubbish! I've told you before, all you need is that little glint in your eye and you could get anyone you wanted.

TONY. A little glint!

WILLIAM. Just a hint of a smile around the eyes.

TONY. A hint of a glint.

WILLIAM. That's right.

TONY. Which I don't have.

WILLIAM. Only when you're not concentrating.

TONY. So how do I normally look?

WILLIAM. Fucking miserable.

TONY. Thanks a lot. William, don't you think you ought to use a plate?

WILLIAM. I like men in construction helmets. As long as they don't wear them in bed.

TONY. He did look good, didn't he? So arrogant. God, he could've done anything he liked with me . . . I wish I could have met him at a dinner party or something, had a chat, got to know each other a bit. In that situation, I do far more justice to myself, rather than leaning against a bar, trying to look like Burt Reynolds. Glinting.

WILLIAM. So why do you carry on going?

TONY. Because it's addictive.

WILLIAM. And you enjoy it.

TONY. Well . . . yes. Sometimes. Anyway, I don't go that often.

WILLIAM. You don't need to. I don't think I'd go at all if I had Greg to fuck me every night.

TONY. He doesn't fuck me every night. Not after five years.

WILLIAM. He could fuck me every night after ten years.

TONY. You'd soon get itchy feet. One-night stands don't suddenly lose their appeal when you fall in love. The prospect of a new body's always exciting. Mind you, it is a transitory excitement, and it doesn't change my feelings for Greg.

WILLIAM. A transitory excitement . . . I saw this guy who looked so – terribly transitory, and he took me back to his place and gave me a transitory rogering on the carpet, and after we'd spent our lust all over the Axminster, we lay transitorily in each other's arms, and he looked into my eyes and said, 'How was it?', and I looked back at him, somewhat sultrily, and said, 'My God, that was – transitory!'

TONY. Have you ever considered sending your jaw on holiday?

WILLIAM. Five years! Who'd have thought it? A paragon of domestic bliss! A man, a flat, a car, and now – a houseboy!

TONY. He's not a houseboy. He's a cleaner. Actually, he's not even a cleaner. He's an actor.

WILLIAM. An actor! No wonder he's a cleaner. I've yet to meet an actor who actually acts. And Greg hates actors.

TONY. We're hiring him to clean, not perform. Whether Greg likes him or not is irrelevant. As long as he's good at cleaning.

WILLIAM. I wonder if he's good at acting.

TONY. Please try not to be too disgusting when he's here. Not everyone wants to know about the workings of your insides – or other people's insides, for that matter. (*He looks at his watch.*) He's late. (*He lights a cigarette.*)

WILLIAM. So how are you going to celebrate your anniversary?

TONY. What?

WILLIAM. Your anniversary!

TONY. We haven't talked about it.

WILLIAM. You've got to do something.

TONY. What can we do? Greg's such a difficult sod. He hates parties, hates eating out –

WILLIAM. Hates paying for it. Tight-fisted bugger.

TONY. We could have dinner here, I suppose, but I'd end up having to do it all, and that's not my idea of a celebration.

WILLIAM. I'll cook for you.

TONY. I wouldn't trust you with boiling the kettle.

The doorbell rings.

WILLIAM. It's the slave.

TONY. William, please . . .

TONY *goes into the hall. Sound of front door opening.*

(*Off.*) Hello.

ROBERT (*off*). Hello. I'm Robert.

TONY (*off*). Tony. Pleased to meet you. Come on in.

Enter ROBERT *and* TONY.

This is William . . . and William, this is Robert.

ROBERT *and* WILLIAM *shake hands.*

WILLIAM. Hello.

ROBERT. Hello.

TONY. William's a neighbour. Well, almost a neighbour. Often pops round. Sort of a – permanent fixture, really. Did you find it alright?

ROBERT. Yes. No trouble.

TONY. Would you like some coffee?

ROBERT. Thank you.

TONY. I'll make a pot.

WILLIAM. A pot!

TONY. William.

WILLIAM. Yes?

TONY. Would you like some coffee?

WILLIAM. Yes, please.

TONY. I won't be a minute. Do sit down. (*He goes into the kitchen.*)

WILLIAM. Make yourself at home.

ROBERT. Thank you.

ROBERT *sits.* WILLIAM *starts a roll-up.*

WILLIAM. Would you like a roll-up?

ROBERT. No thanks.

WILLIAM. Don't you smoke?

ROBERT. Sometimes. I have the odd Silk Cut, but then only on social occasions.

WILLIAM. Strictly business, is it?

ROBERT. No . . . yes. I suppose it is.

WILLIAM. You don't mind if I do, do you?

ROBERT. No. Not at all.

Pause.

WILLIAM. I used to smoke Silk Cut, but I found they made me very chesty. I used to wake up with a very tight feeling just here – (*Pats chest.*) – and I'd cough and cough, but it wouldn't budge. Nothing'd come up.

ROBERT. Did you smoke a lot?

WILLIAM. About fifty. But then I decided to roll my own, cos I thought it'd make me smoke less.

ROBERT. And did it?

WILLIAM. No, but it's shifted the phlegm. Now when I wake up and have a really good cough, it all comes up. Great gobfuls of the stuff. Much more satisfying than having it sit on your chest all day.

ROBERT. I'm afraid they're too strong for me. Although they do have – quite a flavour.

WILLIAM. Yes. (*Beat.*) This stuff's repulsive. Like rimming a camel. Not that I ever have, but I can imagine. I suppose I'm just a glutton for punishment. Do you want a jammy doughnut?

ROBERT. No thank you.

WILLIAM. Well, it's there for the eating. Madam didn't feel like it. She suffers very badly from morning sickness. I wish you would, cos I'll only eat it if you don't.

ROBERT. I'm really not hungry.

WILLIAM. I don't blame you. They're not very nice. I like the sort which are really squidgy, that you bite into and the jam squirts out all over the place, and drips down your chin, and gets everywhere. With these, you're lucky if you find a pinprick in the middle.

Enter TONY. WILLIAM *devours the doughnut.*

TONY. It won't be long. Are you alright?

ROBERT. Yes, thank you.

TONY. It's quite a mess, as you can see. I'll show you round in a minute. I'm afraid Greg and I have been pretty slack about it all. We're both rather . . .

WILLIAM. Filthy.

TONY. We hate cleaning, and any that was done I did. I think Greg thinks flats clean themselves. And it's all got a bit out of hand. So . . . I'll just . . . (*He returns to the kitchen.*)

WILLIAM. Do you like cleaning?

ROBERT. Yes. Yes, I do.

WILLIAM. Mm. (*Beat.*) I don't. I can always find something better to do.

ROBERT. It's a case of having to. I need the money.

WILLIAM. Are you very domestic?

ROBERT. In other people's houses. I think I'm quite good at it. I also do the occasional bit of cooking from time to time. All helps to bring in the cash.

WILLIAM. What else do you do for cash?

TONY *enters with the coffee.*

TONY. Here we are . . .

ROBERT. What do you do?

WILLIAM. I'm a proofreader for Yellow Pages.

TONY. Black?

ROBERT. White, please.

WILLIAM. I wish I could afford a cleaner. One day, I hope to live in Kentish Town. But for now, the lower reaches of Tufnell Park will have to suffice. (*To* ROBERT, *about* TONY.) He's very grand, this one, y'know. He thinks he lives in an After Eight commercial.

TONY. White?

WILLIAM. Yes, please. Have you met Greg yet? Oh no, of course you wouldn't have. You'll like him . . . Robert. He's very nice, very warm. A most gregarious, outgoing sort of a person. And generous to a fault, isn't he, Tony?

ROBERT. Where's the bathroom?

WILLIAM. You're not sick, are you?

ROBERT. No. I want to pee.

TONY. It's through there. On the right.

ROBERT. Thanks. (*He exits into the hall.*)

TONY. William . . .

WILLIAM. I'm off. I've got loads to do. And I want to get some sleep before tonight. I have to look rested and serene if I'm going to score. At the moment I feel like a bucket of horseshit.

TONY. Cruising again!

WILLIAM. Of course.

TONY. You never stop.

WILLIAM. Well, you know what it's like. Once you've had a taste, you keep wanting more. Like Chinese food. Talking of which, I've thought of a brilliant solution to your anniversary problem. Equity's answer to Mrs Beeton also hires himself out for dinner parties. And I'm sure he's very cheap.

TONY. What makes you so sure you'd be invited anyway?

WILLIAM. To make up the numbers. As ever. The day I'm invited to a dinner party and find an odd number of guests, I'll know I'm loved.

TONY. William, you are loved.

WILLIAM. You sweet thing!

They embrace.

I'll buy you something really special for your anniversary.

TONY. There's no need. Without you, there wouldn't be one.

WILLIAM. Oh! D'you know, I think I could fall in love with you, if I didn't find you so sexually uninteresting.

TONY. You break my heart.

They kiss affectionately. Enter ROBERT.

ROBERT. Oh sorry . . .

WILLIAM. That's alright. I'm just saying goodbye. Lovely meeting you, Robert. I'm sure we'll meet again.

ROBERT. Yes. Goodbye.

WILLIAM. Tara, Tony. I'll see myself out.

TONY. Bye.

WILLIAM *exits. Sound of front door opening and then shutting. Pause.*

So.

ROBERT. So.

They smile.

TONY. I'll show you round, shall I?

ROBERT. Yes. (*Beat.*) I like your stereo.

TONY. Good, isn't it?

ROBERT. I've always wanted one like this.

TONY. I'll play something, if you like.

Beat.

ROBERT. Shall we get the business out of the way first?

TONY. Okay.

ROBERT. Where's Greg?

TONY. At a conference. For the weekend.

ROBERT. Oh.

Beat.

TONY. After you.

> ROBERT *notices something behind the sofa. He picks it up. It's* TONY*'s dressing-gown. He offers it to* TONY.

(*Taking it.*) You don't waste any time, do you?

ROBERT. Oh sorry . . .

TONY. No, no. I'm impressed. Shall we . . . ?

ROBERT. Yes.

> ROBERT *goes into the hall, as* TONY *holds the door for him. As* TONY *exits, he throws the dressing gown across his shoulder.*

SCENE TWO

Morning. A vacuum cleaner is heard offstage. GREG (*from New York*) *is reading through a manuscript, trying hard to concentrate. Eventually he looks up and sighs with frustration. He sits back. After several seconds the vacuuming stops. With relief,* GREG *returns to the manuscript. He begins annotating. The vacuum starts up again.* GREG *buries his face in his hands, then he composes himself, puts his hands over his ears and attempts to resume his work. The vacuum gets closer. Soon the door opens and* ROBERT *appears, pushing the vacuum cleaner, covering every square inch of carpet with concentrated thoroughness. He doesn't seem to be aware of* GREG. GREG *has sat back from his work and fixes a beady eye on* ROBERT.

GREG. Excuse me.

> ROBERT *doesn't hear.*

Excuse me.

ROBERT *looks across, smiles shyly and continues his vacuuming.*

Hey!

ROBERT *looks across and turns off the cleaner.*

ROBERT. Sorry?

GREG. Would you mind?

ROBERT *looks slightly puzzled.*

I am trying to work.

ROBERT. Oh. I'm so sorry. I wasn't thinking.

GREG. Do you have to use that thing?

ROBERT. Oh . . .

GREG. Couldn't you do something else? Elsewhere?

ROBERT. I've only got this room left to do.

GREG. Well, is there anything you could do that doesn't involve noise?

ROBERT. I should think so.

GREG. I don't wanna be difficult, but I'm finding it totally impossible to concentrate.

ROBERT. I'm so sorry.

GREG. There's no need to be sorry. You're doing your job. The only problem is I'm trying to do my job too.

ROBERT. I could do the dusting.

GREG. Yeah. Do the dusting.

ROBERT. Would that put you off?

GREG. No. That would not put me off. Dusting's fine. (*Beat.*) So long as it's not loud.

GREG *has returned to his manuscript and* ROBERT *pushes out the vacuum cleaner. He returns with a duster and starts dusting. After a while, he stops, wanting to say something.*

ROBERT. I'm sorry to bother you again but . . . are you going to be here for the rest of the morning?

GREG. If that's alright with you.

ROBERT. Yes of course, but I was just wondering when I could do the vacuuming.

GREG. Next week. (GREG *is still working.*)

ROBERT. Okay. (ROBERT *dusts.*)

GREG. I'm sure the carpet will survive.

They continue working. ROBERT *stops and looks across at* GREG. *He's about to speak, then thinks better of it. He continues dusting. He stops again and plucks up the courage.*

ROBERT. Would you mind if I interrupted again?

GREG. What is it?

ROBERT. Well, I just wanted to say how pleased I am to have met you at last.

GREG. Uh-huh.

ROBERT. Because I've read your book . . . quite a while ago, actually, and I enjoyed it very much.

GREG. Thanks.

ROBERT. It meant a lot to me.

GREG. Yeah?

ROBERT. You see, I come from Shrewsbury.

GREG *looks blankly.*

Have you ever been?

GREG. No.

ROBERT. I don't recommend it; it's very dull. I lived there until I was eighteen, and nothing goes on there, nothing at all, and I found it very difficult – being gay. In fact, I began to think that I was the only gay in the country, let alone Shrewsbury. But your book made me realise I wasn't. It gave me a bit of confidence. It really helped.

GREG. Good.

ROBERT. Never looked back since.

Pause. He returns to his dusting.

GREG. You're an actor.

ROBERT. Yes.

GREG. Ever work?

ROBERT. Oh yes. But it's a bit of a bad time at the moment.

GREG. From what I understand, it always seems to be a bit of a bad time.

ROBERT. I suppose so.

GREG. Dunno how you do it.

ROBERT. It can be difficult.

GREG. Ever done television?

ROBERT. Oh yes.

GREG. What?

ROBERT. Bits and pieces. Nothing very much.

GREG. You work mainly in theatre?

ROBERT. Well, that's where the opportunities have presented themselves, so far. Do you go much?

GREG. No. I prefer the movies.

ROBERT. So do I.

GREG. Uh-huh.

GREG *returns to the manuscript.* ROBERT *dusts. Pause.*

ROBERT. You're from New York, aren't you?

GREG. Yes.

ROBERT. I've always wanted to go there.

GREG. What's stopping you?

ROBERT. Don't know. Money?

GREG. You should go. It's very exciting. I love it.

Beat.

ROBERT. Why do you live here then?

GREG. Well, when I'm in London, I sometimes wonder why I don't live in New York, and when I'm in New York, I realise why I live in London. (*Beat.*) My work's here. And of course Tony.

ROBERT. Do you go back much?

GREG. Once a year.

ROBERT. Tony's very excited about the autumn.

GREG. Yeah. It'll be his first visit. I'm looking forward to it.

ROBERT. I really must get it together. One day.

Beat. He returns to his dusting.

GREG. Hey, I tell you what?

ROBERT. What's that?

GREG. Why don't you leave that?

ROBERT. I've hardly started.

GREG. I can't concentrate with you here. I've gotta get this finished. It's already overdue. (*Beat.*) Leave it till next time, yeah?

ROBERT. Okay.

GREG continues working. ROBERT goes out and returns, minus the duster.

I'll be going then.

GREG. So long, Richard.

ROBERT. Robert . . . actually.

GREG looks up.

GREG. Then so long, Robert.

Beat.

ROBERT. Tony said you'd have my money.

Pause.

GREG. How much?

ROBERT. Ten pounds.

Beat. GREG *takes out his wallet and hands him ten pounds.*

Thank you.

ROBERT *moves to the door.*

Bye then.

GREG (*working*). Goodbye.

ROBERT *pauses at the door.*

ROBERT. I'm sorry if I've been a nuisance, but I didn't expect you to be here. Tony said you usually . . .

The phone rings. GREG *lifts the receiver.*

GREG. Hello? . . . Hi . . . I dunno . . . About six, I should think . . . Uh-huh . . . So-so . . .

ROBERT *has gone out.*

You wanna word with him?

GREG *looks up.*

Well, he just . . . hang on . . . (*Shouts.*) Robert?

Sound of front door shutting.

He's gone . . . Just now . . . No, I'm not running after him . . . Can't it wait? . . . What the hell do you wanna say to him anyway? . . . I'm sorry . . . Look, I really gotta get on, okay? . . . Yeah . . . See you.

He replaces the receiver. Beat. He returns to the manuscript. Pause. He suddenly throws down his pen.

Twenty dollars!

The Adagio of Mozart's Clarinet Concerto starts playing.

SCENE THREE

As the lights come up, the music transfers to the speakers onstage. Evening. TONY, GREG *and* ROBERT *are sitting round the dinner table. They have eaten the main course. They are drinking wine.* TONY *is smoking. There is an empty, untouched place set for dinner.*

GREG. They're so damned lazy. It's like banging my head against a brick wall. I have to constantly nag to get any work out of them, and when they do get round to handing in an essay, it's like they're doing me a favour, even though it is six months late. And nine times out of ten, the standard is dismal, so I lose my temper, and then they sulk. They're nice enough kids, but I don't understand why most of them are doing the course.

ROBERT. I could never teach.

GREG. I can't tell you how depressing it is standing in front of my classes. They're like the Living Dead, or the Stepford Wives. They just sit there, blankly.

TONY. Maybe you bore the shit out of them.

GREG. I am never boring. I put a lot into it. I just wish they'd give me a little bit back.

ROBERT. It sounds very frustrating.

GREG. I've even resorted to jokes to try and get a reaction, but will they laugh?! Not a glimmer.

TONY. That's because you're not funny.

GREG. Thanks a lot.

ROBERT. What jokes do you tell them?

TONY. He only knows one.

ROBERT. I can never remember them.

TONY. Why don't you tell it, Greg? We could do with a good belly laugh.

GREG. I'm not telling it now.

TONY. Go on. Robert wants to hear it.

GREG. You won't find it funny.

TONY. I haven't the past fifty times, it's true, but –

ROBERT. I haven't heard it.

TONY. We promise we'll laugh, however badly you tell it.
    Won't we, Robert?

ROBERT. Yes.

TONY. Go on.

    Beat.

GREG. Well, do you know anything about American history?

ROBERT. Bits.

GREG. Like you know the names of the presidents?

ROBERT. Some of them.

GREG. Does Calvin Coolidge mean anything to you?

ROBERT. A little.

GREG. Well, he was president during the twenties. And it's
    quite interesting that he should have been because the
    twenties were, culturally speaking, a very exciting,
    flamboyant decade, and Coolidge was anything but exciting
    and flamboyant. He kept himself very much to himself. And
    he was a pretty straight sort of a guy, a traditionalist, and he
    believed very strongly in the American way of life.

TONY. It's the way you tell 'em!

GREG. If you don't know fuck all about Coolidge, the joke
    doesn't mean anything!

ROBERT. Please. Carry on.

GREG. Anyway, d'you know who Dorothy Parker was?

TONY. Greg! He's not stupid.

GREG. Listen, one of my students thought she was a tights
    manufacturer.

TONY. Please tell the joke. The tension's killing me.

GREG. Well, the day Coolidge died, some guy came up to her
    and said, 'Have you heard the news? Calvin Coolidge has
    died – '

ROBERT. Oh, and she said, 'How can they tell?' (*Beat.*) Is that
    the one?

TONY. 'Fraid so.

ROBERT. Sorry.

TONY goes to the stereo.

TONY. Any requests?

ROBERT. Shall I serve the pudding?

TONY. In a minute.

ROBERT. That's dreadful of me.

TONY. Greg. What would you like?

GREG. Whatever.

TONY looks through the records.

TONY. Well, let me see. There's Telemann, Vivaldi, Handel, Corelli, Bach, Village People. You'd like some Village People, wouldn't you, Greg? You're not going to sulk, are you?

ROBERT. I'm so sorry.

GREG. I'm not sulking.

TONY. Or we could even have some more Mozart.

ROBERT. We could hear the end of that concerto.

TONY. I think we've heard the best of that. I'm a sucker for slow movements. (*He takes a record out of its sleeve.*) More Mozart, I'm afraid. But this one's an andante rather than an adagio. I hope you don't find it depressing.

ROBERT. Oh no. I love Mozart.

TONY (*putting record on the turntable*). I have to admit, I am indulging myself. I'm suffering from that well-known after-dinner complaint: Melancholia Hirondelle.

He places the stylus on the disc: the Andante of Mozart's Sinfonia Concertante in E flat (K. 364).

ROBERT. What is this?

TONY. It's here.

He hands the sleeve to ROBERT and points.

That one.

ROBERT. Oh. I haven't heard this before.

TONY. I quite like it. There's a lovely bit that comes up in a minute. A sort of descending – tune, that . . . Anyway, you'll hear it.

He walks behind GREG *and kisses his head.*

Alright?

GREG. Uh-huh.

Beat.

TONY. Well, you could have chosen something.

GREG. I'm okay.

Beat.

ROBERT. When I was at school, there was this master who . . . took me under his wing, you might say. I don't think he was gay, but his interest in me was more than academic. Anyway, I used to write a lot – poetry and things – and one day, I remember, he called me to his room and worked his way through a whole load of stuff I'd given him, line by line, word by word, until he'd completely eroded my confidence, and at the time, I – Sorry, are you listening to the music?

TONY. No. Carry on.

ROBERT. Well . . . at the time, I accepted what he said. I believed him. I could see nothing of value in any of it. And he said what I should do was forget everything I'd written about, and start afresh. Well, the idea was fine, but it's easier said than done. And the unfortunate thing was that his comments had an effect, in that I haven't written anything from that day to this, and I don't think I'll ever forgive him for that. And what really makes me resent him – which is why I thought of him in the first place – is that much later, we were having a chat about music, and I said that Mozart was probably the greatest composer who had ever lived, and he said I was wrong. He said that the greatest composer who had ever lived was Vaughan Williams, and Mozart in comparison was merely a brilliant technician. This man, who had completely crushed my confidence in writing, obviously couldn't tell Stork from butter. To dismiss Mozart as a brilliant technician and nothing more is a travesty. (*Beat.*) Don't you agree?

TONY. Of course.

ROBERT. I presume you both like Mozart.

TONY. We do. Well, I do.

GREG. So do I.

TONY. You prefer Verdi.

GREG. I like Verdi too. I also like Handel and Vivaldi. And Puccini and Bruce Springsteen. But I also like Mozart. I've never said I didn't.

TONY. But you don't like him as much as Verdi.

GREG. I don't know why you say that.

TONY. You don't find him as moving.

GREG. He moves me in a different way.

TONY. Greg's an old softy, really. He listens politely to most music, but what actually gets his juices flowing is a big, thumping tear-jerker, with a tune you can whistle to. A snatch of *Traviata* or *Butterfly,* and he's crying like a baby. Isn't that true, Greg?

GREG. No.

TONY. Hard to believe – such a stern exterior.

ROBERT. I've always loved Mozart. Ever since I was twelve.

TONY. Would you regard yourself as having been a precocious child?

ROBERT. No . . .

TONY. When I was twelve, I was into Helen Shapiro.

GREG. When I was twelve, I was having a nervous breakdown.

ROBERT. Really?

TONY. His Catholic upbringing. Wrestling with the concept of limbo, and he cracked up under the strain. Talking of precocious.

GREG. Fucking nuns.

TONY. Poor thing . . .

He strokes GREG's *head.*

Sorry, you were saying.

ROBERT. It's not important.

TONY. It is. Go on.

ROBERT. Erm . . . I've forgotten where . . .

TONY. You were saying how you'd always loved Mozart.
Since you were twelve.

ROBERT. Oh yes. You see, my piano teacher introduced me to
him.

TONY. Good for him.

ROBERT. She was a woman, actually.

TONY. Oh.

ROBERT. I'd asked her who her favourite composer was, and
she said it was him. I'd never heard his music, but because
I idolised her so much, I gave him a hearing, and liked it.
I'm not saying I completely appreciated it, but I sensed
there was something there, and for quite a few years I went
round saying how much I loved Mozart, whereas in fact
I suppose I was imitating a love for him. But I knew that
one day I'd really love him. And it was when I was taken
to Covent Garden for the first time, by an aunt, to see *Cosi
Fan Tutte,* that I fell head over heels. It was the moment of
'Soave sia il vento'. I'd never heard anything so beautiful.

TONY. Are you sure you weren't precocious?

ROBERT. I don't think so.

TONY. Then maybe your aunt was. Mine used to take me to
Holiday on Ice.

ROBERT. I'll never forget that performance. And in particular,
the moment when that trio started. It was sublime. So when
this master dismissed Mozart as a mere technician, I was
dumbfounded. I find his music deeply moving. Even
sensual. In fact, the most erotic experience I can imagine is

being fucked to him. (*He sips his wine, wishing he hadn't said that.*) I'll get the pudding. (*He goes into the kitchen.*)

TONY. Yes, that'd be lovely.

Beat. TONY *goes to the phone and dials.*

GREG. What's the point?

TONY. I'll try just once more.

GREG. It's so fucking rude.

TONY. It's not like him.

GREG. I bet he's out cruising.

TONY. He must have forgotten.

GREG. At least he could have phoned.

TONY. If he's forgotten, he wouldn't phone, would he? (*Holds on, then replaces the receiver.*) No.

GREG. Great evening.

TONY. Just because he spoilt your joke.

GREG. You know what I'm talking about.

TONY. He's a good cook.

GREG. At that price, he should be.

TONY. It's not my fault.

GREG. Of course it's your fault. It was your idea. You asked him.

TONY. He's alright.

GREG. That's not the point. I just don't want him here.

TONY. So if he hadn't done the cooking, who would have?

GREG. Don't be ridiculous.

TONY. I'm not being ridiculous. If Robert hadn't done the cooking, I would have had to, and I didn't want to. Just for one night, I didn't want to. If you weren't so antisocial, we could've gone to a restaurant, or if you weren't so inept, you could have cooked. But you automatically presume that I will.

GREG. I'm too busy.

TONY. You're too busy! I suppose there are no claims on my time. I have nothing to do but house-cleaning and cooking! It's obvious you regard my attempts at writing as no more than a hobby.

GREG. That is not so.

TONY. It is so. You don't take it seriously.

GREG. I'm being practical.

TONY. So am I. The less I have to do around the flat, the more time I can devote to work.

GREG. I don't have an endless supply of money. I have to be careful. Robert is an extravagance.

TONY. He's not.

GREG. Then why don't you pay for him?

TONY. You know why.

GREG. Because you're broke.

TONY. And I'll stay broke if you treat me as a housewife and not give me the support I need.

GREG. I give you plenty!

TONY. I don't mean money.

GREG. And I don't treat you as a housewife.

TONY. Oh, leave it alone! It's boring.

GREG. It's always boring when you know you're wrong!

TONY. And a happy anniversary to you, too!

Enter ROBERT *with four desserts.*

ROBERT. I did four, just in case William turns up.

GREG. He won't.

ROBERT. Well . . .

TONY. Then there'll be more for us! It looks delicious. Doesn't it, Greg?

GREG. Yeah.

TONY. Where did you learn to cook like this?

ROBERT. I didn't learn. I taught myself. I enjoy it. What about you?

TONY. Oh, I'm not very good at it, and I certainly don't enjoy it. But it's a case of having to.

ROBERT. And what about you, Greg?

TONY. Greg loves cooking, don't you, Greg? Can't keep him out of the kitchen.

ROBERT. Really . . .

GREG. No. He's joking.

ROBERT. Oh.

TONY. I have an irrepressible wit. Forgive me.

They eat.

This is delicious, Robert. You've done very well.

ROBERT. I'm very grateful. I need every penny I can get.

TONY. It must be very hard being an actor.

ROBERT. It must be very hard being a writer.

TONY. Yes.

ROBERT. How long have you been at it?

TONY. Difficult to be exact. I've always scribbled away, but I plunged myself into it full-time – a few years ago.

ROBERT. What did you do before?

TONY. A mind-crushing job in computers. I had to give it up. And I felt I had to put myself to the test as a writer. What's the point of talking about something if you never do it?

ROBERT. I agree. And how's it going?

TONY. Okay.

ROBERT. What have you had published so far?

Beat.

TONY. Oh . . . one or two things. A short story . . .

ROBERT. Really. What was it in?

TONY. Nothing important.

GREG. The *New Review.*

ROBERT. Oh. (*Beat.*) Could I read it?

TONY. If you like. I'll look it out for you sometime.

ROBERT. And what else?

TONY. Why do you want to know?

ROBERT. I'm interested.

TONY. Well, I've written a few articles for a friend who edits
this trade magazine –

ROBERT. What were they about?

TONY. A variety of things. In the first one I wrote, I took a
hard-hitting look at the advances made in the design of
typists' chairs, another was an in-depth analysis of the
problems of hiring conference rooms, yet another put
forward new ideas for things to do at the office party . . .
(*Beat.*) Impressive, isn't it? I hasten to add I wrote them for
pocket-money. My real interest is a collection of short
stories which I'm trying to finish at the moment.

ROBERT. And what are your chances of getting them
published?

TONY. Surprisingly enough, there is a slight chance. (*Beat.*)
I know a publisher who's quite interested.

GREG. You can say that again.

TONY. Greg thinks he's more interested in me than my work.

GREG. I know he is.

TONY. He isn't. He actually believes I can write.

GREG. So do I. But it doesn't alter the fact that that guy is a
fat, slimy lecher.

TONY. He's not fat.

ROBERT. Do you have an agent?

TONY. What?

ROBERT. An agent.

TONY. No. (*To* GREG.) I don't know what you've got against
him.

ROBERT. Mine's hopeless.

TONY. Sorry?

ROBERT. He doesn't get me any work. I complained to him
the other day that I'd been unemployed for months and he
got quite shirty with me. He told me my availability was my
greatest asset. I think I ought to leave him.

TONY. I think you should.

Beat.

ROBERT. So what do you live on?

TONY. Well, I do the occasional bit of temp work . . . and sign
on. More wine, Robert?

ROBERT. Gosh, it sounds just like me. You ought to take up
cleaning.

TONY. Wine.

ROBERT. Oh. Yes, thank you.

TONY *pours, then his own glass. He is about to put down
the bottle when he notices* GREG *holding out his glass for
a refill. He looks at* GREG, *then pours him a glass.*

GREG. Thanks.

ROBERT. Cheers!

GREG. Cheers!

TONY. Cheers.

ROBERT. To success . . . and a happy anniversary!

GREG. Yeah . . .

They drink.

ROBERT. At least with writing, you can do it by yourself.
What I mean is, you can't act by yourself – you have to
wait for someone to employ you – whereas with writing

you can . . . get on with it. Regardless. (*Beat.*) Although it must be difficult. (*Pause.*) Do you find it difficult, Greg?

GREG. It depends. It's vital to have a routine.

ROBERT. Five thousand words before breakfast and all that sort of thing.

GREG. Not quite. It's a case of working out a timetable. The days I'm not lecturing at college I devote to writing. It seems to work.

ROBERT. And what about you, Tony? Do you have a similar routine?

TONY. I write when I write.

Beat.

ROBERT. I envy you. Both. Perhaps I ought to try my hand at it again. (*Beat.*) I read a lot. I've just read *The Woman in White.* Have you read it?

GREG. Yes.

ROBERT. Marvellous, isn't it?

GREG. I used to think so, but I reread it a few years back and didn't like it as much.

ROBERT. Why's that?

GREG. I guess I just changed my mind, that's all. It's happened before. I'd have a first impression of something and go around saying how fantastic it was, but if I went back to it, I'd often find I didn't feel the same. It's important to reassess your opinions – and few people are prepared to. I always suspect those who say, 'I adore so-and-so,' or, 'I loathe what's-'is-name.' The chances are they don't. They just haven't bothered to think about it recently. Like their opinion's locked in a time warp. Intellectual idleness – I guess that's it. It's hard work keeping your mind open.

Beat.

TONY (*to* ROBERT). And what other books have you read recently?

GREG. Excuse me. (*He leaves the room.*)

ROBERT. Is he alright?

TONY. Not as a comedian.

ROBERT. He seems a bit pissed off.

TONY. He's okay.

ROBERT. Would you like coffee?

TONY. I'm fine at the moment. Thanks.

ROBERT. I'd better clear away . . .

TONY. No. Leave it. There's time for that later.

   Pause.

ROBERT. Could I have a cigarette, please?

TONY. Help yourself.

   TONY *offers him a cigarette.* ROBERT *takes one.* TONY
   offers him a light.

ROBERT. Thank you. (*Beat.*) Five years!

TONY. Sorry?

ROBERT. Five years. That's quite an achievement.

TONY. I suppose it is.

ROBERT. Have you lived together all that time?

TONY. Nearly. We moved in together after a month. Well, I
suppose I should say, I moved in. It's Greg's flat.

ROBERT. Quick work! Love at first sight!

TONY. For me. It took Greg a bit longer. He doesn't fall in
love easily.

   Pause.

ROBERT. Don't you get jealous of each other?

TONY. There's no point.

ROBERT. I would.

TONY. Have you ever had a relationship?

ROBERT. Yes. Once. And the thought of him screwing around
would have driven me mad.

TONY. Why did you split up?

ROBERT. He met someone else.

TONY. Oh.

ROBERT. But while we were together, if he'd have felt the need to have other men, I'd have felt such a failure. If I couldn't have satisfied him, then what price our relationship?

TONY. It can be tricky, but infidelity is a fact of life. We both enjoy the occasional one-night stand. We don't do it all the time, and we'd never bring anyone back if the other one was here. Perhaps it's not ideal, but I think it's realistic. I'd much rather have that than be deceitful to one another – pretending we were faithful when we weren't.

ROBERT. I'd find it difficult.

TONY. Well . . . if you believe in someone, then the odd stray fuck shouldn't be a threat. It's just sex. Gratifying the libido. And if that is a threat, then one's belief must be pretty weak to begin with.

ROBERT. I wish I could think like that. I'm too possessive.

TONY. You'd probably cope. Who knows? Each relationship has its own rules. Mind you, I've yet to see one which convinces me that monogamy isn't abnormal.

ROBERT. But it isn't.

TONY. Do you know, the only animals that are monogamous are jackals? And they eat each other's vomit. Hardly a good example to model oneself on.

Enter GREG *in a dressing gown.*

You alright?

GREG. Yes.

TONY. Good.

ROBERT. I wonder what's happened to William?

TONY. No idea. (*Beat.*) You didn't take to him, did you?

ROBERT. I've only met him once.

GREG. That should be enough.

TONY. He's sweet.

ROBERT. Sweet William!

He giggles. TONY *smiles.* ROBERT *registers* GREG *isn't smiling.*

TONY. That was a joke, Greg. You see, Robert was using a horticultural analogy to pun on the names of both the person and the –

GREG. Tony, give it a rest.

TONY. Sadly, Americans don't have a sense of humour. They tend to be far too serious about everything. It's all the fault of those fucking Pilgrim Fathers. Dull old cunts.

GREG. You know I hate that word.

TONY. No wonder they all mug each other and drop bombs on people.

ROBERT. Shall I make some coffee?

GREG. Not for me.

TONY. I'd love some. Thanks.

As ROBERT *rises, the doorbell rings. Freeze. Then* TONY *gets up,* ROBERT *picks up a few dishes and exits into the kitchen.*

Better late than never, I suppose.

He goes into the hall. Sound of front door opening.

(*Off.*) William.

WILLIAM (*off*). Happy anniversary.

Front door closes. Beat. Enter WILLIAM. *His face is bruised and cut.* TONY *follows.*

Sorry I'm late. I got held up.

TONY. What on earth's happened?

WILLIAM. Nothing. Just a little hitch. I see you started without me. I'm only three hours late.

TONY. William.

GREG. Sit down. Like some brandy?

WILLIAM. You think I should on an empty stomach? Oh go on. Force me.

He hands a long, oblong package to TONY.

Here's your present. It's basically for Tony, Greg, but I'm sure you'll benefit from it in the end. (*To* TONY.) It's got a battery in it. (*He sits.* GREG *gives him a glass of brandy.*)

TONY. William.

WILLIAM. It was only a bit of rough trade.

TONY. Oh Christ.

WILLIAM. He was gorgeous. Absolutely gorgeous.

GREG. Have you phoned the police?

WILLIAM. What's the point?

TONY. Your face . . . I'll take you to the hospital.

WILLIAM. I don't need to.

TONY. Why didn't you phone?

WILLIAM. It's tricky in a pair of handcuffs. He wouldn't even let me answer the phone. That was the worst thing – I can't bear not knowing who's ringing me up.

Enter ROBERT *with a tray of coffee.*

ROBERT. Here's the coffee . . . oh . . .

WILLIAM. Hello, Robert. Excuse the face. I slipped with the blusher.

ROBERT. Would you like some coffee?

WILLIAM. That'd be nice. Getting their money's worth, are they?

TONY. But why did you bother to come over? We'd have come to you.

WILLIAM. I didn't want to miss out on anything. I'd have been here a bit earlier, but it took me ages to squeeze out of those fucking handcuffs.

GREG. What happened?

WILLIAM. I just popped into the cottage for a tea-time quickie, and I couldn't believe my luck when this guy gave me the eye – big, brawny, smothered in leather –

TONY. Psychopathic.

WILLIAM. – and so we went back to my place. It started out quite promisingly. He told me to take my clothes off and lie face down on the bed, then he put the handcuffs on and I resigned myself to a slightly heavier session than I ideally would have wished for at that time of the day. I was more in the mood for a light snack than a full meal, if you take my meaning, but then I began to have my doubts, cos he didn't do anything, he just stood there, and after a while he started muttering under his breath, saying really nasty things, and then he started to go through all my belongings, throwing them all over the place, tearing up this and that, and he'd go for occasional wanders around the flat, and then come back in and threaten me some more, and I thought, 'Christ, if it wasn't for you, I could have my feet up in front of *Coronation Street.*'

TONY. But your face –

WILLIAM. That was his way of saying goodnight – several belts across the face. That and smashing my record player. Oh, and pissing over the carpet. He stood there waving his cock around, saying, 'I bet you'd like to suck on this, you filthy little queer.' Trouble is, I would've.

TONY. For Christ's sake . . .

WILLIAM. He was there for ages. I thought he was going to kill me. Still, I shouldn't complain. At least he behaved like he looked.

GREG. I bet he wasn't gay.

WILLIAM. I think you're probably right. Anyway, it's his loss. He doesn't know what he's . . .

Suddenly stops. Beat.

TONY. Are you alright?

WILLIAM (*very quietly*). I'm sorry.

He exits through the hall door. TONY follows. Pause.

ROBERT. Would you like some coffee?

GREG. No. Thank you.

Beat.

ROBERT. I suppose . . . I might as well . . .

He clears more things from the table and goes into the kitchen. GREG pours himself a brandy. He goes over to the phone and lifts the receiver. Beat. He replaces it. ROBERT comes back in, clears more things from the table, and returns to the kitchen. Pause. TONY enters.

TONY. I think I'll take him to the hospital.

GREG. Yeah. Do you think I should phone the police?

TONY. No. I wouldn't bother. There's not much point now. We'll sort that out tomorrow.

GREG. You want me to come with you?

TONY. No. It's probably better if it's just me. (*Beat.*) So I'd better . . .

GREG. Yeah . . .

They're looking at each other.

TONY (*quietly*). See you.

GREG (*quietly*). Sure.

TONY *exits.*

SCENE FOUR

Night. The room is lit by the street light. GREG is sitting listening to 'Soave sia il vento' from Cosi Fan Tutte *playing quietly on the stereo. He's wearing a dressing gown. The front door opens quietly. After several seconds, TONY walks in.*

TONY. Greg?

GREG. Hi.

TONY. I thought you'd be in bed.

GREG. I couldn't sleep. How's William?

TONY. Okay.

GREG. What did the hospital say?

TONY. We didn't stay long enough to find out. There were loads of people in front of us, and William was behaving rather badly.

GREG. How do you mean?

TONY. He was trying to chat up one of the orderlies. Are you alright?

GREG. Sure.

Beat.

TONY. So I thought I might as well take him home to bed.

GREG. Will he be alright by himself?

TONY. He's out for the count. I gave him hot milk, and Mogadon, and then he asked me to read to him.

GREG. Really?

TONY. Yes. A Barbara Cartland novel. Still, I didn't have to read for very long. The combination of Mogadon and Barbara Cartland is enough to knock anyone out.

GREG. What if he wakes up?

TONY. He won't. And I'll pop round first thing. He's not in that bad a state. Just shaken up. (*Beat.*) Haven't heard this for ages.

GREG. Do you want a drink, or . . . ?

TONY. No, I'm fine. (*Pause.*) Actually, I didn't want to stay with William. I wanted to come back here. Spend the night with you.

GREG *looks at him. He takes his hand.*

Did Robert get off okay?

GREG. Yeah.

TONY. Did you give him his cab fare?

GREG. Sure.

TONY. I bet he had to remind you.

GREG. He didn't give me a chance to forget.

   TONY *goes over to the stereo.*

   Next year, just the two of us. Okay?

TONY. Okay.

GREG. Even if it means a takeaway.

   TONY *puts the record back in the sleeve.*

TONY. I'm sorry I got ratty at dinner.

GREG. That's okay.

TONY. No it's not. It's ungrateful. I don't mean it. But
   sometimes, it's hard to . . .

   Beat.

GREG. It doesn't matter.

TONY. When Robert asked me about my writing, I felt rather
   stupid. I've achieved absolutely nothing.

GREG. You have.

TONY. But it's all so slow. I see you churning out one thing
   after another, while I just sit around –

GREG. There's no comparison. I'm doing something entirely
   different from you.

TONY. And some days, I feel I have nothing to say, nothing
   worth writing.

GREG. So do I. It's hard work.

TONY. Yes, I know. (*Pause.*) But it is difficult.

GREG. It's late, baby. Why don't we go to bed?

TONY. In a minute.

   He goes to the sofa and settles between GREG*'s legs.*

   Happy anniversary.

GREG. That was yesterday.

Pause.

TONY. When you arrived at that party, I thought to myself,
'I am going to get that man, if it's the last thing I do,' and
I dragged you out into the garden away from everyone, and
sweated blood trying to think of things to talk about, but
you didn't give an inch. You're such a difficult bastard.

GREG. God, that party.

TONY. It was pretty awful, wasn't it? I didn't want to go, but
William insisted. And I'm glad he did, cos otherwise . . .

GREG *strokes* TONY*'s hair.*

GREG. I thought you dragged me into the kitchen.

TONY. Then suddenly, I noticed a little gleam in your eye, and
you smiled and brushed my hand, and I knew it wasn't
accidental, and it was at that moment that I thought: 'I've
got him!' It was a pity the sex was so disastrous.

GREG. You behaved like a virgin.

TONY. I was tense! And if you remember, you threw up in the
bathroom.

GREG. At least it wasn't in the bedroom.

TONY. I might not be able to turn men's heads, but I can
certainly turn their stomachs.

GREG. I'd drunk too much.

TONY. Oh, I wish we were going away sooner.

GREG. It's not that long.

TONY. Five months . . .

GREG. Four.

TONY. Well . . . I wish we were going tomorrow. You've got to
take me everywhere. I want to go to the Empire State
Building –

GREG. Maybe.

TONY. And the Statue of Liberty –

GREG. Well –

TONY. We've got to!

GREG. I've already decided the places we're going to go.

TONY. Where?

GREG. Lots of places! I wanna show you where I lived as a kid. There's a little place nearby called Carl Schurz Park looking out over the East River – I spent a lot of time there; go to Central Park and take you out on Rowboat Lake, Bethesda Fountain on a Sunday. I'll take you to the promenade on Brooklyn Heights, in the middle of the night, and look out over Manhattan –

TONY. Is that where Woody Allen and Diane Keaton sat when they – ?

GREG. No, and I'll take you to the Village – Christopher Street, we gotta go there, and – oh, I'll take you places. I'll show you New York. Screw the Statue of Liberty!

Pause.

TONY. Greg.

GREG. Yeah?

TONY. You must fuck me tonight. We must have an Anniversary Fuck. And you absolutely mustn't take 'no' for an answer.

Beat. GREG *leans down to him,* TONY *moves up to him, and they kiss.*

GREG. It's very late. And I'm very tired.

They kiss again, then TONY *nestles into his lap. Pause.*

TONY. If you want to get rid of Robert, I'll understand. Honestly. I won't mind.

GREG. We'll talk about it some other time.

He strokes TONY*'s hair.* TONY *turns into* GREG*'s lap. He opens his robe slightly and begins to blow him off.* GREG *leaves his hand resting on* TONY*'s head and his eyes close. He moans quietly. Suddenly,* TONY *stops. They* *are both completely still. Then* TONY *raises his head and gently slides round into his previous position between* GREG's *legs.*

TONY. Maybe you're right. It is a bit late.

SCENE FIVE

Afternoon. TONY *is sitting at the table, surrounded by pieces of paper and notebooks. He is sharpening pencils.* WILLIAM *is sitting on the sofa, eating a huge cream cake. They both have mugs of tea.*

TONY. It was a miserable evening.

WILLIAM. I thought you were enjoying yourself.

TONY. How would you know? You deserted me as soon as we arrived.

WILLIAM. I wanted to get straight down to business.

TONY. I'm giving up discos. I don't see the point any more. Everyone standing around, trying to look cool and disinterested. End up looking lobotomised.

WILLIAM. The cabaret was fun.

TONY. The cabaret was disgusting. Unamusing, unentertaining, mindless, sexist crap. Repressive drivel!

WILLIAM. You go to discos to be political?! No wonder you have such a good time!

TONY. Simply because I'm surrounded by attractive men, deafened by loud music, blinded by the strobe . . . just because they offer the possibility of a fuck doesn't exempt them from criticism. Not in my book, anyway.

WILLIAM. Have an éclair. Calm yourself down.

TONY. I'm not hungry.

WILLIAM. Well, if I had to choose between political principles and discos, it'd be discos every time.

TONY. That's because you haven't got any political principles.

WILLIAM. I have. I've always been vaguely left-wing. Ever since I had a crush on Tariq Ali. But I can't bring myself to join any party. I've looked through hundreds of manifestos –

TONY. Hundreds!

WILLIAM. I have! And if gays are mentioned at all, it's usually ninety-seventh down on the list of priorities. I reckon there's as much homophobia among Socialists as anyone, made worse by the fact that they won't admit to it. I prefer downright hostility to hypocrisy. I mean, if I lived in Tehran, as opposed to Tufnell Park, there'd be no mistaking what people thought of me. If you're buried up to your neck in the ground, having boulders hurled at your head, at least you know where you stand. By the way, who was that little guy you were talking to?

TONY. He wasn't little. He was a dwarf.

WILLIAM. Why didn't you go off with him?

TONY. Because I wouldn't have known what to do with him – whether to fuck him, or sit him on the pillow next to my teddy bear.

WILLIAM. Tony! If I didn't know you better, I'd say you were becoming bitter and twisted.

TONY. I'm fed up.

WILLIAM. Why?

TONY. I don't know.

WILLIAM. Is it your writing?

TONY. Well, that's always a problem. Mind you, I've just finished a story.

WILLIAM. Have you?

TONY. Yes. This morning.

WILLIAM. I want to read it.

TONY. You can't.

WILLIAM. Why not?

TONY. Not until Greg's read it, anyway.

WILLIAM. What do you want to give it to him for? He'll only tear it to pieces.

TONY. But that's what I need. Greg knows what he's talking about.

WILLIAM. You have to say that.

TONY. I don't.

WILLIAM. And it's right that you should. It's very loyal. Wrong, but loyal. Are you missing him?

TONY. He only went yesterday! And he's coming back tonight.

WILLIAM. I reckon what you need is a good fucking.

TONY. I had a 'good fucking' two nights ago.

WILLIAM. Well then, you've got no reason to be fed up.

Beat.

TONY. Actually, it wasn't so good.

WILLIAM. How do you mean?

TONY. I had to ask him to stop.

WILLIAM. I bet Greg wasn't too happy about that.

TONY. He's used to it.

WILLIAM. I've told you before, if you don't give your man your cherry –

TONY. It's easy for you. You've got a cast-iron arsehole. Mine's very sensitive.

WILLIAM. Temperamental, more like. It's all in the mind. You can take it if you really want it.

TONY. I know I can, but that doesn't always help. He can use a ton of grease and it's agony, and other times, with only a dab of spit, I've opened up a mile and felt ecstatic. Stupid, isn't it? Still, he's always been very patient with me.

WILLIAM. Then what are you worried about?

TONY. Because I feel inadequate. As if I'm failing him. I suppose I'm terrified of losing him.

WILLIAM. Losing him? Do you think Greg's likely to leave you because occasionally your arsehole's a bit tight? After five years? I've never heard such rubbish!

TONY. I can't help how I feel.

WILLIAM. Well, if you're so worried, why not do something about it? Practise on the vibrator I bought you.

TONY. I do, sometimes. I used it last night, actually. But I got a complaint from the woman downstairs.

WILLIAM. Why?

TONY. Well, I put it on the floor, impaled myself on it, switched it on, and the next thing I knew, she was hammering on the front door, and said would I please be more considerate and not use the Hoover at such a late hour.

WILLIAM. You need a silencer.

TONY. Anyway, I don't like vibrators very much. I'm very grateful; don't think I'm not. But – well, you can't talk to them. They don't whisper sweet nothings into your ear. And you certainly can't suck them.

WILLIAM. You should broaden your horizons.

TONY. I suppose I just don't get turned on by throbbing plastic.

WILLIAM. You're too romantic, that's your trouble.

TONY. I am. You're right.

Pause.

WILLIAM. Have you heard from Robert?

TONY. Not a word. He's too busy being successful.

WILLIAM. When's his series come out?

TONY. Oh, not for ages. He won't have finished filming it yet. Lucky sod.

WILLIAM. Well, it solved the problem for you. You didn't have to go through the messy business of sacking him.

TONY. True. But the flat's not getting any cleaner.

WILLIAM. I've noticed. Still, what's it matter, if it's stopped Greg moaning on about the extravagance. (*Beat.*) You know, dirt's never bothered me. I'd be happy living in a pigsty, if I was sharing my slops with someone I loved. Good orgasms are much more important than clean surfaces, don't you think?

TONY. Maybe.

WILLIAM. I thought it was unnecessary hiring Robert in the first place. I've always suspected couples who live in spotless flats. It's like they're compensating for something – all bra and no tits. But you walk in here and you think –

TONY. All tits and no bra.

WILLIAM. Yes. You know there are more important things going on than squirting Pledge all over the place or wiping down the rubber plant. You love each other. That's what's important. Not how versatile you are with a duster. And I tell you, so many people envy you.

TONY. What on earth for?

WILLIAM. Cos you've got it sussed. You're both happily married, you both fuck around, and it doesn't bother you. How many people do you know who cope with that?

TONY. Quite a few, I should think.

WILLIAM. Sometimes I wish I was in your position. Don't get me wrong – I'm quite happy. But there are times when I'd like a bit more. A chance to get to know someone in a relationship. Stability, I suppose.

TONY. Why presume a relationship provides that?

WILLIAM. And occasionally – not often – but occasionally, a one-night stand can be a real downer, when you suddenly catch a glimpse of what that person's really like. I wonder what impression I give? (*Beat.*) Still, most times it's fun.

TONY. You make us sound like an ideal couple. We're not too ideal at the moment.

WILLIAM. How do you mean?

TONY. Well . . . we're not getting on too brilliantly. Greg's a bit cool with me. And we're not making love as often as we used to. Actually, I'm a bit worried.

WILLIAM. If you've been together for five years, you can't expect every day to be magic, can you? You go through phases. You have to have your ups and downs. Changes, even.

TONY. I suppose so.

WILLIAM. You're probably overreacting. As usual. Always worrying over nothing, you daft sod!

TONY. Maybe. I'm just down at the moment – you know what I'm like. As you say, it's probably just a phase.

WILLIAM. Why don't you plan a wonderful weekend together? Eat yourselves stupid, get pissed, and fuck twice an hour.

TONY. Unfortunately, I can't. I've got to go away this weekend to a family christening. Actually, I think that's what's depressing me. I loathe family occasions.

WILLIAM. Then what about tonight? Make it really special. Cook him his favourite meal, put candles on the table, have a really romantic evening. Tell you what, I'll help you shop – I love spending other people's money. When's he due back?

TONY. About eight.

WILLIAM. Well, when he walks in, have that piece of music playing – you know, the dreary piece, the one that you both call 'our tune' . . . the Barbirolli –

TONY. Barber.

WILLIAM. That's right. Have that playing and drape yourself across the sofa in a jockstrap. Get it just right for when he arrives. Oh, I can see it now! It'll do you the world of good. And by tomorrow morning, you won't know what you've been worrying about! I reckon I've got more faith in you both than you have.

SCENE SIX

Evening. Light from the street and through the hall door, slightly ajar. The Adagio from Barber's String Quartet is playing on the stereo. The phone rings.

GREG (*off*). Shit.

Movements off. A door opening.

(*Off.*) Okay, okay . . .

Enter GREG, awkwardly pulling on a dressing gown. He switches on a lamp. As he's about to lift the receiver, the phone stops ringing.

Great! Jesus . . . If you're gonna interrupt a fuck, at least have the courtesy to wait! Who the hell hangs on for eight rings?

He goes into the kitchen, talking the while.

I always let it ring at least ten times. At LEAST ten times! Jesus . . . You have to allow for people who don't have extensions, for Chrissake. You have to allow for people screwing, or taking a crap. You can't expect everyone to be sitting on top of the goddamn phone.

By now, he's back in the room at the drinks table, with two glasses with ice in them.

You wanna drink?

No reply. Raising voice:

I said, d'you wanna drink?

Enter ROBERT, naked.

Oh, you're here . . . I'm fixing a drink. D'you want one?

ROBERT. Yes. (*He sits on the sofa.*) Thank you. Who was it?

GREG. Didn't hang on long enough for me to find out. How many times do you let a phone ring before hanging up?

ROBERT. Oh . . .

GREG. You gotta let it ring at least ten times. At least! That's only reasonable.

Hands him drink.

Baby, you'll catch your death of cold.

ROBERT. Turn the heating on, then.

GREG. It's not cold enough yet. November, I'll turn it on.

ROBERT. Then I'll catch my death of cold.

GREG. Then wear a robe! It's cheaper.

ROBERT. Haven't got one.

> GREG *sighs with impatience and exits through the hall
> door.* ROBERT *walks to the window. He stands to the side,
> looking down into the street, sipping his drink. Enter* GREG
> *carrying a dressing gown. He notices* ROBERT *at the
> window.*

GREG. You ever thought that might be a little indiscreet . . . ?

> *He walks up behind* ROBERT *and wraps the robe around
> his shoulders. Then he puts his arms around him.* ROBERT
> *rests his head back against* GREG*'s face.*

ROBERT. I'm sure this smells of me by now.

GREG. He doesn't notice. He wears too much scent.

> *Beat.*

ROBERT. Our first weekend together.

GREG. Uh-huh.

ROBERT. I've always hated Sunday nights. I think it's a hang-
over from schooldays. The prospect of Monday morning.
Back to reality. My father always woke me up at seven-
fifteen with a cup of tea. I hated it. It was very sweet of
him, but I hated it.

GREG. Would you mind if I turned this off? It's like a fucking
funeral.

> GREG *takes the stylus off the record.*

ROBERT. I can't bear the thought of tomorrow morning.

GREG. It's still only eight o'clock.

ROBERT. When's he due back?

GREG. Not until lunchtime.

ROBERT. So I leave . . .

GREG. Ten o'clock.

ROBERT. Ten o'clock. That leaves us fourteen hours. Well, I'm
not working tomorrow, so I don't need much sleep. In fact,
I don't need any. So assuming we make it twice an hour,
you can fuck me twenty-eight times between now and then.

GREG. I *am* working tomorrow, and I *do* need sleep.

They kiss.

But not that much.

ROBERT. This is such a treat. Makes a change from snogging
in the lavatory of the British Museum, or screwing round at
my place at nine-thirty in the morning, or having a quick
one here while Tony's in Tesco's.

GREG. Are you complaining?

ROBERT. No. Well, a bit. It is difficult, at times. (*Beat.*) I was
defending you the other day.

GREG. Oh?

ROBERT. I was having lunch with this actor, who plays the
lead in the thing I'm doing. He's very nice. We get on well.
Quite attractive, actually. Unfortunately, he's irredeemably
straight. Anyway, he was asking me about myself, and said,
did I have anybody, and I said, yes. And he asked if I lived
with this person, and I said, no, and he wanted to know
why not. So I told him that my lover lived with somebody
else and didn't want to leave him. And he said, but if he
loves you, why does he still live with this other person?
And I said, because he loves him as well. And he said, but
you can't love two people, and I said it would appear that
you could. He was quite put out by this. He reckoned that
I was getting a raw deal, and that this lover of mine was
obviously a two-timing, greedy bastard. (*Pause.*) That's
when I attempted to put up a defence on your behalf, but
I wasn't very convincing. It's very difficult explaining about
us. You invariably come out of it looking like a shit, and I
come out of it dripping behind the ears.

GREG. Is this actor guy married?

ROBERT. Oh yes. Of course, the irony is that he hasn't left a vagina intact within a four-mile radius of the studios. The odd deceitful fuck's alright, but falling in love – that's really bad.

GREG. Did it bother you – what he said?

ROBERT. Only to the extent that I don't like to hear you being slagged off. I'll keep my mouth shut from now on. People don't understand. Why should they? Only those involved know what's really going on.

GREG. I am a shit.

Beat. He smiles. Then ROBERT *smiles.*

But I'm not a liar. I love you, Robert. I wish I could make it easier. But I don't know how.

Pause.

ROBERT. From the very first moment I saw you, I wanted you. But I didn't think I had a hope in hell of getting you. Now I have, I'm prepared to put up with anything to keep you.

Pause.

GREG. What say you take off that robe?

Pause.

ROBERT. What say I do?

Beat.

GREG. Get one of those cushions – put it on the floor. (*Beat.*) Kneel down. Then lie down over it. With your ass in the air. Slowly. And see what I won't do to you.

Beat. ROBERT *sips his drink, then kneels on the floor, positions a cushion, lets his robe slip to the floor and slowly lowers himself over the cushion.* GREG *looks at him, then kneels over him, and kisses his back and buttocks. He buries his face in the side of his back and growls.* ROBERT *giggles.*

ROBERT. So – what won't you do to me?

*Sound of front door opening. GREG and ROBERT freeze.
Front door shuts. GREG and ROBERT leap to their feet
and awkwardly attempt to get ROBERT's dressing gown
back on. GREG goes towards the door, but turns in his
tracks as it opens and TONY enters. He turns on the lights.
He is carrying an overnight bag and a carrier bag. He stops
as he notices ROBERT, who's holding the robe around him,
untied. A moment of stillness.*

TONY. Hello, Robert.

Beat.

ROBERT (*just audible*). Hello, Tony.

Pause.

TONY. How's the series going?

ROBERT. Oh, it's . . . (*Tailing off.*)

Beat.

TONY. Look, I tell you what . . . I'll go and . . .

*He turns towards the door, stops, turns back and looks at
ROBERT. Beat.*

Suits you better than it does me. (*He walks out.*)

ROBERT. My clothes are in the bedroom.

GREG. I'll go fetch them.

*He exits. ROBERT picks up the cushion and puts it back on
the sofa. He's not sure what to do. He drains the remains of
his drink. Enter GREG with ROBERT's clothes and bag.
ROBERT hurriedly starts dressing.*

ROBERT. There's all my stuff in the bathroom. Would you . . .
er . . .

GREG. Yeah.

*GREG exits. ROBERT continues dressing. GREG returns
with a toilet bag. He puts it in ROBERT's bag.*

Was there anything else?

ROBERT. I don't think so. No. (*He finishes dressing. He puts his bag over his shoulder.*) Will you phone me?

GREG. Yeah.

ROBERT. Tomorrow morning?

GREG. Sure.

> ROBERT *goes towards the door. GREG stays where he is. ROBERT stops before exiting. He goes back to GREG, quickly kisses him on the cheek, and walks out. Pause. GREG goes to the drinks and pours out two. Enter TONY with the carrier bag.*

I've fixed you a drink.

TONY. Thank you.

He puts the carrier bag on the table and starts unpacking. GREG takes the drink to him.

GREG. More booty, huh?

TONY. It's getting embarrassing. I keep telling her not to, but she insists. I reckon she'll still be giving me food parcels when I'm sixty-five.

GREG. She's very generous.

TONY. Yes. (*He looks into an aluminium packet.*) Look at this . . . a joint of beef. She can't afford it.

GREG idly inspects a jar which TONY has unpacked.

That's from Aunty Ruth. Gooseberry jam. She grows them on her allotment. (*He takes a few things into the kitchen.*)

GREG. Bad weekend, huh?

TONY (*off*). Pretty bad. (*He comes back in.*) Actually, it was the worst ever. I've had an awful time. I couldn't face the thought of staying another night, so I made up a rather weak excuse . . . (*He lights a cigarette and sips his drink.*)

GREG. How was the christening?

TONY. It was . . . Okay. I imagine. I've never been to a Catholic one before, so I've nothing to compare it with. All my relatives looked pretty glum, and the other lot – the

Catholics – looked pretty smug. And I guess I looked fairly indifferent. (*He starts taking out more things from the bag.*)

GREG. Is your mother alright?

TONY. She's fine. Thank you. Sends her love.

GREG. That's nice.

TONY (*holding up a packet of biscuits*). Chocolate-chip cookies. She knows you like them.

GREG. Tony, I'm terribly sorry. I wouldn't have wished this on you for the world.

TONY. The fucking baby wouldn't stop crying. Ugly little tyke. Mind you, I pity him, having those two as parents. Chances are, he'll end up taking after them, or looking like them – or both, God forbid. If I'd have been him, I'd have dive-bombed straight into the font and had done with it. Did you have a good weekend?

GREG. Please . . .

TONY. Try as I might, I can't like any of them. And yet there's a bit of me that envies them. Funny, isn't it? (*He takes out a cake tin – the final item.*) Oh, here's the big treat. Again, especially for you. Chocolate layer cake. 'Greg's Gateau', as she rather tweely calls it.

GREG. Thank you.

TONY. I didn't bake it. (*He takes more things into the kitchen. Off.*) She's threatening to come up for a weekend. Wants to see some shows. And she's complaining that you never go up to see her.

GREG. Let's arrange it . . .

TONY (*off*). Okay. (*He re-enters.*) Well, my weekends are free. How about yours?

GREG. Tony . . .

TONY. What?

Beat.

GREG. Aren't you going to say anything?

TONY. What would you suggest?

GREG. Well, you can't just ignore it. We've gotta talk about it.

Beat.

TONY. Do you know, a weekend return is now fourteen pounds, sixty pence? Unbelievable, isn't it? Fourteen pounds, sixty! And all for a christening! I think I'll invoice the Pope. One of the other mob did offer me a lift back – well, as far as St Albans, but I thought, by the time I've got from there to – Euston, if that's where you go to from St Albans. Or is it King's Cross? Anyway, I thought by that time, I might just as well get the Inter-City, especially as I'd paid the fare, and I didn't really want to have to – I didn't want to have to speak with him all the way. He's an estate agent. His wife's the shyest person I've ever met. He speaks for her all the time. She's Cornish. So he says. Have you always used the flat? Or was it just this weekend, and the rest of the time you've used his place? Or do you go somewhere else? (*Pause.*) You do it here, don't you? In the bedroom, in here . . . everywhere. I've never noticed any stains. Mind you, he has made a living out of cleaning up. (*Beat.*) So you've obviously planned it very well, cos I've never . . . Does he watch me leave? Is he hiding somewhere, lurking behind the hedge, and as soon as he sees me turn the corner, he leaps up the stairs, tearing off his jeans for a quickie? Am I right? And all those nights when we haven't made it, was that cos you'd been with him and you'd fucked yourself dry?

GREG. Tony.

TONY. You wanted me to talk – I'm talking. When was the first time? No, don't tell me. The night of our anniversary, wasn't it? Or was it before?

GREG. No. It wasn't before.

TONY. *Cosi Fan Tutte.* I thought it rather odd you should be listening to that – you hardly ever play Mozart. Was he right? Is it the most erotic experience you can imagine, fucking to Mozart? Maybe we should try it. A quick blast of *The Magic Flute* and you'd be up me like a rat up a drain.

I thought I smelt something on your cock. But I stopped myself saying anything, because I thought well, even if he has, what's it matter? That's the name of the game. He's allowed to. So am I. The occasional bit on the side. All part of the arrangement. But I didn't think that arrangement provided for a . . . four-month affair. It is four months, isn't it? (*Beat.*) Why didn't you tell me?

GREG. How could I tell you?

TONY. You should've told me. It's ridiculous.

GREG. Is it? You think I should have told you? 'Hey Tony, I'm screwing Robert, so whadda ya know?' Is that what you wanted? That's what you wanted me to tell you? I think *that's* ridiculous.

TONY. But the whole point is that we shouldn't have to lie to each other.

GREG. The whole point is that we should stick together! And if that means we have to lie to each other, then that's fine by me!

TONY. Don't include me in that. I don't lie to you.

GREG. Oh no, you're so fucking virtuous! So paranoid about the truth. It's not such a big deal.

TONY. You really mean that?

GREG. Yeah.

TONY. Well, I don't believe you. You're kidding yourself. Anything to resist feeling guilty. It is a big deal, and you know it.

GREG. Maybe talking about it's not such a good idea.

TONY. Jesus Christ, it makes me look so stupid! How many people know about this? Does William?

GREG. No. No one.

TONY. Is that the truth?

GREG. Of course.

TONY. Of course! Sorry – I'm just being paranoid.

GREG. Of course it's the truth. No one knows.

TONY. Is he the only affair you've had while we've been together?

GREG. Yes.

TONY. Are you sure?

GREG. For Christ's sake!

TONY. How do I know you're telling the truth? Is he the only affair you've had while we've been together? I want to know.

GREG. I've told you – he's the only one.

TONY. You're sure about that, are you?

GREG. Will you stop this?

TONY. Do you love me?

GREG. What?

TONY. I said, do you love me?

GREG. You're gonna carry on like this all night?

TONY. Answer me.

GREG. Cos if you are, I'm going out.

TONY. I've asked you a question.

GREG. Okay, I'm going out.

TONY (*barring his way*). Do you love me?

GREG. Get out of my way.

TONY. Do you love me?

GREG. You know I do.

TONY. But really – do you love me?

GREG. Yes, I really love you. Now get the fuck out of my way.

TONY. No.

GREG. Tony!

TONY. I want to know if you love me.

GREG. I've told you.

TONY. Do you love him?

GREG. Oh shit –

TONY. Do you love him? Tell me.

GREG. Get out of my way, Tony.

TONY. Tell me! Do you love him?

GREG. Move, for fuck's sake!

TONY. Do you?

GREG. Yes.(*Beat.*) Yes, I do.

They are still.

TONY. Well, that certainly has the ring of truth.

TONY *goes to the sofa and sits.* GREG *stays at the door.* TONY *lights a cigarette. Then he half looks back at* GREG.

I thought you were going out.

GREG *goes to him and puts a hand on his shoulder.* TONY *tenses up.* GREG *takes his hand away.*

Is he a good fuck? Is he a better fuck than I am? Is that what it is? I bet he is. I bet he's got a really slack arsehole, hasn't he? I bet he can't get enough of it. Like a cat on heat, waving it around, begging for more. That's it, isn't it?

GREG. No.

TONY. I mean, that's what it basically comes down to, doesn't it?

GREG. It has nothing to do with that.

TONY. And you're prepared to jeopardise our relationship for the gratification of your cock. Because you've found an easier lay than me, you're prepared to ditch us. Who'd have thought that our five years together would eventually stand or fall on the elasticity of my sphincter?

Beat. GREG *returns to his papers. Pause.*

You can go out if you want to. I won't stop you.

GREG. I don't want to go out.

TONY. You said you did.

GREG. Well, now I don't.

Pause.

TONY. I don't feel very well. I feel a bit sick.

GREG. Go to bed, then.

TONY. No. The room'd start spinning. It'd make me throw up. I don't want to spend all night hanging over the lavatory.

Pause. TONY *looks across at* GREG.

You're not concentrating on that. You're only pretending to. (*Beat.*) Aren't you?

GREG. I certainly can't concentrate if you carry on talking.

TONY. You wanted me to talk.

GREG. I think it'd be better if we talked tomorrow.

Pause.

TONY. Greg?

GREG. What?

Beat.

TONY. Are you going to carry on seeing him?

Pause.

GREG. Yes.

TONY. I see. (*Beat.*) So that's it then.

GREG. What do you mean?

TONY. I mean, I'm not going to share you with that little jerk. I want you for myself.

GREG. You want me for yourself?

TONY. Yes.

GREG. How can you say that? You've never had me for yourself, and I've never had you for myself, and I don't want that. I don't want that from anyone. We haven't been faithful to each other ever since we met, and we've both accepted that. At least, I have. So why have you suddenly decided you're not in the mood for sharing? We've shared each other around half the gay scene in London!

TONY. But we haven't fallen in love with half the gay scene in London, have we? They were one-night stands, and that's different from having a four-month affair with a cleaner! You know it is.

GREG. You still think it's just a case of turning a blind eye to one-night stands, don't you? You've never been able to think further than that.

TONY. You seem to have changed the rules somewhere along the line. Since when has it been a case of turning a blind eye to a grubby little liaison –

GREG. Changed the rules? What rules? What rules are you talking about? You want rules? You want us to make promises? Okay, we'll make promises. So we'll never sleep around again. You'd like that, wouldn't you? You'd like not to be able to go to discos and bars with William, wouldn't you?

TONY. I thought you'd have to bring him up.

GREG. Well, he's not exactly a celibate influence, is he? You think I enjoy the prospect of what you two get up to when I have to go away?

TONY. Brilliant! You're the one who's wrecking our relationship and of course it's William's fault!

GREG. I am not wrecking our relationship! Would you think for one minute! There's always been the possibility that things'd change, and you've never been able to accept that. You've said you can, but you can't. But just because they are changing, it doesn't mean they're coming to an end. We can't chuck the whole thing out!

TONY. I am not prepared to share you with anybody. Take it, or leave it.

GREG. I leave it.

TONY. Fine. That's how much you love me!

GREG. You haven't understood a word I've said.

TONY. I've understood everything.

GREG. You're not even trying.

TONY. You're prepared to give me up, and you're not prepared to give him up. That's all there is to understand! But what you'd really like is for me to say, fine, go ahead, have Robert as well, I don't mind, so that you can have your cake and eat it. (*He's on his feet, heading for the drinks table.*)

GREG. Oh shit!! You're not making it any easier for me!

TONY. Was that a cry for sympathy? That really is too much to ask! I seem to remember I'm the one who walked into this room not ten minutes ago to be confronted by our ex-skivvy. Why should it be my responsibility to make anything easier? You should be down on your fucking knees, not standing there giving me lectures on how to conduct relationships.

GREG. Tony –

TONY. Your teaching credits aren't exactly shit-hot at the moment. Why should I listen to someone who thinks with his cock?

GREG. Tony –

TONY. You really are an arrogant bastard! Make it easier for you? Jesus Christ . . . !

They embrace, holding each other tightly.

The only thing I've ever wanted is to be with you. I could do without anything as long as I have you. I can't bear the thought of you looking at anyone else, let alone making love to them. Every time I knew you were with a trick, I felt sick. I tried not to think about it, but I couldn't get it out of my mind. That you'd whisper the same things as you whisper to me, moan in the same way when you came, kiss like you kiss me after it's all over, and hold him in your arms and close your eyes. I can't cope with it any more. I'm tired of all the bars and clubs, tired of looking around, of competing, pretending I need other men when all I want is you. Why don't we stop it now? Why don't we start all over again? We don't need anyone else. Sitting here, cuddled up together, making love. That'd be so nice, wouldn't it, Greg? Wouldn't that make you happy? Just the two of us, together? He wasn't even a good cleaner!

GREG (*still embracing* TONY). You haven't enjoyed me making love to you for the past twelve months –

TONY. That's not true –

GREG. – maybe longer. You used to. It used to be fantastic. But not any more.

TONY. It's just a phase –

GREG. Tony –

TONY. It is. Relationships go in phases. They have their ups and downs. And we're having a down.

GREG. A pretty long down.

TONY. It'll soon go up again.

Beat. They smile.

GREG. Tony, it doesn't bother me, but it bothers you, and it shouldn't. It's making you so unhappy. And that touching little domestic scene you describe, I don't want that – I never have – and you know that. I'm not that person. You've got to accept things as they are, not kid yourself they're like they were, or pretend they're what they've never been. I still love you. I still want us to be together. But I'm not suddenly going to ask you to lay out my pipe and slippers. And I doubt that Robert will suddenly disappear into thin air.

TONY. I can but hope.

GREG *kisses his forehead.*

It's certainly taught me one thing: from now on, I'll always do my own housework! (*Beat.*) Listen, why don't we have a romantic moment on the sofa? Stuff our faces with chocolate cake, wash it down with a large drink, and listen to our favourite music. (*Beat.*) Yes?

GREG. Okay.

TONY. You get the cake. I'll sort it out in here.

GREG *goes into the kitchen.* TONY *pauses a moment. Then he looks through the records. He can't find what he wants. His search becomes more animated. Then he notices the sleeve he's looking for, lying empty. The record is already on the turntable. As he picks up the sleeve,* GREG *comes in from the kitchen, having suddenly realised something.*

GREG. Tony . . .

He stops as he sees TONY *with the sleeve.*

TONY. Obviously, a popular choice.

The phone rings. TONY *leaps to it.*

If that little bastard dares . . . (*He lifts the receiver.*) Yes? (*Beat.*) Oh yes, hello, how are you? . . . No I'm fine, fine . . . Lovely to hear from you . . . You phoned earlier? . . . Ah well, I was out – we were out . . . Yes, just got back in . . . It's going alright – slowly but surely, yes . . . Oh, I can't wait . . . Yes I know I've left it too long but – it's only a few weeks now . . . I'll see you then . . . Yes . . . Yes he is, I'll . . . and to you, yes . . . Hang on . . .

He holds out the receiver to GREG. GREG *takes it.*

GREG. Hello? . . . Mom, hi, how are you? Is anything wrong? . . . No, everything's fine . . . Is Dad okay? . . . Uh-huh . . .

TONY *takes the record off the turntable, replaces it in its sleeve, and puts it back on the shelves as* GREG *continues talking.*

. . . He won! That must be the first time in his life. How much? . . . Twenty dollars, huh? Well, it's a start . . . It'll all go on this call if you're not . . . Hi, Dad, congratulations! . . . Yeah, that's great . . . I know she doesn't approve but . . . You gotta give her some of it . . . Uh-huh . . . Well, if it blocks you up, don't eat it, she won't mind . . . No, no, look this is using up all your money . . . Yeah, we're looking forward to seeing you too . . . Tony's very excited . . . You're gonna meet us at the airport? . . . That's great . . . We'll speak before then, okay? . . . Love to Mom . . . and to you . . . Yeah, I will . . . Bye now.

He replaces the receiver. Pause.

TONY. I'm going to bed. How about you?

GREG. In a while. (*Beat.*) You want some cake?

TONY. No. I'm not hungry. Thank you.

GREG *goes to his papers.*

How long are you going to be?

GREG. Not long.

TONY. See you in a bit, then.

GREG. Yeah.

TONY *goes to the door.*

Oh, by the way, I read your story.

TONY. You did?

GREG. Yeah.

TONY. I didn't think you'd have had the time.

Beat.

GREG. It's quite good. (*Pause.*) I think the central character suffers from being too narrowly defined. He needs a certain – fleshing out. I didn't quite believe in him as a person. (*Beat.*) I think if you're gonna have a character behave so – extremely, you have to have established him sufficiently; you have to – deserve, if you like, the taking of that liberty – with your material. (*Pause.*) You really think I'm like that?

Pause.

TONY. So you think it's only quite good.

GREG. There are many excellent things in it –

TONY. But all these excellent things add up to only quite good.

GREG. Oh shit, Tony, what do you want me to say? It needs more work. You're maybe a little too close to your material. But for Christ's sake, you haven't written that much, so what can you expect? As an early effort, it is quite an achievement.

Pause.

TONY. Well, thank you for having bothered to read it.

GREG. Oh, come on –

TONY. No, no, really. I'm – quite grateful. (*Beat.*) Sorry.
(*Beat.*) So. I'll get ready then.

*As he turns to leave, he notices the dressing gown on the
floor. He picks it up.*

Greg?

GREG. Yeah?

TONY. What you were saying earlier . . . I did understand.
(*Beat.*) But I really don't think I can . . .

Beat.

GREG. What?

Beat.

TONY. It doesn't matter.

*He puts the dressing gown over his shoulder and walks out,
as Voggue's 'Dancin' the Night Away' starts playing.*

SCENE SEVEN

*Voggue fades as the lights come up. Night. The only light
spills in from the street through the window. The front door is
heard being opened. The sound of people entering and walking
along the hall. The door opens. Enter* TONY. *He motions in*
JÜRGEN (*from Hamburg*), *who's dressed entirely in leather.*

TONY. Kalt.

JÜRGEN. Bitte?

TONY. Ja. Sehr kalt.

JÜRGEN. Ach ja.

TONY. Er . . . möchtest du ein . . . er . . . du möchtest . . . er . . .
do you want a drink?

JÜRGEN. Ja.

TONY. Was?

JÜRGEN. Whisky?

TONY. Visky – whisky, ja. Yes. Eissen?

JÜRGEN. Eissen?

TONY. Ice . . . brrr.

JÜRGEN (*shivers*). Ja.

TONY. Nein. In the drinken. The whisky.

JÜRGEN. Ach ja. I want . . . straight up. Not on the rocks.

TONY. Ja. Gut. (*Starts fixing the drinks.*) Du setzest? (*He motions to the sofa.*)

JÜRGEN. Bitte?

TONY. Do you . . . er . . . want to setzen?

JÜRGEN (*sitting on sofa*). Ich verstehe nicht.

TONY. Bitte?

JÜRGEN. Not understand.

TONY. Oh, but you have. You've just done exactly what I wanted you to.

JÜRGEN. Bitte?

TONY. Don't worry. Das ist gut.

JÜRGEN. Ja.

TONY. Ja.

TONY *hands him a drink.*

JÜRGEN. Zum Wohl!

TONY. Cheers!

They drink.

Music . . . Musik?

JÜRGEN. Ja.

TONY. What do you like? Was . . . do you like? Disco?

JÜRGEN. Nein, nein. Zuviel Disco . . . quiet . . .

TONY. Quiet. Ja.

JÜRGEN. Und langsam . . . slow.

TONY. Slow. Quiet and slow. I've got loads of that.

He chooses a record and puts it on – the Adagio of Schubert's Quintet in C (D. 956).

Tell you what . . .

He produces a small electric fire from a corner and sets it up in front of the sofa.

. . . rather than freezing to death . . . The central heating's broken down. Too fucking mean to have it mended. Well, that's his problem . . .

He sits next to JÜRGEN.

Better? Ja?

JÜRGEN. Ja.

TONY. Gut. (*Pause.*) You like this? Musik gut? Ja?

JÜRGEN. Ach ja. Schubert.

TONY. That's right.

JÜRGEN. Sehr schön. Sehr traurig.

TONY. Traurig?

JÜRGEN (*trying to explain*). Ach . . .

TONY. Oh, it doesn't matter. I'm sure you're right.

JÜRGEN looks across at TONY. *He chuckles. He slaps* TONY*'s leg affectionately.* TONY *smiles back, although the slap was somewhat harder than he would have liked.* JÜRGEN *drains his glass.*

Another? . . . ein anderer?

JÜRGEN. Ach . . . nein.

JÜRGEN puts down his glass and puts his arm along the back of the sofa. TONY *looks at him.* JÜRGEN *draws* TONY *into him and kisses him. As he does so, he gradually envelops* TONY. *The kiss goes on for a long time. As their lips part,* TONY *is limp with desire.*

Wohnst du hier allein?

TONY. Pardon? Bitte?

JÜRGEN. You . . . live . . . alone?

TONY. No. Well, yes. Sort of.

> JÜRGEN *doesn't understand.*

> I'm alone . . . allein . . . jetzt . . . at the moment. My
> landlord . . . em . . . nicht hier. Er ist . . . erm . . . on holiday.
> In New York.

JÜRGEN. Ach. New York. Ja. Sehr gut. Grosse Schwänze!
Gute Fickerei! Ja.

TONY. Mmm . . .

JÜRGEN (*trying to explain*). Big cocks . . . good fucking . . .
in New York.

TONY. Yes, I'm sure there is.

JÜRGEN. Ja! Sehr gut! I . . . love . . . New York.

TONY. Anyway, I'm not here for much longer. Ich gehe –

JÜRGEN. New York?

TONY. No. Ich gehe . . . from hier . . . next week. Ich . . . move
in with . . . a friend . . . mit einem Freunde. Ja! Ich . . . move
in with a friend . . . next week. Oh fuck it, it doesn't matter.

JÜRGEN. Ja.

> TONY *kisses him. During the kiss,* JÜRGEN *fondles*
> TONY*'s crotch and arse. Their lips part.*

TONY. You, and Schubert – who needs conversation?

JÜRGEN. Bitte?

TONY. You don't understand a word I'm saying, do you?

JÜRGEN. Verstehe nicht.

> *He chuckles and starts kissing* TONY*'s neck. During the*
> *following speech, he works thoroughly over* TONY*'s body,*
> *and even though* TONY *continues speaking, with hardly*
> *any inflection, it obviously turns* TONY *on a lot.*

TONY. I could say – you're faintly ludicrous . . . You leave me
cold . . . (*Moans with pleasure.*)

JÜRGEN (*briefly taking his mouth from* TONY's *body*). Gut . . .
gut . . .

TONY. Ja . . . oh ja . . . If you don't get off me this instant,
I am going to break that glass and rub it into your neck –
you disgust me . . . oh . . .

JÜRGEN. . . . Gut . . . gut . . .

TONY. Oh ja . . . mm . . . You think you're so good, don't
you? . . . I wonder how many arses you've fucked . . .
hundreds . . . thousands . . . and mine will be one more
notch on your cock – if you're lucky . . . Oh . . .

JÜRGEN. . . . Ja . . .

TONY. Mm . . . I think you once appeared to me – during a
wank . . . And very like what I dreamt of – when Greg
was making love to me . . . Oh . . . I could even say I love
you –

Suddenly JÜRGEN *lifts his head.*

JÜRGEN. Was?

TONY. What is it?

JÜRGEN. Du liebst mich? You . . . love . . . me?

TONY. Oh no! I mean, I like you. But no, I don't love you.

JÜRGEN. Gut! Me . . . no love . . . I don't like.

TONY. No. It is a nuisance, isn't it?

JÜRGEN. I had . . . love. He . . . verheiratet, verheiratet . . .
ach . . . eine Frau . . . woman.

TONY. Went off with a woman?

JÜRGEN. Ja.

TONY. How irritating!

JÜRGEN. Und ich . . . ich . . . (*Mimes slashing wrists.*)

TONY. Oh no! It's never worth it. (*Looks for the scars.*) I can't
see any scars . . .

JÜRGEN. Nein. Ich war . . . scare?

TONY. Scared?

JÜRGEN. Ja.

TONY. Frightened. You were too frightened. Thank God for that, otherwise I'd have been at a loose end tonight –

JÜRGEN. Und now . . . no more love . . . never!

JÜRGEN holds TONY's head between his hands and kisses him. He pulls TONY into him. Pause.

TONY. You can't say that. I can see why you should but – no, you can't say that.

JÜRGEN: 'Ich liebe dich.' Die ganze Zeit, hat er gesagt, 'Ich liebe dich.' Ich liebe dich!

He runs his fingers through TONY's hair. Pause.

TONY. Ich liebe dich.

Pause.

JÜRGEN. Schubert hat dieses Stück in seinem letzten Lebensjahr geschrieben, als er erst einunddreissig war. Unglaublich, nicht?

Beat.

TONY. Now you've completely lost me.

Beat.

Sorry, I don't know your name.

JÜRGEN. Bitte?

TONY. It's not important.

The lights are fading as the music plays on.

This is so nice.

JÜRGEN. Gut, ja?

TONY. Oh yes. Sehr, sehr gut.

They remain still and close together in the warm red glow of the electric fire. And, slowly, that fades to black.

End.

MY NIGHT WITH REG

For

Michael Burlington
(1949-1985)

and

Andrei Tooth
(1950-1987)

By eight o'clock all was over, and nothing remained
except darkness as on any other night, always.

Giuseppe di Lampedusa, *The Leopard,*
translated by Archibald Colquhoun

My Night with Reg was first performed at the Royal Court
Theatre, London, on 31 March 1994. The cast was as follows:

JOHN	Anthony Calf
GUY	David Bamber
ERIC	Joe Duttine
DANIEL	John Sessions
BERNIE	Roger Frost
BENNY	Kenneth MacDonald

Director Roger Michell
Designer William Dudley
Lighting Designer Jon Linstrum
Sound Designer Paul Arditti

The production transferred with the same cast to the Criterion
Theatre, London, produced by Royal Court Theatre Productions
in association with Bill Kenwright, on 15 November 1994.
The following cast took over on 15 May 1995:

JOHN	Richard Lintern
GUY	Jason Watkins
ERIC	Scott Ransome
DANIEL	Hugh Bonneville
BERNIE	Roger Sloman
BENNY	Kenneth MacDonald

The production transferred to the Playhouse Theatre, London,
on 27 June 1995.

Characters

JOHN, *mid-thirties*

GUY, *mid-thirties*

ERIC, *eighteen*

DANIEL, *mid-thirties*

BERNIE, *mid-forties*

BENNY, *late thirties*

Setting

Guy's flat. Ground floor. Sitting room. A conservatory adjoins it, leading into the garden.

SCENE ONE

*'Every Breath You Take' by The Police starts playing. As
the lights come up, the music fades. Late afternoon. Cloudy.*
ERIC *is painting a window-frame in the conservatory. He's
listening to a Walkman.* JOHN *and* GUY *are standing in the
sitting room.* GUY *is wearing an apron.*

JOHN. Am I early?

GUY. No.

JOHN. I couldn't remember what time you said.

GUY. You're not, really.

> JOHN *glances at the apron.* GUY *suddenly remembers he's
> wearing it.*

> (*Taking it off.*) I was just stiffening some egg whites.

JOHN. You look well.

GUY. Do I?

JOHN. Yes.

GUY. I've been to Lanzarote.

JOHN. Oh.

GUY. You look well, too.

JOHN. Thanks.

GUY. You don't look a day older.

JOHN. Well –

GUY. You don't, honestly. You're just the same.

JOHN. It's been a year or two, hasn't it?

GUY. Nine-and-a-half, actually.

JOHN. God!

GUY. When we passed each other on the escalator at Camden Town.

JOHN. Yeah.

GUY. I'm so surprised to see you.

ERIC (*singing along with his tape*). 'Baby, baby, please . . . '

GUY. He was supposed to have finished yesterday.

JOHN. I've got the right day, haven't I?

GUY. Oh yes. It's just that when I phoned, it sounded like you weren't going to be able to make it. I'm really pleased you have. Would you like a drink?

JOHN. Scotch. Thanks.

> GUY *puts the apron in a drawer on his way to the drinks table.*

GUY. Anything with it?

JOHN. As it comes.

GUY. Ice?

JOHN. No.

GUY. Straight?

JOHN. Yes.

GUY. Right.

> *He pours two scotches.*

JOHN. Is it one of the Balearics?

GUY. What?

JOHN. Lanzarote.

GUY. Canaries.

JOHN. Oh.

GUY. But I know what you mean. Sort of interchangeable, aren't they?

JOHN. Was it fun?

GUY. Yes. Well, sort of.

He hands him a drink.

JOHN. Cheers!

GUY. Cheers!

They drink.

I've got a bit of bad news, actually.

JOHN. Have you?

GUY. I'm afraid Daniel's had to cry off at the last minute. I'd have let you know, but as it seemed unlikely you were going to come –

JOHN. It's okay. I know.

GUY. Do you?

JOHN. I bumped into Reg last night. At a film.

GUY. Oh.

JOHN. He's gone to Sydney, hasn't he?

GUY. Yes. Some sheep-farmer reckons he's found a Pissarro in his shed. At least, Daniel thinks that's what he said. So you don't mind?

JOHN. No.

GUY. Good. It'd have been fun, though, wouldn't it? The three of us together after all this time. You don't feel you're here under false pretences, then?

JOHN. Of course not. Why should I?

GUY. Well, Daniel's your old mate, isn't he? You've kept in touch –

JOHN. On and off.

GUY. Whereas we . . . How was the film?

JOHN. It wasn't up to much. Two hours of French people talking. I couldn't see the point.

GUY. What was it?

ERIC (*singing with his tape*). 'I'll be watching you . . . '

GUY. Would you like a nut?

JOHN. I'm okay, thanks.

GUY. No, I meant to put them out.

> *He goes out.* JOHN *glances at* ERIC. GUY *enters with a bowl of nuts which he puts on the coffee table.*

> Help yourself.

JOHN (*taking out a packet of cigarettes*). Do you?

GUY. No.

JOHN. Do you mind if I do?

GUY. Not at all. I'll find the ashtray.

> *He goes out again as* JOHN *lights a cigarette.* GUY *returns with an ashtray.*

> Anyway, Reg is still coming, so . . . He's not exactly the life and soul, but I sort of like him. Do you?

JOHN. Yeah.

GUY. And they seem very happy together. What did he make of the film?

JOHN. I'm not sure. It's a nice flat.

GUY. Do you think so?

JOHN. Yes.

GUY. I must say, I'm really quite pleased with it. In fact, I was thinking the other night, I don't see why I should ever have to move again.

JOHN. I could never think that.

GUY. You're not the settling type though, are you? Well, you weren't. Sit down, please.

JOHN. You don't have to be polite, you know.

GUY. No. Sorry.

> JOHN *flops into an armchair.*

> You always used to do that.

JOHN. What?

GUY. Sort of hurl yourself at furniture.

JOHN. Oh, I'm sorry –

GUY. No, no. It's just – seeing it again . . .

ERIC (*singing with his tape*). 'I feel so cold and I long for your embrace . . . '

GUY (*sidling towards the conservatory*). Eric.

No response.

Eric.

ERIC (*lifting his earphones*). Eh?

GUY. How's it going?

ERIC. Done in a tick.

GUY. Only it's getting on –

ERIC. No worries.

He replaces his earphones and carries on. Meanwhile, JOHN's been fidgeting in his chair. He feels behind a cushion and produces a long, tubular piece of knitting. GUY clocks this.

GUY. Oh –

JOHN. I thought I felt something.

GUY (*taking it off him*). Sorry.

JOHN. What is it?

GUY (*putting it in a drawer*). A cover for my door-sausage, actually.

JOHN. Oh.

Beat.

Do you do a lot of knitting?

GUY. No. Well, from time to time. I find it quite therapeutic.

JOHN. Really?

GUY. A sort of lust-depressant.

JOHN. Why would you need that?

GUY. Well . . . with things as they are . . .

JOHN. You haven't given it up, have you?

GUY. No, no. I think it's given me up, to tell you the truth. But one does need to be careful. Don't you think? You didn't mind me ringing, did you?

JOHN. No.

GUY. Only I remember Daniel saying you'd popped round for dinner some months ago and, as I was having this little do, I thought it'd be nice if you came, so I got your number off him. I was quite surprised to get you. Daniel said you've been difficult to get hold of recently. He thought you may have gone away.

JOHN. No. I've been around. But I'm not that clever at keeping in touch.

GUY. He said you weren't – disappearing for a few years, then suddenly reappearing on the doorstep.

JOHN. Yeah.

GUY. So what have you been up to?

JOHN. In what way?

GUY. Any way, really.

JOHN. Travelled a bit, hung around a bit. Fuck all, actually. And you?

GUY. Oh, plodding along – as you do . . .

Beat.

JOHN. I was thinking – on my way over . . .

GUY. Yes?

JOHN. That play we did for DramSoc –

GUY. *The Bacchae*?

JOHN. Yes.

GUY. Christ!

JOHN. It was good.

GUY. Did you think so?

JOHN. Well . . . it was a laugh.

GUY. You were ever so good as Dionysus.

JOHN. Oh –

GUY. No, you were. Especially as it was your first role.

JOHN. And last! That bloody jockstrap you made me do it in! My balls kept falling out.

GUY. Oh yes . . .

He sips his drink.

JOHN. And the chorus! Finished me every night. All those Danny La Rues miming to a tape.

GUY. Marlene Dietrichs, actually.

JOHN. Were they?

GUY. A Classics professor thought it was 'truly Euripidean'.

JOHN. Daniel thought it was crap. Wrongly, in my opinion.

GUY. That was sour grapes. He was so cross I didn't give him Agave.

JOHN. I'd forgotten that.

GUY. It was such a coup getting you.

JOHN. Why?

GUY. Well, you know . . . Do you still play rugby?

JOHN. No.

GUY. You look fit.

JOHN. That's because I go to the gym. I can't face getting old.

GUY. You're not old. None of us are.

ERIC (*singing with his tape*). 'I hope my legs don't break . . . '

JOHN *glances at* ERIC.

GUY. We're not.

JOHN (*referring to his glass*). Could I?

GUY. Please.

He takes the glass to the drinks table.

JOHN. I'll go and get some. I forgot.

GUY. There's no need to. I've got loads.

JOHN. No, I will.

GUY. There's no need, really. So what are you actually up to now? Workwise.

JOHN. Nothing much. Well, nothing at all. I'm not sure I see the point if you don't have to.

GUY. Of course, your father died, didn't he?

JOHN. Yeah, and Mum died a few years ago.

GUY. I'm sorry.

JOHN. Just in time, really, cos I'd nearly got through what Dad left me.

GUY. Oh.

He hands him a drink.

Cheers!

JOHN. Cheers!

He drinks.

I sometimes think about investing in a pub – or a restaurant, maybe.

GUY. You need something, don't you?

JOHN. I dabbled in sports gear for a while. Ages ago. But I couldn't get into it. Got a bit restless. Of course now I've got a stake in the Holland Park pad. We'll probably sell it; it's too big for me, and my brother and sister don't want it: they're both very respectably married and into heavy breeding. They see me as the family reprobate.

GUY. Do they?

JOHN. Which I am. And what about you, workwise?

GUY. Oh, it's not very interesting. I did a bit of this and that and ended up as a copywriter, which is what I still am. Well, you probably know through Daniel.

JOHN. Yeah . . . And what about the sentimental side of things?

GUY. The odd near-miss. I thought we might eat outside.

JOHN. It's going to piss down.

GUY. Daniel mentioned you'd met someone.

JOHN. Did he?

GUY. Yes. An air-steward?

JOHN. Oh! That was way back. He pissed off with a pilot. I don't know why I bothered. I fucking hate air-stewards at the best of times: false tans, false smiles, wiggling their bottoms in everyone's face.

GUY. And that's before they get on the plane.

JOHN *laughs.* ERIC *looks round. They drink.*

JOHN. So do you enjoy living alone?

GUY. Yes. Do you?

JOHN. Yes.

Beat.

Guy?

GUY. What?

Beat.

JOHN. I'll go and get a bottle.

GUY. No, don't. There's plenty. Really.

Beat. JOHN *lights a cigarette as* ERIC *appears at the conservatory entrance.*

ERIC. Got any turps?

GUY. Turps. Yes.

He goes out.

ERIC. Only I left in a bit of a rush. Forgot me rags an' all.

Beat.

JOHN. What you listening to?

ERIC. The Police.

JOHN. Oh.

ERIC. D'you like them?

JOHN. I think I did . . .

ERIC. They're great.

Beat.

JOHN. Birmingham?

ERIC. How did you know?

JOHN. Been down here long?

ERIC. Six months nearly. I live with my aunty.

Beat.

I don't see her much. (*Re. the conservatory.*) Nice, isn't it?

JOHN. Yes.

ERIC. I've painted all this, you know.

Enter GUY *with turps.*

GUY. That's it, I'm afraid.

ERIC. Ta.

GUY. Would you like a drink?

ERIC. Not while I'm on the job. But thank you for asking.

He returns to the conservatory, replaces his earphones and starts clearing up.

GUY. He's a bit slow, but very good. There's nothing he can't put his hand to. It's quite a small do. I hope you don't get bored.

JOHN. Course I won't.

GUY. It's funny – glancing through the names in my address book, I realised I didn't like most of them and the ones I did like had either split up or died – well, one of them had. Of the ones who'd split up, I couldn't decide which partner to invite and the dead friend – she was no problem at all, so we're down to five. Apart from us two and Reg, there'll be

Benny and Bernie. You won't know them. Neither does Reg.
Daniel's met them a few times, but . . . I met them at The
Frog and Trumpet, where Eric works part-time. In fact, they
put me onto him. Bernie's quite nice. A bit odd, mind you.
He sells plastic cups. I think you'll like Benny, though. He
drives a bus. It's more of a token gathering, but I thought
it'd be nice to – wet the baby's head, so to speak. My little
flat. It's such a shame Daniel can't make it.

JOHN. Yeah.

GUY. God, the two of you!

JOHN. A bit out of order, weren't we?

GUY. It never seemed to stop.

JOHN. Should've graduated in shafting. I might have got a
First, then.

GUY. And the rivalry! Whoever you had, Daniel had to have,
and vice versa.

JOHN. Yeah.

GUY. Anyway . . .

Beat.

Would you like to see the garden?

The doorbell rings.

(*Looking at his watch.*) I don't believe it!

JOHN. I knew I'd got it wrong.

GUY. No, no, you haven't. Honestly.

He goes out. JOHN *gets up and checks himself in a mirror.*
The sound of the front door being opened.

(*Off.*) Daniel!

JOHN *freezes.*

DANIEL (*off*). Gert!

GUY (*off*). You're supposed to be in Sydney.

DANIEL (*off*). I know!

GUY (*off*). Guess who's here!

DANIEL bursts in with a bag. JOHN opens his arms.

JOHN. Dan!

DANIEL. Juanita!

They embrace extravagantly. ERIC clocks this.

What the fuck are you doing here? Don't tell me – you got the time wrong.

JOHN. I knew I had.

GUY. You haven't.

DANIEL. Very early, very late or very absent. You old poof!

JOHN. Not old!

They embrace again. DANIEL mauls JOHN's backside.

DANIEL. Darling, it's dropped!

JOHN. Fuck off.

DANIEL. Dropped, dropped, dropped! At least two inches! It'll be dragging on the floor before the night's out.

JOHN tweaks one of DANIEL's nipples. DANIEL shrieks. ERIC looks on.

No, it hasn't. It's perfect. I promise!

JOHN lets go.

The Flying Fuck of the First Fifteen!

They embrace again.

Darling, be gentle. I'm still intacta.

JOHN. How are you?

DANIEL. Earthbound. The plane wouldn't work. Why haven't you phoned?

JOHN. You know what I'm like.

DANIEL. It's months. You promised faithfully. (*To* GUY.) It's a miracle he's here. (*Extending an arm to* GUY.) Gertie!

GUY goes to DANIEL, who puts his arms round them both.

The Beverleys live! I've got just the thing.

He goes to his bag and clocks ERIC.

(*Mouthing.*) Who is that?

GUY. Eric.

DANIEL (*mouthing*). To die!

He takes a bottle of champagne from his bag and starts to open it.

Gertie, get the glasses! Warm as shit, but fuck it!

GUY *grabs three glasses.*

(*Re.* ERIC.) Would your friend like some?

GUY. He's busy.

The cork pops and champagne sprays.

DANIEL (*to* JOHN). Always reminds me of you.

He starts pouring.

Hideously naff to do it like that, but why drink it if you don't flaunt it?

JOHN. I ought to get some.

GUY. There's no need.

DANIEL. Don't tell me, you forgot to bring a bottle. Quelle surprise! Well, at least you got the right address.

JOHN *cuffs his ear.*

Ow! (*Raising his glass.*) Gross indecency!

JOHN & GUY. Gross indecency!

They drink.

GUY. I can't believe this. We were just saying what a shame you couldn't be here. Actually, why are you here?

DANIEL (*singing*). 'Didn't know what time it was, the lights were low-oh-oh, I leaned back on my radio-oh-oh . . . '

JOHN *picks it up.*

DANIEL & JOHN. 'Some cat was layin' down some rock'n'roll, lotta soul, he said . . . '

DANIEL (*con emozione*). 'There's a starman waiting in the sky . . . '

JOHN. You've skipped a bit.

DANIEL (*regardlessly*). 'He'd like to come and meet us . . . '

JOHN *rejoins. Also* GUY, *tentatively.*

DANIEL, JOHN & GUY. 'But he thinks he'd blow our minds, There's a starman waiting in the sky . . . '

DANIEL (*refilling their glasses*). This is heaven on a stick. My little playmates! (*Raising his glass.*) Sodomy!

JOHN & GUY. Sodomy!

They drink.

DANIEL. Colston Hall!

JOHN. Jesus!

DANIEL. You were with Freddie –

JOHN. No, you were with Freddie. I was with Barry.

DANIEL. No, I was with Barry. We'd done a swap. I was with Freddie the night before.

JOHN. Were you?

DANIEL (*to* GUY). Who were you with?

GUY. I was in the gallery. We could only get two pairs and a single –

DANIEL. Then we all went on to the Moulin Rouge –

JOHN. And you lost a contact lens!

DANIEL. That's right!

GUY. And you brought the club to a halt crawling around on all fours in your Ziggy gear –

DANIEL. And I found it in my gin-and-tonic!

JOHN. Jesus!

DANIEL (*singing*). 'If we can sparkle he may land toni-i-ight . . . '

GUY. But why aren't you in Sydney?

DANIEL. We were stuck on the runway for three hours, then shoved into an hotel that made Treblinka seem like paradise, with the promise of a morning take-off. But when I woke up, I thought fuck this for a game of old fairies, got myself on a flight this evening and popped back home to give Reg the most gorgeous surprise which, of course, I did. He was like a startled rabbit and up me before I'd grounded my Gucci. What am I like? It's nearly a year and I'm still besotted. (*To* JOHN.) You've got that look about you.

JOHN. What do you mean?

DANIEL. Don't you think, Guy? I could always tell when you'd been at it. Have you just left a trick panting for more?

JOHN. Have I fuck!

DANIEL. You can't fool me. You have the most lingering post-coital glow of anyone I know. It's absolutely unmistakable. At university you were glowing for three solid years.

GUY. You both were.

DANIEL. I bet my bippy you've had it off in the past twenty-four hours.

JOHN. I wish I had, but believe it or not, I do occasionally do other things. Like seeing my accountant who's just spent the past few hours giving me a gentle bollocking.

GUY. And going to the cinema. You were there last night, weren't you?

JOHN. That's right.

GUY. Reg can vouch for it.

DANIEL. Reg?

JOHN. We bumped into each other.

DANIEL. Really?

JOHN. Yeah.

DANIEL. He never said. Mind you, we didn't talk much. Major rogering, then he had to piss off. What the fuck were you doing at a Rohmer retrospective? I thought you only liked films with naked men and gratuitous violence.

JOHN. I do. It bored my bum off.

GUY. How long have you got?

DANIEL. About forty years, God willing!

He checks his watch and goes to his bag.

(Mouthing – re. ERIC.) Gorgeous!

He takes out a gift and gives it to GUY.

Happy flatwarming, pet!

He kisses him.

GUY *(opening it)*. Thank you. *(Taking out a glossy hardback.)* *Solo Banquets*. You are sweet.

He kisses DANIEL.

DANIEL. Not that you need it; you're the best cook I know. But look who wrote it.

GUY. Gertrude Pinner. *(Laughing.)* Daniel!

DANIEL. And look at the back.

GUY *does so.*

She's doing something ferocious with a meringue and a pile of kumquats.

GUY. Shit! The egg whites! Oh, they'll have to wait.

JOHN. Is that my fault?

GUY. Of course not.

DANIEL. It's bound to be. I don't know what you're talking about, but it's bound to be.

JOHN *cuffs him again.*

Would you stop that? I'll get Reg onto you.

GUY. I'm afraid I haven't got any more champagne, but I think I've got most other things.

JOHN. I wouldn't mind another scotch.

DANIEL. I'll have whatever the big boys are having.

GUY *prepares three scotches.*

(*To* JOHN.) So what've you been up to? Don't tell me –
counting the wrinkles, trying to shed a few years at the gym
and squandering the family fortune. The idle rich!

JOHN. You can talk!

DANIEL. Some of us have to work. We're not all Harriet
Inheritance.

GUY *distributes the drinks.*

JOHN. Cheers!

GUY. Cheers!

DANIEL. Indecent exposure!

JOHN & GUY. Indecent exposure!

They drink.

DANIEL. Are you cooking something simply sensational?

GUY. It's nothing much.

DANIEL. You're the only person I know who could do a
Sunday roast on a Baby Belling.

JOHN. You made us some great meals.

GUY. Someone had to feed you. Beans and beer were all you
ever seemed to have – foodwise.

DANIEL. I wish I could stay. Who else is coming?

GUY. Just Benny and Bernie.

DANIEL. Treat in store! Bernie redefines boredom –

GUY. He's not that bad.

DANIEL. Completely barking, but Benny! The Dick of Death!

JOHN. How do you know?

DANIEL. Impossible not to. You could tell his religion through
a kaftan. That man is awash with testosterone. And you
should see him drive his bus! I had the misfortune to be on
it once. Never again! I was sitting on top, screaming.

JOHN. Wouldn't be the first time.

DANIEL (*hitting him*). Harlot!

> *The phone rings.* DANIEL *instantly answers it.*

> Our Lady of Sorrows STD clinic. Can I help you?

GUY. Daniel!

DANIEL. Yes, he is. Who shall I say's calling? . . . Oh! (*Passing the phone to* GUY.) It's Brad.

GUY. Hello . . . It's a bit difficult at the moment . . . Have you? . . . I'll phone later, alright? . . . Bye.

> *He replaces the receiver.*

> Drinks alright?

DANIEL. So that was Brad, eh?

GUY. Yeah.

DANIEL. Sounded a bit breathy to me.

GUY. Did he?

JOHN. Who's Brad?

GUY. He's no one.

DANIEL. Come on, Gert!

GUY. Daniel!

DANIEL. They talk to each other. Over the phone.

JOHN. Talk to each other?

DANIEL. You know.

JOHN. Like dirty?

DANIEL. Would you say dirty, Gertie?

GUY. No. Well, yes. Filthy, actually, but there's more to it than that. Well, a bit more. He lives in Theydon Bois.

DANIEL. I've heard it's charming.

GUY. A lorry-driver, so he says. I suspect he's a florist, but what's it matter?

JOHN. Have you met him?

GUY. No. Probably never will. Would you like a top-up?

JOHN. What do you talk about?

GUY. Nothing, really.

DANIEL. Gert!

GUY. Daniel, please!

DANIEL. Brad wants to be housetrained.

JOHN. Housetrained?

GUY. Daniel!

JOHN. How can you housetrain him over the phone?

GUY (*to* DANIEL). You bastard!

DANIEL. Do share!

GUY. I just tell him what to do and he does it, alright?

JOHN. Like what?

GUY. I don't want to talk about it.

JOHN. And how do you know he's doing what you've told him to?

GUY. I don't. But I do hear a lot of panting and he has been known to let out the occasional bark.

JOHN *and* DANIEL *burst out laughing.*

It's a fantasy, for Christ's sake! I'm not entering him for Crufts.

DANIEL (*putting his arm round* GUY). Darling, don't be cross! You know we love you. And I must say, you're looking gorgeous. Isn't he, Jonty? Lampedusa obviously did you the world of good.

GUY. Lanzarote.

DANIEL. That's right. Did you manage to get your end away?

GUY. That's not why I went.

DANIEL. I know, but did you?

GUY. I'm not telling you.

DANIEL. So who was it with?

GUY. Daniel!

DANIEL. He's practically taken the veil, you know.

GUY. I haven't.

DANIEL. He's taking safety to an extreme. You know he masturbates in Marigolds?

GUY. This isn't true –

DANIEL. And he won't look at pornography without a condom over his head.

GUY. I'm just trying to be careful, that's all. And I'm trying not to think about it all the time, which is why I find things to distract me.

JOHN. Like knitting.

DANIEL. And a man who thinks he's a dog.

GUY. I wouldn't expect you to understand. And at least it's safe.

DANIEL. Meanwhile, back in Lanzarote –

GUY. Honestly –

DANIEL. You met this man –

GUY. Daniel –

DANIEL. Mm?

GUY. Well, if you must know . . .

DANIEL. Yes?

GUY. I did.

DANIEL. Oh!

GUY. Only for one night, mind you.

DANIEL. And?

GUY. That's it.

DANIEL. What happened?

GUY. It wasn't very pleasant, actually.

DANIEL. Why not?

GUY. He took advantage of me.

JOHN. How?

GUY. Well, I was a bit drunk, you see, and he forced himself on me. I couldn't do much about it.

JOHN. What a bastard!

GUY. And the worst thing was, he didn't use any protection. Can you imagine? I mean, how irresponsible! I couldn't stop thinking about it. It spoiled the rest of my holiday.

DANIEL. Was he a native?

GUY. No. A mortician from Swindon.

DANIEL and JOHN giggle.

It isn't funny, Daniel!

DANIEL. Fancy dying in Swindon!

JOHN. Only thing to do there.

GUY. Swindon's hardly the point.

ERIC has appeared at the conservatory entrance.

ERIC. 'Scuse me.

GUY. How are you getting on?

ERIC. No worries. I've just wound my tape back.

GUY. Oh.

ERIC (*to* JOHN). If you wanted to have a listen. Just the first track, like. It's great.

Beat.

JOHN. Okay.

Looks are exchanged between him, DANIEL and GUY, as he goes to ERIC. ERIC leads him into the conservatory and puts the earphones on him. He starts the tape and watches JOHN's reaction. Meanwhile:

GUY. I can't believe he's here! When I asked him, he more or less said no. I nearly died when he turned up. He's just the same, isn't he?

DANIEL. Is he?

GUY. Twelve years! Apart from that time we passed each other in Camden Town. He's exactly as I remember him.

DANIEL. Have you told him you've still got his jockstrap?

GUY. Of course I haven't.

DANIEL. It must be dreadfully rancid by now.

GUY. I can hardly breathe.

DANIEL. Pull yourself together, Gert! It was a post-schoolboy crush. You can't spend the rest of your life lusting after someone you never see.

GUY. I know it's stupid, but . . . You don't really believe me, do you? You don't think it's possible.

DANIEL. And he's hardly reliable. Adorable, but completely irresponsible. The last person to have a relationship with.

GUY. That's not even on the cards.

DANIEL. Then what is on the cards?

GUY. I don't know!

DANIEL. Are you going to tell him?

GUY. No. I can't.

DANIEL. Why not? He can only tell you to fuck off or laugh in your face.

GUY. That party.

DANIEL. What party?

GUY. The last night of *The Bacchae*.

DANIEL. Did I ever tell you how vile I thought it was?

GUY. It was the only time he really talked to me. It wasn't like when the three of us were together. We were sitting up in the flies with a bottle of wine and he just opened up. He talked about everything and then he said something that . . . I just know he was hinting that we should do it and – I don't know why – I hedged around, probably because I was so taken aback. I mean, I was being offered the only thing in the world that I've ever wanted.

DANIEL. And then Pentheus found you and proceeded to puke up, if memory serves. Hardly surprising, considering the production he'd just been in.

GUY. I go over that moment again and again. The biggest regret of my life.

DANIEL. Well, maybe there'll be another moment tonight. You're the host – assert yourself. I doubt you'll end up wed, but if you get him pissed enough, he might let you blow him off behind the Yucca.

JOHN *removes the earphones.*

ERIC. What d'you think?

JOHN. It's nice.

ERIC. D'you like it?

JOHN. Yeah.

ERIC. I told you it was good.

JOHN. Thanks.

ERIC. Cheers.

ERIC *returns to his clearing up, while* JOHN *returns to the sitting room.*

DANIEL. Life-changing moment?

JOHN. Quite cute, isn't he?

DANIEL. I'd eat his shit for breakfast. No, I didn't mean that. Well, not really. You are looking at a new man: Monica Monogamy, that's moi. (*To* GUY.) You will look after Reg, won't you? You know he's a bit shy. My little Rinaldo.

GUY. Who?

DANIEL. Reg.

GUY. Rinaldo?

DANIEL. That's his name. Isn't it sweet? But he hates it. Insists on being Anglicised. Well, that's Americans for you. Tell him I love him. Appassionatamente!

GUY. Alright.

DANIEL. The Antipodes beckon.

GUY. I'm so pleased you came.

DANIEL. Gert!

They embrace.

GUY. And thanks for the book.

DANIEL. Major pleasure.

GUY. I hope the sheep-farmer doesn't disappoint you.

DANIEL. If he does, there's always the sheep. And fuck it, it's a trip. Juanita!

He embraces JOHN.

JOHN. It's great to see you again, Dan.

DANIEL. If you don't keep in touch –

JOHN. I will. Honestly.

DANIEL. I've never believed a word you've said, but I still adore you.

They kiss.

JOHN. Have a good time!

DANIEL. And you. Both of you.

He picks up his bag and goes to the conservatory entrance.

(To ERIC.*)* Bye!

ERIC. See you.

DANIEL. I think you're doing the most marvellous job.

ERIC. Ta.

DANIEL. My pleasure.

He goes to the door, GUY *following.*

Just one word, Gert.

GUY. What's that?

DANIEL. Yucca!

GUY *pushes him out.* JOHN *lights a cigarette. He and* ERIC *glance at each other. The sound of the front door being opened.*

(*Off.*) I'll phone you when I get back. Happy flatwarming, darling!

GUY (*off*). Bye.

DANIEL (*off*). 'There's a starman waiting in the sky . . . '

GUY (*off*). You'll miss your plane.

DANIEL (*off*). Ciao!

The front door's closed. GUY *re-enters.*

GUY. Well!

JOHN. Look out, Sydney!

GUY. Unbelievable! I mean, just when I was saying what a shame it was the three of us –

JOHN (*re. his glass*). Could I?

GUY (*going to take the glass*). Of course.

JOHN (*going to the drinks table*). It's okay.

He pours a scotch.

Would you like one?

GUY. No. I think I'm alright, thanks.

JOHN. If you want to get on –

GUY. It's fine. All in hand.

JOHN. Don't let me stop you.

GUY. No, it's fine.

JOHN *suddenly covers his face with his hand.*

John?

He seems to be crying.

Are you alright?

ERIC *glances at* JOHN, *then carries on with his work.*

JOHN. Christ, I haven't . . .

GUY. What?

JOHN. For years . . .

GUY. John, what is it?

JOHN. Guy . . .

> *Beat. Then* GUY *goes to him and tentatively puts an arm round him.* JOHN *instantly embraces him, crying freely.* GUY *returns the embrace.*

> You're the only one . . . Guy . . . you're the only one . . .

GUY. What are you er . . . ?

JOHN. The only one, Guy . . .

GUY. John . . . ?

> JOHN *can't speak for crying.* GUY *doesn't know what's happening. Then he cautiously strokes* JOHN's *hair.*

> It's alright . . . (*Getting tearful himself.*) It's alright . . .

> *He strokes* JOHN's *hair more confidently as* JOHN *tries to speak. Then:*

JOHN. Last night . . .

GUY. Yes?

JOHN. Last night . . .

GUY. You were at the pictures.

JOHN. Yeah, and er . . .

GUY. What?

JOHN. Reg . . .

GUY. You bumped into him.

JOHN. Yeah . . . No, I . . .

GUY. You didn't bump into him.

JOHN. No . . . Shit!

GUY. It's okay . . .

JOHN. We met . . .

GUY. Yes?

JOHN. Like, we meant to . . .

GUY. Yes?

JOHN. We spent the night together . . .

Beat.

I haven't cried for years . . . not for years . . .

Beat.

GUY. You spent the night together?

JOHN. Yes . . . Oh, Guy . . . I love him . . .

GUY. After one night?

JOHN. After nine months –

GUY. Nine months?

JOHN. We've been seeing each other since that dinner party – when we first met . . .

Beat.

You're the only one, Guy . . . the only one I could tell this to.

Beat.

GUY. Oh. I see.

Beat. They gradually get out of the embrace. JOHN searches his pockets.

JOHN. Fuck!

GUY (*searching his own pockets*). It's okay.

Finding nothing, he goes to a drawer and pulls out the apron. He hands it to JOHN.

Sorry, it's . . .

JOHN (*taking it and wiping his eyes*). Thank you. I only came because I thought he was in Sydney. He's my best mate. I know I never see him – well, hardly ever, but . . . I can't face him.

Beat.

GUY. Then why don't you er . . . you and Reg . . . stop it?

JOHN. We've talked about it, but it's not that easy, Guy . . . when you're in love . . . to let go.

Beat.

GUY. No. I suppose not.

JOHN. You won't tell Reg, will you?

GUY. What?

JOHN. That I've told you. He doesn't want anyone to know. So you won't, will you?

Beat.

GUY. No. Look, I'd better go into the kitchen.

JOHN. Your egg whites.

GUY. Yes . . . and I've got to skim the consommé.

JOHN *suddenly embraces him tightly.*

JOHN. You're a friend.

Beat.

GUY. Yes.

ERIC*'s standing at the conservatory entrance.*

ERIC. All done.

They look at him. GUY *walks out.*

Have I . . . ?

JOHN. No. So you're not joining us?

ERIC. 'Fraid not. I'm standing in for Eric.

JOHN. Eric?

ERIC. He lets me run it when he's off. He's very good like that.

JOHN. I thought you were Eric.

ERIC. I am. He's the landlord. Frog and Trumpet.

JOHN. Doesn't that get confusing?

ERIC. We've got two Normans an' all.

Beat.

JOHN. Things are working out, then.

ERIC. Sort of. Better than Brum, anyway.

Beat.

I used to stack shelves in Fine Fare.

JOHN. Did you?

ERIC. Then I was a meat-packer in Nechells Green.

Beat.

When I moved down here, I tried to get into security at
Marks and Spencer, but they said I didn't have the qualifica-
tions. Then my aunty put me in touch with this friend of hers
who does interior decorating and I'm managing okay . . .

JOHN. Good.

ERIC. . . . what with The Frog and Trumpet an' all, but what I
really want to do is join the police.

JOHN. Are you musical, then?

ERIC. No. I just want to be a policeman.

Beat.

The way they go on in the pub! Can't understand it. They
only think about one thing and they don't seem to care
much who they do it with, either. I don't want to be like
them. There's more to life than that, isn't there?

Beat.

JOHN. Yes.

ERIC. I can wait. I'm quite happy.

GUY *appears, crying.*

JOHN. What's wrong?

GUY. I've run out of vinegar.

JOHN. What?

GUY. I've run out of pissing vinegar.

He's crying helplessly. Beat. JOHN *puts an arm round him.*

JOHN. I'll go and get some. I was going to get some booze
anyway.

Beat.

ERIC. Well, I'll be off, then. It's all done.

GUY (*through tears*). Thank you. It's very nice.

ERIC goes to the door and turns.

ERIC. Enjoy the party.

He leaves. Beat.

JOHN. Was there any particular vinegar you wanted?

GUY. No. Anything except malt.

JOHN. Right.

GUY. I'm sorry. Must be all the excitement.

JOHN goes to the door.

JOHN. Oh. I forgot.

He takes a smallish bag from his jacket pocket and hands it to GUY.

For your flatwarming.

GUY. You shouldn't have.

JOHN. It's nothing very much – at all, really . . .

GUY looks in the bag.

You could save it for later . . .

GUY takes out a paperback.

I'm afraid I didn't get round to wrapping it.

GUY. *Cooking for One.* Thanks.

JOHN. Just a gesture.

GUY. No. Thank you.

*JOHN leaves. GUY wipes his eyes. He goes to the
conservatory entrance and looks at it. Then he sits down.
He touches the cover of* Cooking for One. *Beat. He picks up
the phone and dials. He waits, then:*

Brad? . . . It's Guy. How are you? . . . Fine. Sorry about
earlier . . . Yes . . . Anyway, I just felt like a bit of a chat.

The doorbell rings.

Shit! . . . No, I didn't mean you! . . . I've got to go . . . Brad, I'm sorry . . . I'll call you soon . . . Sorry . . .

He replaces the receiver and gets up as rain suddenly starts pelting down onto the conservatory roof. He looks out.

Oh no!

The doorbell rings again.

Blackout as the rain continues.

SCENE TWO

Dusk. The rain is still pelting down onto the roof of the conservatory. BERNIE *stands at the entrance, inspecting it.* BENNY *and* JOHN *are seated.* GUY *is hovering. All have drinks. A bowl of nuts sits on the coffee table.*

BERNIE. Nice. Very nice. He's a good little worker. This is the year, Benny, for our conservatory. Adds thousands, you know. I saw a very smart one in a magazine. Reasonable, too. Lots of stained glass – not too garish, but not dull, either – and garlands moulded all the way round with the odd cherub and bird dotted here and there. Very smart it was, with a fountain in the middle. Did I show it you, Benny?

BENNY. Yeah.

BERNIE. I like the sound of water. Very relaxing.

A clap of thunder as the rain becomes torrential.

GUY. Nuts?

Beat.

I planned on eating outside.

JOHN *lights a cigarette.*

BENNY. Could I?

JOHN *offers him one and lights it.* GUY *provides them with a fresh ashtray.*

BERNIE. That's your third.

BENNY. Who's counting?

BERNIE. I am. He gave up for two-and-a-half years, you know. Have you ever given up, John?

JOHN. No.

BERNIE. I used to smoke like a chimney as a kid, up until I was about twenty-one, twenty-one-and-a-half or thereabouts. But I asked myself, 'Bernard, is a nicotine hit more important than life itself?' and I had to answer, 'No.' So I stopped there and then. The best decision I've ever made.

GUY. Are everyone's drinks alright?

BENNY. Wouldn't say no.

GUY *goes to take his glass.*

It's okay. I'll do it.

GUY. Yes, help yourselves. That's best.

BENNY *pours himself a drink.*

BERNIE. Good job we didn't bring the car.

More thunder as the rain continues.

Funny thing is, Benjamin and I have never been happier – isn't that right, Ben? We see more of each other, find time to do things we'd never done before. I've read more books these past few years than in my whole life! We've been to the cinema – well, once or twice. Of course, with a video . . . In fact, we saw a film only last week at that cinema in erm . . .

BENNY. East Finchley.

BERNIE. That's the one. French thing. People sitting around talking about this and that . . . well, about themselves, really. Quite interesting.

BENNY. You dropped off.

BERNIE. I'd had a hard day.

BENNY. We thought we were going to see *Robocop*.

BERNIE. Well, if they do insist on changing the programme halfway through the week!

BENNY. I told you it was French.

BERNIE. Why they can't recognise weeks like the rest of us – i.e. beginning on Sunday and ending on Saturday – is beyond me. But the point is, we saw it and we wouldn't have dreamt of going a couple of years ago. We'd have probably found ourselves in a smoky bar, drinking a lot and spending too much. I can't help thinking it's brought us to our senses, made us realise what we've got going for us.

The doorbell rings. JOHN *stands up.*

GUY. Are you alright?

JOHN. I'm going to the toilet.

He exits.

GUY. I won't be a minute.

GUY *exits.*

BENNY. Why do you always go on about fucking conservatories?

BERNIE. You'd like one, wouldn't you?

BENNY. There's a time and place.

BERNIE. Talking of which, you might have worn a looser pair of trousers.

BENNY. This is the only suit I've got.

DANIEL *enters, followed by* GUY. *Beat.*

DANIEL. Where's John?

GUY. In the loo.

BENNY. Hello, Dan.

He goes to DANIEL *and they embrace. Then* DANIEL *goes to* BERNIE *and embraces him. He starts crying.* BERNIE*'s unsure how to cope. He pats his back.*

BERNIE. Oh dear . . . dear me . . .

For several seconds, the sound of DANIEL *sobbing and the rain outside. Then he releases himself from the embrace and dries his eyes.*

GUY. Alright?

DANIEL. Yes.

He suddenly retches. GUY *darts across to him.*

GUY. Dan!

DANIEL *breathes deeply.*

DANIEL. I'm alright. Really. Could I have a brandy?

BENNY *indicates he'll deal with it and pours a brandy.*

Oh, Jesus! Nothing in there.

GUY. Maybe you should try and eat a little something.

DANIEL. Was the music alright?

GUY. Of course it was.

DANIEL. He loved it. Never stopped playing it.

GUY. And you bought it me.

DANIEL. That's right.

BENNY *gives him a brandy.*

Thanks.

He takes a sip.

Oh! Divine! I mustn't stay long cos of his mother.

GUY. She's not alone?

DANIEL. No, but I said I'd get back.

GUY. I did ask her.

DANIEL. She thought you were very sweet, but she wanted to stay at the flat.

He takes another sip.

He didn't want a funeral, you know, but I couldn't not for her . . . for me . . . I didn't follow his wishes. Pretty appalling, isn't it?

GUY. You did the right thing.

DANIEL. He'd have been furious.

GUY. It's you who has to deal with it. You've done nothing wrong.

The rain has been easing off.

DANIEL. How long's he going to be in there?

GUY. Shall I give him a shout?

DANIEL. He's probably transfixed in front of the mirror. Give him another half-hour.

He has another sip.

I think I'll pop into the garden for a minute. Get a bit of air.

BERNIE. Would you mind if I joined you? Bit smoky, isn't it?

DANIEL. As long as you keep your hands to yourself, Bernard. No funny business in the shrubbery, now!

BERNIE (*unsure how to react*). No . . .

They go into the garden as BENNY *replenishes his glass.*

BENNY. Want anything?

GUY. I'm fine, thanks.

BENNY. I think I'll join them. What about you?

GUY. In a minute. I need to check the food.

BENNY. Right.

He goes into the garden as JOHN *enters.*

GUY. Okay?

JOHN. Yeah.

GUY. They're in the garden.

JOHN. Right. (*Re. his glass.*) May I?

GUY. You know you don't have to ask.

JOHN *pours himself a scotch.* GUY *sips his drink.*

All pretty difficult, isn't it?

JOHN. You could say that.

GUY. For everyone, really.

JOHN. Mm.

He gulps his drink.

Maybe I should go.

GUY. You can't do that! It'd look so odd. Well . . . I suppose if
you want to –

JOHN. No, you're right.

Beat.

GUY. I know it's the wrong time to say this and it's not really
my business, but – I can't help feeling that, in the long run,
it might be easier for you both if you – actually got round to
telling him sometime. Obviously not today, but – sometime.
I'm speaking out of turn, aren't I? But it seems so unfair –
to both of you, not just Daniel. I mean, you're friends, John.
You just can't have that sort of secret and the longer it goes
on . . . I'm sorry.

JOHN. You're right.

GUY. After what you've been through, I really shouldn't . . .
I'm sorry.

Beat.

JOHN. The last time I saw him – it's funny, but I knew it was
the last time . . . One minute – that's all I had. Dan had
popped out the room for some reason or other and . . . Cos
the rest of the time, Dan was at the bedside, holding his
hand . . . which is as it should be, isn't it? And me pretending I was just a friend. I couldn't even see his fucking
corpse.

Enter BENNY.

BENNY. Bernie's so fucking boring sometimes, I don't know
how I've put up with him all these years. He's twittering
on about fuck-knows-what out there. I've had to come in,
else I'd have whacked him with a spade. Sorry, am I
interrupting?

GUY. No.

JOHN. I'll be in the kitchen.

   JOHN *exits.*

BENNY. I'm not, am I?

GUY. No.

BENNY (*Re. his glass*). May I?

GUY. Of course.

   BENNY *replenishes his drink.*

BENNY. What a cunt! Garbage by the fucking yard! But the
   funny thing is, I only seem to notice what a complete prick
   he can be when other people are around. Want anything?

GUY. I'm fine, thanks.

BENNY. Cheers!

GUY. Cheers!

   They drink. BENNY *lights a cigarette.* GUY *gets him an
   ashtray.*

BENNY. I dunno! Fucking turn-up, isn't it?

GUY. Yeah.

BENNY. Why do they have to play that bloody music? It's
   upsetting enough as it is.

GUY. It was one of Reg's favourites.

BENNY. He wasn't there to hear it, was he?

GUY. It's difficult knowing what to do. There's no time,
   everyone's distressed.

BENNY. I want to be put in a bin-liner and chucked out with
   the rubbish.

GUY. It's the people left behind, though, isn't it?

   Beat.

   It was funny seeing everyone in suits. Especially when
   you're used to them in more recherché gear.

BENNY. Do you think mine's too tight?

GUY. No.

BENNY. Bernie thinks so. The trousers, anyway.

GUY. It looks fine.

BENNY (*inspecting himself*). I suppose my cock does stick out a bit.

GUY *sips his drink.*

Reg used to love it.

GUY. Italian, isn't it?

BENNY. My cock. Couldn't get enough of it.

He grabs a handful of nuts and starts eating them.

GUY. You had it off with Reg?

BENNY. A few times. Started a couple of years back. At your flatwarming, actually. That's where Bernie and I met him – well, you know that; you introduced us. Made a date for the next night and Bob was your uncle. Cos Daniel was in er . . .

GUY. Sydney.

BENNY. That's the one. He's always somewhere, isn't he? Nice job! Better than the 134, I can tell you!

GUY. I didn't know . . .

BENNY. Why should you? No one does. And Bernie certainly doesn't, so I'd appreciate it if you kept your mouth shut. He's trying to make me a good boy. Thinks we should stay home nights with our feet up. Not really me, though, is it? Don't get me wrong – Bernie and I get on fine. Like a fucking institution after all these years. He'd never leave me.

GUY. Would you leave him?

BENNY. No, but sometimes he gets on my tits. I gotta prowl around a bit, haven't I? Go mad otherwise. Did you like Reg?

GUY. Yes. And he made Daniel happy.

BENNY. He was a good fuck. Bit noisy, though. Not very keen on that; are you? Tends to put me off my stroke. Enjoyed the sound of his own vice, you might say.

He has more nuts.

Between you and me, I thought he was a miserable sod. We never really talked. Just got down to business, then pissed off. But he certainly got my nuts twitching. You don't mind me telling you, do you?

GUY. No.

BENNY. I needed to tell someone and you're the obvious person. I'm pretty fucking worried, I don't mind admitting.

GUY. Did you take any precautions or anything?

BENNY. Of course we did! Sometimes. Well, you didn't really think about that then, did you?

GUY. Some of us did.

BENNY. Every fucking morning, I wake up and check my body, inch by inch, to make sure something hasn't appeared during the night, and when I get back from work, the same routine. And any little cough, twinge or itch brings me out in a cold sweat. And then I start panicking about the fucking cold sweat. I tell you, if I haven't caught anything, it'll be a fucking miracle.

Enter BERNIE.

BERNIE. I was thinking, Guy, it might be possible to eat outside after all.

GUY. Is Daniel alright?

BERNIE. Oh, yes. I've been singing the praises of conservatories, actually. It wouldn't surprise me if he ended up getting one.

BENNY. I don't know where he'd put it. He lives on the top floor.

BERNIE (*re. the glass in his hand*). And he said he'd like a triple, then he'll shoot off.

BENNY. I'll do it.

BENNY *takes the glass and pours a brandy.*

BERNIE. It's not cold. Just a bit damp.

BENNY. That's summer for you. I'd rather be anywhere than here – Paris, New York, Rome.

BERNIE. You sound like a perfume bottle, Benny.

BENNY *glances at him as he takes the brandy out into the garden.*

It's very kind of you to do this, Guy. Very decent.

GUY. I just thought people might want somewhere to go after the wake. It's nothing.

BERNIE. It's very nice of you, though. Very nice.

GUY. I think I ought to see Daniel –

BERNIE. We don't get much of a chance to chat, do we, Guy?

GUY. Don't we?

BERNIE. Benny's the one people warm to. He's more gregarious than me. One of the lads, and I don't begrudge it. It's a sort of compliment, if you think about it, because I do love him. Could I hold you, Guy?

GUY *is momentarily thrown.*

Just for a second?

GUY. Yes.

BERNIE *gauchely puts his arms round him.* GUY *can't relax. A moment's awkwardness, then* BERNIE *lets go.*

BERNIE. Thank you for that. I'm scared to death, Guy.

GUY. Why?

BERNIE. I don't want to lose him.

GUY. Why should you? You said everything was fine.

BERNIE. He's always been something of a free spirit, you might say. Amazing we've lasted as long as we have. If I dwell upon what he's got up to, what he might still be getting up to . . . breaks my heart, Guy, it does really. I put up with it, of course, and most of the time, I'm probably imagining it. Do you think I am?

GUY. I'm sure you are.

BERNIE. I could kill him sometimes. Doesn't take me
   seriously, Guy.

GUY. Of course he does.

BERNIE. Doesn't seem to realise that I have feelings too.
   I still fancy him, you know, but we haven't done it in a long
   time. He'll play around once too often, he will really, and
   I'd show him the door, Guy. I would. It's the last thing I
   want, but I'd do it. Maybe I'm a little naive, but I like to
   think two people should be sufficient unto themselves, so to
   speak.

   Beat.

GUY. I really ought to go and see Daniel.

BERNIE. I spent a night with Reg.

GUY. What?

BERNIE. I did, Guy. I spent a night with him. The only time
   I've done such a thing and he's dead!

GUY. When?

BERNIE. Just after your flatwarming. I say a night – forty-five
   minutes, actually, and I have to admit I'd never felt like that
   before and doubt I will again, but now I have to ask myself,
   'Was it worth it?' and I have to answer, 'No'. It certainly
   was not, Guy. Once, that's all! Just the once! And I might
   die because of it.

   Enter DANIEL through the conservatory.

DANIEL. He's not still in the bog?

GUY. He's in the kitchen. I'll get him. I've got to check the
   food, anyway.

BERNIE. Need a hand?

GUY. No, I'll be fine.

   He exits. Beat.

BERNIE. I'm sure he could do with a spare pair. Better go and
   see.

He exits. DANIEL *sips his drink. Enter* JOHN.

DANIEL. Where have you been hiding yourself?

JOHN. I haven't.

DANIEL. I've got to go in a minute.

JOHN. How are you?

DANIEL. Marvellous. I've just cremated my lover. What a fucking nightmare!

JOHN. Yeah.

Beat.

DANIEL. Thanks for going to the hospital. I'm sure he appreciated it.

JOHN. Good.

DANIEL. I don't know what I'm going to do. Everything, the smallest thing'll make me miss him. (*He has another sip.*) Do you want a drink?

JOHN. I'll do it.

DANIEL. No, let me. Scotch?

JOHN. Yes. Thanks.

DANIEL *pours a scotch.*

DANIEL. Isn't it incredible? After all these years, the three of us can still be here for each other. It's the best thing in the world. Guy's such a sweetie, isn't he?

JOHN. Yes.

DANIEL. One of the nicest people I know.

He hands JOHN *his drink.*

Cheers!

JOHN. Cheers!

They drink.

DANIEL. I'm off to Spain next week.

JOHN. Whereabouts?

DANIEL. Seville. Some art fair or other. Maybe I'll cancel.

JOHN. It might do you good.

DANIEL. Would you come with me?

Beat.

We could go together. I mean, the art-fair business – I can get through that in a matter of hours. And we could have a car – go into the mountains. Or just stay in the city. Whatever.

JOHN. I'm not sure . . .

DANIEL. No. Well.

Beat.

Don't lose touch. Not again.

JOHN. No.

DANIEL. I think he was having an affair.

JOHN. Was he?

DANIEL. The last year or so. Something wasn't right. I should have sorted it out. Too late now. I got it in my head that he was being unfaithful. Not the odd bit on the side – I don't think there was and I never asked because I didn't want to know – but that he was actually having an affair.

JOHN *lights a cigarette.*

And it got to the point where I'd convinced myself he was in love with somebody else. The stupid thing is – and this is what I regret – I couldn't confront him about it, I suppose because I couldn't face it and was hoping he wouldn't do that to me. Then when he was dying and the things he was saying to me, I felt ashamed. He wouldn't have done that to me, would he? You don't think he was having an affair, do you, John?

Pause.

JOHN. I'm sure he wasn't.

DANIEL *breaks down.* JOHN *puts his arms round him.*

DANIEL. Even when he was lying there, all skin and bones, looking like his grandfather, I couldn't stop myself thinking about it, staring into those half-dead eyes, wondering if he'd cheated.

JOHN. Daniel . . . Dan . . .

DANIEL. He told me he loved me over and over again. I suppose that's what matters, isn't it?

Beat.

JOHN. Yes.

DANIEL. Oh, John . . .

Enter BENNY *from the garden.*

BENNY. It's quite nice out there now – sorry.

DANIEL *and* JOHN *disengage as* BERNIE *enters with an air freshener.*

BERNIE. It's quite a spread, I must say! I don't know about you boys, but I could eat a scabby horse, as my Aunty Jean used to say. She was Scottish.

He starts spraying.

BENNY. What the fuck are you doing?

BERNIE. Smells like an ashtray.

BENNY. Smells like a brothel now.

The doorbell rings.

DANIEL. I'm off.

BERNIE. You should eat something, you know. Keep your strength up.

DANIEL. Later, maybe. Thanks.

He kisses BERNIE, *then* BENNY.

Thank you.

BENNY. See you.

DANIEL *kisses* JOHN.

DANIEL. Bye, darling.

JOHN. Bye.

GUY *leads* ERIC *in, who's carrying a bottle of wine.*

BENNY. Hello, Eric.

ERIC. Hello.

DANIEL. I'm off.

He kisses GUY, *as* JOHN *goes into the garden.*

GUY. I'll see you out.

DANIEL. Don't bother. Thank you.

GUY. We'll talk later.

DANIEL. Yeah.

He exits.

BERNIE. Poor Daniel.

ERIC (*handing* GUY *the bottle*). I brought you this. I thought you might need cheering up.

GUY. That's sweet of you. Thanks.

BERNIE. Did you know Reg?

ERIC. No, but Guy mentioned last night he had a funeral on today. Anyway, I'm not stopping.

GUY. Are you working tonight?

ERIC. No.

GUY. Then stay. At least have a drink.

BENNY (*going to the drinks table*). What do you fancy, Eric?

ERIC. Dunno. Coke?

BENNY. Have something stronger! What about a scotch?

BERNIE. Eric's allowed to have a soft drink if he wants, Benny.

ERIC. Alright then. With Coke in.

BENNY (*pouring*). This'll put hair on your chest. Or maybe you don't need it.

ERIC. Someone's parked outside without a permit.

BERNIE. It doesn't apply after six-thirty, Eric.

ERIC. It's eight o'clock in this area.

GUY. You're not a policeman yet.

BENNY. But when you are, will you promise me something?

ERIC. What?

BENNY. That you'll let me see your helmet.

He hands him the drink.

Bottoms up!

ERIC. Ta.

GUY. Anyway, whoever the culprit is can't be here. No one's come in their car.

BENNY. Speak for yourself!

BERNIE. Benny! I think you've had enough.

GUY. Food should be about ten minutes.

BERNIE. How's The Frog and Trumpet, Eric?

ERIC. Alright. I haven't seen you in there for ages.

BERNIE. We don't go out as much as we used to.

ERIC. It's still the same.

BERNIE. Becoming quite a permanent fixture there, aren't you?

ERIC. Not for much longer, I hope.

BERNIE. My father wanted to join the force, you know, but he didn't have the feet for it. Took up chiropody instead.

ERIC. Someone was asking after you a few weeks ago.

BERNIE. Really? Who?

ERIC. Posh bloke. Robert something-or-other?

GUY. Ford?

ERIC. That sounds right.

BENNY. Robert Ford?

BERNIE. I don't know him.

ERIC. Maybe it was Benny.

GUY. A few weeks ago?

ERIC. A month or so.

BERNIE. Do I know him, Benny?

BENNY. How the fuck should I know? If you don't know who
you know, no one else fucking will. (*To* ERIC.) He's a lord,
you know.

GUY. That's not true. We just called him that because he had a
receding chin and a stupid accent.

BENNY. And a fucking prodigious ejaculation! He was in a
Chinese restaurant once –

GUY. Benny –

BERNIE. What Chinese restaurant?

BENNY. I don't fucking know. What the fuck do you ask me
that for?

BERNIE. Because I haven't heard this before, Benny, that's
all. You've never mentioned it.

BENNY. I don't have to tell you everything, do I?

BERNIE. There's no need to be obstreperous.

BENNY. But it's such a stupid fucking question! 'What
Chinese restaurant?' What's it fucking matter? The Bridge
on the River Kwai in Streatham High Street! Will that do
you?

BERNIE. And who is Robert Ford, anyway?

BENNY. If you don't fucking know him, why the fuck do you
want to know what Chinese restaurant he was in?

BERNIE. It's been a very distressing day, Benny.

BENNY. I've lost my flow now.

ERIC. Chinese restaurant.

BENNY. What?

ERIC. That's where you'd got to. He was in a Chinese
restaurant.

BERNIE. It isn't in China, anyway.

BENNY. What isn't?

BERNIE. The River Kwai.

GUY. Benny –

ERIC. Go on. Tell us.

GUY. He's dead.

Beat.

BENNY. You're kidding!

ERIC. Dead?

BENNY. When?

GUY. Ten days ago.

BENNY. Fuck me!

Beat. BERNIE *starts crying.*

What's up? You didn't even fucking know him!

BERNIE. How did you know him?

BENNY. What d'you mean?

BERNIE. How did you know him!

BENNY. I met him in the pub.

BERNIE. Is that all?

BENNY. Give it a rest, Bernie!

BERNIE. I want to know!

BENNY. What's it matter? He's fucking dead!

Beat

BERNIE. Goodbye, Guy. Thank you.

BENNY. What you doing?

BERNIE. Eric, see you again, no doubt.

BENNY. Where you off to?

BERNIE. Has it ever crossed your mind that some people
might find even me a little bit attractive? One or two have in

the past, you know, Benny. And he made me feel a darned sight better than you do most of the time! I really don't want to lose you.

He leaves. Pause. BENNY *replenishes his glass.*

BENNY. Bit of air.

He goes into the garden. Beat. ERIC *wanders over to the conservatory entrance and casts his eye around.*

ERIC. It'll need a fresh coat soon.

GUY. Do you think so?

ERIC. Got a bit flaky at the edges.

GUY. It'll have to wait, I'm afraid.

ERIC. You shouldn't play around, should you?

GUY. What do you mean?

ERIC. If you're with someone, you shouldn't do it. Eric's Norman's playing up.

GUY. Eric's Norman . . . ?

ERIC. Landlord at The Frog. He should never have asked him to move in. I think he's starting to regret it now an' all. I quite like Norman, but he's a bit of a slut.

GUY. Which Norman do you mean? I always get confused.

ERIC. Short hair and no knickers.

GUY. That's the entire clientele.

ERIC. The other Norman's black.

GUY. Yes, of course.

ERIC. Anyway, Eric's Norman's turned the whole place into a knocking-shop. I don't know how Eric puts up with it cos he must've noticed. I've seen Norman take blokes up to the flat, down to the cellar, into the bogs. I couldn't stand for that, could you?

GUY. I shouldn't think so.

Beat.

ERIC. You ever had a bloke? In a relationship, like?

GUY. No. I haven't.

ERIC. I'm surprised.

GUY. Why?

ERIC. You're nice.

GUY. I could say the same about you.

ERIC. I'm young, though. I've got loads of time. Can I have a
   top-up?

GUY. Help yourself.

ERIC. What about you?

GUY. I'm fine, thank you.

   ERIC *pours a drink.*

ERIC. Have you ever been in love?

GUY. Have you?

ERIC. There was this girl called Janice from Handsworth. I
   was eight, but we didn't do much about it. Then there was a
   bloke at school called Dwight, but he'd have smashed my
   face off as soon as look at me, and since then, well . . .

   Beat.

   Cheers!

GUY. Cheers!

   They drink.

ERIC. So have you?

   Beat.

GUY. I met someone . . . oh, nearly fifteen years ago now at
   university. We've seen each other only a handful of times
   since then. I don't even know him that well. Yet hardly a
   day's passed without me thinking about him. He doesn't
   feel the same about me. I know he likes me, but then quite a
   few people do. I sometimes think I'd rather be fancied than
   liked.

ERIC. You wouldn't if you were.

GUY. I'd like the chance to find out.

ERIC. It's John, isn't it?

GUY. Yes.

ERIC. I could tell by the way you are with him.

GUY. That obvious, am I?

ERIC. No. I could just tell.

GUY. The first time I saw him was in a queue in the Refectory. He was wearing a rugby shirt and jeans and a pair of dirty plimsolls. He ordered sausages, beans and a double portion of chips, gooseberry crumble and ice cream, and a carton of milk. He was with a couple of mates who were a bit loud, but there was something about him – the way he picked up his cutlery, handed over his money, the smile he gave the cashier . . . I was in such a state, I put custard on my quiche. And that was it! Not long after, we became friendly through Daniel, who spotted him in a gay pub. Imagine the hysteria that caused! You see, John was incredible. He didn't seem to care. One minute, he'd be playing rugby, the next, he'd be tonguing a fresher in the Union loo. He got a bit of aggro, but he could certainly stand up for himself and eventually, people thought twice. He's always had a reserve; something untouchable.

Beat.

He's the only one. Can you understand that? Daniel thinks I'm mad and occasionally I've wondered if I'm imagining it. But it's stood the test of time and I have to believe it. It sounds stupid, doesn't it? Do you think it sounds stupid?

ERIC. Have you ever told him?

GUY. No.

ERIC. But you've got to! Just think if you were run down by a bus tomorrow!

GUY. That's hardly likely. Unless Benny were driving it.

ERIC. Hang on.

He goes into the garden.

GUY. Eric, what are you doing? Eric!

He sips his drink.

Jesus!

He takes another sip. Enter JOHN.

JOHN. Eric said you wanted a word.

GUY. Did he? Are you alright?

JOHN. Yeah.

He lights a cigarette.

He's cute.

GUY. Yes. Yes, he is.

JOHN. So what did you want?

GUY. Nothing really.

JOHN. Up to my eyes in it, aren't I?

Beat.

GUY. If you want a bit of company, if you ever want to stay, you know you're welcome.

JOHN. Yeah. Thanks. Do you know, I've never understood why someone hasn't snapped you up?

GUY. Really?

JOHN. Yes. I mean, you're such a nice guy, you're so . . . It's not fair, is it? Still, it'll happen one day, I'm sure. Do you see much of him?

GUY. Who?

JOHN. Eric.

GUY. From time to time. Mainly at the pub.

JOHN. What about him?

GUY. What do you mean?

JOHN. Have you ever thought about giving Eric a go?

GUY. As you say, he's . . . cute, but –

JOHN. He can only say no and he likes you, doesn't he?

GUY. I think so, but 'like' isn't the issue.

Beat.

The way some of these young ones look at me, or not, as the case may be! I know I'm nearly forty, but my dick hasn't dropped off.

Beat.

But yes, he's cute. You're right.

JOHN. You should tell him.

GUY. Yes, maybe I should.

JOHN. Anyway, you deserve someone.

GUY. John?

JOHN. Yes?

Beat.

GUY. You remember *The Bacchae*?

JOHN. Mm?

GUY. And the last-night party, when we were up in the flies?

JOHN. Up in the flies . . . Yes! I remember! That little scumbag playing – whatever it was –

GUY. Pentheus.

JOHN. That's it! He chucked his ring, didn't he?

GUY. Yes, but I meant before that.

JOHN. Before he threw up?

GUY. Before he arrived.

JOHN. Right.

Beat.

GUY. We were having a bit of a chat.

JOHN. Uh-huh.

GUY. We were . . . Well, you said something –

JOHN. Do you know, some bastard nicked my jockstrap?

GUY. Did they?

JOHN. Yes! Not that I wanted it, but . . . Sorry, what were you saying?

GUY. Up in the flies, we were having a chat and a bottle of wine and you were telling me about yourself.

JOHN. What did I say?

GUY. Lots of things.

JOHN. Was I pissed?

GUY. Not particularly. And after a while, you said something to me that I thought meant that you might want to . . .

JOHN. What?

GUY. That I thought meant you might . . .

Beat.

Do you remember?

JOHN. I remember Pentheus throwing up.

Beat.

GUY. He was a bit of a pain, wasn't he?

JOHN. Yeah.

Beat.

He's left me nothing, you know.

Beat.

GUY. Well, it'd have been a bit difficult, wouldn't it? Daniel not knowing and everything.

JOHN. But I can't help wondering. I haven't loved anyone before. He knocked me for six. The first time in my life when I felt I wasn't in control. Do you think he loved me?

GUY. I wouldn't know. I hardly ever saw you together and he never talked about it because he didn't know I knew.

JOHN. Did you like him?

GUY. Yes.

JOHN. Really?

GUY. Yes. Well, I suppose my opinion of him went down a bit after you'd told me about the two of you.

JOHN. Did your opinion of me go down a bit?

GUY. No.

JOHN. Why not? We were both shitting on Daniel.

Beat.

GUY. To be honest, I did think you should've told him, but you're going to, aren't you?

JOHN. It's over now. Why disillusion him?

GUY. But in one sense, it's not over, is it? Dan'll carry on talking about him and we'll carry on lying.

JOHN. That's better than spoiling it for him. He was happy with Reg. So was I. Why fuck it up?

GUY. Maybe this isn't the best time to talk about it. You've had the most awful day –

JOHN. And if I do tell him – and I'm not saying I never will – how much should I tell him? All of it? Part of it? Once I'd started, where would I stop?

GUY. But I can't help feeling that Reg was having his cake and eating it.

JOHN. What's it matter?

GUY. Quite a few cakes, by all accounts.

Beat.

JOHN. What?

GUY. Well . . . he wasn't exactly a saint, was he?

JOHN. What do you mean?

GUY. I'm not telling you anything new.

JOHN. What are you telling me?

GUY. Nothing.

JOHN. Guy!

GUY. I suppose all I'm saying is that if he could do that to Daniel, why couldn't he do it to you?

JOHN. He was having an affair?

GUY. No, no! I'm just telling you what you already know.

JOHN. And what's that?

GUY. That fidelity wasn't exactly his strong point.

JOHN. Wasn't it?

GUY. For Christ's sake, John, the very fact that he had an affair with you!

JOHN. Who else?

GUY. I don't know.

JOHN. Who?

GUY. No one!

JOHN pours a scotch.

I'm sorry. It's not my place . . .

He gulps it down.

I just didn't like the way he treated you – both of you. That's all.

JOHN pours another.

You just can't carry on like that.

He gulps it down.

This is the wrong time. We really shouldn't be talking about it.

JOHN. Even if he did . . . a bit on the side . . . what's it matter? It doesn't take anything away . . . What the fuck's it matter?

GUY. But it does matter! What the hell was he playing at? It was so irresponsible. Even the vicar told me what a good fuck he was outside the crematorium! God, I'm sorry. I'm sorry. I didn't mean to say that. I'm sorry. It's because I'm worried about you, about Daniel and the lot of you. I'm sorry. I really didn't mean to.

JOHN. One minute! I mean, what do you say to someone when you know it's the last time?

GUY. John –

JOHN. What do you say? I leant over, smelt his hair, kissed his cheek, managed to say, 'I love you' and before he could say anything, Daniel had come back. He told me hundreds of times he loved me, but the one time that would've mattered was the last and Daniel came back to the bedside. Maybe he didn't in the end. When you're dying, maybe things fall into place and Dan was the only person who counted –

GUY. John –

JOHN. And now I'll never know.

Beat.

You're probably thinking, 'I could have told you so.' But those few years – it could've been a night and it'd have been worth it.

Beat.

I'm frightened.

GUY. Yes.

Beat. He touches JOHN's *arm.* JOHN *doesn't respond.* BENNY *and* ERIC *come back in.* GUY *starts sniffing.*

Oh God! I'm sorry. Something's burning. Sorry.

He dashes out. The rain starts again. BENNY *goes to* JOHN.

BENNY. Do you want a drink?

JOHN *shakes his head.* BENNY *puts an arm around him.*

Fucking summer!

ERIC *goes to the door.*

ERIC. Do you want any help?

GUY (*off*). No. No, thanks.

ERIC *glances at* JOHN *and* BENNY. *He's not sure what to do. Then he looks through* GUY's *records.*

BENNY. Can I bum a fag?

JOHN offers him one. BENNY takes two and puts them in his mouth. JOHN lights them, then BENNY puts one in JOHN's mouth, keeping the other for himself.

I owe you 'undreds.

BENNY saunters over to the conservatory entrance.

I kinda see what Bernie's talking about. Nice, isn't it?

JOHN goes over and stands next to him.

Like your own fuckin' jungle.

JOHN's crying quietly.

Oh dear. Got you bad, hasn't it?

He puts his arms round JOHN. JOHN puts his round BENNY, still crying.

There you go. That's right.

ERIC looks at them, then returns to the records. BENNY strokes JOHN's hair. JOHN's crying begins to subside.

That's right.

BENNY rubs his face against JOHN's hair. He gently kisses it. JOHN raises his face and brushes it against BENNY's.

Yeah. That's right.

BENNY takes a drag on his cigarette and throws it into the conservatory. He gently takes JOHN's cigarette off him, drags on it, then throws that into the conservatory. He kisses JOHN's face several times, ending up at his mouth. They kiss gently on the lips, then passionately. ERIC watches them, then goes to the drinks table and pours himself a stiff one. GUY enters, distressed.

GUY. A complete fucking incineration! It'll have to be a takeaway –

He clocks BENNY and JOHN. BENNY gently ends the kiss and, still in the embrace, looks at GUY.

BENNY. He's alright. Don't worry. He'll be fine.

His arm round JOHN, *he leads him into the conservatory.*
GUY *watches them.*

ERIC. Can I get you something?

GUY. No. Gin. Thank you.

ERIC obliges.

I can't believe it. The timer didn't go off. Cost me a fortune.
It hasn't quite worked out as planned. I can't believe it. You
can't trust anyone. They only installed it last week.

He looks towards the conservatory.

Are you hungry? The salad and cheese are still intact.
Would you like some?

ERIC (*handing him his drink*). I'm fine, thanks.

GUY. Are you sure?

ERIC. I picked up a burger on the way.

GUY. Just as well. Cheers!

ERIC. Cheers!

They sip their drinks. GUY *glances again at the
conservatory.*

Nice records.

GUY. Oh. Yes.

ERIC. I haven't heard of most of them.

GUY. Play one if you like.

ERIC. Did you tell him?

GUY. What?

ERIC. What you were going to?

GUY. No. Not exactly.

He sits on the sofa.

Fuck it, I'm nearly forty! What if I reach fifty and still
haven't met anyone? I'm nothing to write home about now
– God knows what I'll be like then. Dogs'll probably bark
at me in the street.

ERIC. You're not that bad.

He glances into the conservatory.

Funny, isn't it? Just when you think you've got a handle on
things, it all pisses off in another direction.

GUY. What?

ERIC. I'm a bit rat-arsed.

He sits next to GUY.

GUY. Are you?

ERIC. When you work in a pub, people think you drink all the
time, but you don't. Except for Norman. He's always
shoving one up the Optics. But I'm not used to it. I stick to
Coke. Haven't had this much in ages.

*He rests his head back and closes his eyes. GUY looks at
him, then towards the conservatory, then back at ERIC. The
rain is still pouring down onto the conservatory roof. GUY
tentatively moves a hand towards ERIC's knee.*

(*His eyes still shut.*) D'you know something?

*GUY instantly withdraws his hand, having not made
contact.*

GUY. What?

ERIC. I like you.

GUY. Do you?

ERIC. You're not like the others, thinking about sex all the
time. I mean, how can you judge a bloke by the shape of his
bum or the size of his packet?

GUY. You can't.

Beat.

Well, maybe not the whole person.

He looks back to the conservatory.

I hope they're not killing my plants.

*He looks back at ERIC whose eyes are still closed. His gaze
works slowly down his whole body.*

ERIC. I was a choirboy.

GUY. Were you?

ERIC. I did solos. The organist was very encouraging. Gave
me the odd private lesson.

GUY. Really?

ERIC. He had incredible hands. Small, but versatile. Comes
with the job, I suppose. You can't just die, though, can you?
There must be something else.

GUY. Do you think so?

ERIC. Wouldn't make sense, otherwise. Like, while we're
pissing around, getting our knickers in a twist, it's all going
on anyway, isn't it? Whatever we do.

Beat.

Like, it's night now, then it'll be morning.

Beat.

I'm pissed.

GUY. Can I kiss you? I'm sorry, I didn't mean that. Can I? I
shouldn't have said that. I'm sorry.

He puts his hand on ERIC's *knee, then withdraws it.*

Sorry.

He looks towards the conservatory. ERIC *looks at him.*
Beat. Then GUY *looks at* ERIC.

ERIC. It's like me mum asking for a snog.

Beat.

I didn't mean that nastily. Just a bit surprised. I've never
thought of you like that. I don't think I can.

Beat.

Mum's dead, actually.

Beat.

Sorry.

Beat.

GUY. Would you stay the night? Not to do anything. Just lie together. Would you do that?

Beat.

ERIC. You mean, just sleeping in the same bed?

GUY. Yes. Would you?

Beat.

ERIC. Yeah.

GUY. Good. Thanks.

He looks at the conservatory, then back at ERIC.

Can I get you anything?

ERIC. I spent a night with someone once. Year or so ago. It was the first time I really did it. Properly, you know. It was very nice. I thought, I've saved myself up for this and I've made the right decision. What he said to me, what he did to me, even though it was only the first time we'd met, I thought, this is the one. But he never saw me again and I got the impression he wasn't telling me the whole story. Some people don't have any scruples, do they?

GUY. What was his name?

ERIC. He said names didn't matter, I could call him anything I wanted. So I called him Dwight, after that boy at school. The only other name I could think of was Janice, but that'd have been a bit daft.

Enter BENNY *and* JOHN *from the conservatory.*

JOHN. We're off.

GUY. Right. I could rustle something up. You haven't eaten anything.

BENNY. I'm not hungry.

GUY. The timer went all to fuck.

JOHN. Thanks, Guy.

He embraces him, then:

GUY. Bye, Benny.

GUY *kisses* BENNY.

BENNY. Thanks a lot. Tara, Eric.

ERIC. Bye.

JOHN. Bye.

They've gone. Beat.

GUY. How about a cup of tea?

The phone rings. GUY *answers it.*

Hello? . . . (*Quietly.*) Oh . . . Yeah . . . Look, Brad, I'm a bit tied up . . . Tomorrow . . . Brad, it's not . . . (*Very quietly.*) Down, boy! . . . Okay? . . . Bye.

He replaces the receiver.

Tea?

ERIC. Ta.

GUY *exits.* ERIC *goes to the records and looks through them again. He picks one out. He takes it out of the sleeve and puts it on the turntable. He puts the stylus on the record. The second movement of Ravel's Piano Concerto in G Major starts playing.* GUY *enters almost immediately.*

GUY. Why have you put that on?

ERIC. It was Dwight's favourite. He played it to me when the sun was coming up. He said it'd always remind him of me.

Beat.

It'd be nice to see him again, even from a distance.

Beat.

Wonder what he's up to?

The music continues as the rain keeps falling and the lights fade.

SCENE THREE

The music continues. Dawn. The rain has reduced to a drizzle pattering onto the roof of the conservatory. ERIC *leans against the conservatory entrance, naked, looking out at the garden and listening to the music. At one point, he slowly, elegantly raises his arm as if executing a dance movement. Then he continues listening.* JOHN *appears at the doorway, naked and dishevelled, just roused from sleep.* ERIC *doesn't notice him. He seems disturbed. He glances round the room, then focuses on the record player. He takes the record off.* ERIC *looks round.*

ERIC. What did you do that for?

JOHN. Why are you playing this?

ERIC. It's nice.

> *Beat.*

> Are you alright?

JOHN. I was dreaming, then heard that. I got a bit confused.

> *Beat.*

> What time is it?

ERIC. Dunno. About five, I think.

JOHN. Why are you up?

> ERIC *shrugs.* JOHN *retrieves a dressing gown from a pile of clothes and puts it on.*

> You'll catch cold.

ERIC. It's summer.

> *Beat.*

JOHN. I'm sorry I wasn't . . . The booze and everything . . .

ERIC. I was pissed an' all.

JOHN. Yeah.

ERIC. I didn't want to anyway.

JOHN. Didn't you?

ERIC. No.

JOHN. Why not?

ERIC. I'd have felt guilty, wouldn't I? Cup of tea?

JOHN. Yes.

> ERIC *goes out.* JOHN *searches for a cigarette. He looks through a few empty packets before finding one. He lights it, inhales, coughs, grimaces, then inhales again. He takes a pile of photographs from a drawer and slowly looks through them.* ERIC *returns.*

ERIC. Done in a tick.

> *Beat.* ERIC *looks through the pile of clothes, finds a pair of underpants and puts them on.*

> Can I have a fag?

JOHN (*pointing to the packet.*) There's some in there.

> ERIC *takes one.*

ERIC. Got a light?

JOHN (*giving him a light*). I didn't think you smoked.

ERIC. I don't, but everyone I know who doesn't's dead. What are those?

JOHN. A few photos of university. I came across them a day or two ago.

ERIC. Let's have a look.

> JOHN *gives them to him.*

JOHN (*pointing to a photo*). There's Dan, Guy, and there's me.

ERIC. Had people used to look like that?

JOHN. What does that mean?

ERIC. Isn't Guy's hair long? Ugh! Daniel's wearing flares! Don't he look horrible! Is that you?

JOHN. Yes.

ERIC. God, you look young!

> JOHN *takes them off him.*

> I was enjoying them.

Beat.

I wonder if I'd've enjoyed university. No one ever went from our school. I got four CSEs, mind you. Did you enjoy it?

JOHN. Yes, I did.

ERIC. Which school did you go to?

JOHN. Marlborough.

ERIC. Is that a public school?

JOHN. Yeah.

ERIC. I guessed as much.

JOHN. Why?

ERIC. You're that sort, aren't you?

JOHN. Am I?

ERIC. I don't mean it nastily. Did you see *Another Country*?

JOHN. Yes.

ERIC. I loved that film. All them posh blokes bonking. Was it like that at your school?

JOHN. A little bit.

ERIC. You didn't get it at Erdington Comprehensive. If they thought you were a poof, they chucked you in the canal and pissed on you.

JOHN. Did they do that to you?

ERIC. No. They never found out. I got thrown out of a window.

JOHN. Why?

ERIC. I think they were a bit bored.

JOHN. Did you get hurt?

ERIC. No. It was only the first floor. I'll get the tea.

He goes out. JOHN *glances at a few more photos, puts them aside and sits down.* ERIC *returns with two mugs of tea and gives one to* JOHN.

JOHN. Thanks.

ERIC *sits next to him. They sip their tea.*

ERIC. Everyone was arseholed, weren't they?

JOHN. Yes.

ERIC. Bernie was on another planet! He's like this woman
I knew when I was a kid. She hung around outside the
playground singing at the top of her voice – opera and stuff
– and she always had a bunch of lilies. If you got too close,
she hit you on the head with them.

JOHN. I don't think Bernie's got to that point.

ERIC. Well, he's not singing yet, but I didn't know where to
put myself when he ran up to the coffin and chucked a lily
on it. Just when it was going through the doors an' all! I
thought he was going through with it for a minute. Benny
should never have brought Conrad. I mean, he didn't even
know Guy and he must've realised that Bernie was going to
take the hump. I hate that Conrad. Can't understand what
Benny sees in him.

Beat.

Benny's changed, hasn't he? He's like a little wife. Just
what Bernie always wanted him to be. He should never have
kicked him out. Doesn't know what to do with himself now.
Lonely as fuck and miserable as sin! I found him in the
garden at one point chatting up the oleander. Then he told
me he was thinking of joining the Salvation Army. I reckon
he's two bricks short of a load.

Beat.

He was so fond of Guy! He came in the pub after he'd
heard Guy'd been taken ill. He was in such a state, Eric and
I had to take him upstairs.

Beat.

Can't believe it, can you? It just doesn't make sense. I
mean, it's not as if he put it around a lot. He didn't seem to,
anyway. Mind you, I suppose I didn't know him that well.

JOHN. Neither did I.

ERIC *looks at him.*

You're right. He didn't put it around. He was extremely careful. In fact, when I went to see him in hospital, he put it down to an encounter he had on holiday . . . oh, years ago now. Not that it matters. But I guess you can't help thinking about it.

Beat.

ERIC. Nice flowers.

JOHN. Yes.

ERIC. Did you see that bouquet in the shape of a bone? I wonder who sent that.

JOHN. He was there, actually. Brad. The one in the leather collar.

ERIC. I thought he was a vicar.

JOHN. Nobody knows what he is. Even Guy didn't; they never met.

ERIC. You won't tell Eric, will you?

JOHN. What?

ERIC. That I stayed the night.

JOHN. That's all you have done.

ERIC. He had his fingers burnt with Norman, I can tell you! Best thing he did giving him the elbow. You mustn't say anything. You won't, will you?

JOHN. Of course I won't.

ERIC. I don't want him getting suspicious.

JOHN. When's he back?

ERIC. When his mother gets out of traction. We're making a go of it, see, and I think it's working out alright. I've got quite accustomed to the idea of running a pub since the police turned me down. I've had a few ideas an' all.

JOHN. I've thought about getting a pub . . . or a restaurant or something.

ERIC. So why don't you?

JOHN. Maybe I will.

ERIC (*looking at him*). You're odd, you are.

JOHN. Am I?

ERIC. Keep yourself to yourself, don't you?

No response.

Do you ever open up?

JOHN. Sometimes.

Beat.

ERIC. You and Guy never sort of . . .

JOHN. What?

ERIC. Had a thing together, did you?

JOHN. No.

ERIC. It's amazing, isn't it? Leaving you his flat and everything.

Beat.

He loved you, you know. He said you were the only one.

Beat.

JOHN. I've found piles of photographs of me; discarded notebooks from university that he must have taken from my room; write-ups of matches that I played; a bottle of aftershave – I still remember missing that; a comb; a shirt; an old biro that I used during Finals with my teethmarks on it; even a leather jockstrap I wore in a play. I found all this stuff in a case on top of the wardrobe. It was the weirdest thing.

ERIC. He'd have only done it cos of what he felt for you. And you felt nothing for him?

JOHN. Of course I did. He was a mate. The nicest man.

ERIC. But you didn't love him or anything?

JOHN. He should've said something.

ERIC. What would you have done?

JOHN. I don't know.

Beat.

ERIC. Have you ever been in love?

JOHN. Yes.

ERIC. Who with?

JOHN. Nosey little fucker, aren't you?

ERIC. Sorry.

JOHN holds his hand.

JOHN. A man called Reg.

ERIC. Reg?

JOHN. Yes.

Beat.

ERIC. You mean . . . ?

JOHN. Yes.

Beat.

ERIC. Oh.

JOHN lifts ERIC's hand to his lips and kisses it.

When?

JOHN. The last few years of his life.

ERIC. And did you actually – do it, like?

JOHN. All the time.

ERIC. Oh.

He licks ERIC's fingers.

Did Daniel know?

JOHN. Not a clue.

ERIC. Did anyone?

JOHN. Guy. He was the only one.

ERIC. Oh.

JOHN *touches* ERIC*'s knee.*

John . . .

JOHN. What?

He slides his hand up ERIC*'s thigh.*

ERIC. Will you ever tell him?

JOHN. You think I should?

ERIC. Yeah.

JOHN. So did Guy. So do I.

ERIC. So will you?

JOHN*'s hand reaches* ERIC*'s crotch.* ERIC *pushes it away.*

JOHN. I've never faced up to responsibilities.

ERIC. You've got to sometime though, haven't you?

Beat.

You must tell him. It's only fair. You're friends, for Christ's sake! You'd feel better for it, as well.

JOHN. You're right.

He puts his arm round ERIC*'s shoulder.* ERIC *resists.*

Please . . .

Beat. ERIC *stops resisting. Then* JOHN *gently draws* ERIC*'s head onto his shoulder.* ERIC *resists again.*

ERIC. No.

JOHN. It's alright. We're not doing anything.

Beat. ERIC *tentatively submits, letting his head rest on* JOHN*'s shoulder.* JOHN *strokes his hair.*

That's alright, isn't it?

Beat.

ERIC. I've been thinking.

JOHN. Have you?

ERIC. The security at The Frog and Trumpet's rubbish.

JOHN. Is it?

ERIC. Cameras. It's the only way. A kiddie could get in there
at the moment. I'll have a word with Eric.

JOHN runs his hand down ERIC's *back.* ERIC *tenses, then
relaxes.*

I've also had a thought or two about how to boost business.
Cabaret: that's the thing. What do you think?

JOHN. Could be.

ERIC. I haven't told Eric yet, but I'm sure he'll go along with
it. I might give it a go myself an' all. Once or twice,
y'know; we'd get other acts in too. I've been giving it a lot
of thought.

JOHN gently fingers the top of ERIC's *underpants.*

That music I was listening to, what you turned off, I thought
I could start with that and come on as a nymph or
something, like they thought it was going to be ballet –

JOHN. I can't quite see you as a nymph.

ERIC. Why not?

JOHN. You're more of a satyr –

ERIC. A what?

JOHN. Or a fox . . .

He lets his hand run over ERIC's *backside.*

Or a dog.

Beat.

ERIC. I'll stick with nymph. Any road, just when everyone
was getting a bit bored, the music'd change into Annie
Lennox or Dorothy Squires and I'd whip off whatever I had
on and there'd be something else underneath and I'd go into
this big number. What d'you think?

JOHN eases down ERIC's *pants.*

John . . .

JOHN. Please . . .

ERIC. I mustn't . . .

JOHN (*stroking* ERIC*'s arse*). Your skin . . . so young . . .

ERIC. Eh?

JOHN. I used to have a bum like yours.

ERIC. You've got a nice bum. Considering.

JOHN. Considering what?

ERIC. Well, you know . . . If I reach your age, I wouldn't mind looking like you.

JOHN. I'm old enough to be your fucking dad!

ERIC. At least you're still here to moan about it!

JOHN *freezes*.

I'm sorry. I didn't mean . . .

JOHN. Why's he done this? The flat – I don't need it. I don't even want it.

ERIC. He loved you.

JOHN. But I didn't love him. I can't help that, can I?

Beat.

I only visited him a couple of times. Couldn't face it . . .

Beat.

The last time I saw him – lying on his side, shrivelled up like a little old man – he made me lean right down to put my ear against his mouth and he said, 'I love you. I always have,' and I'd never realised before. I must be stupid.

ERIC. No you're not. You can't help not loving him back.

JOHN. That's right, isn't it? I can't help that.

ERIC (*tearful*). We're all going to miss him.

JOHN. The worst thing, Eric – the worst thing of all is that when Guy said he loved me that last time I saw him, all I could think was that I wish it'd been Reg.

The doorbell rings. They jump.

ERIC. Fuck me!

JOHN. Who the hell's that?

JOHN goes out. ERIC rummages through the clothes. The front door's opened.

DANIEL (*off*). Darling!

JOHN (*off*). Daniel!

DANIEL (*off*). I'd kill for coffee.

Enter DANIEL and JOHN before ERIC's found any clothing.

(*Clocking ERIC.*) Sweet! Mm! I sniff tumescence.

JOHN. It's five-thirty!

DANIEL. I knew you wouldn't mind.

JOHN. You only left three hours ago.

DANIEL. I couldn't face going home, so I popped up the Heath.

JOHN. It's raining.

DANIEL. Didn't stop anyone. When I left twenty minutes ago, it was still like Nero's Rome. What is it about summer? Plays havoc with the hormones.

JOHN. You're still in your funeral gear.

DANIEL. I could've been in a body-bag and I'd have got laid.

ERIC. I'll make some coffee, shall I?

JOHN. Yes.

DANIEL. That would be divine.

ERIC goes out.

It doesn't look like you two have been discussing Jane Austen.

JOHN. It's not quite as it might seem.

DANIEL. Pretty damned near, I'd say. (*Re. JOHN's dressing gown.*) Isn't that Guy's?

JOHN. Is it?

Beat.

DANIEL. You managed to get rid of Bernie, then.

JOHN. We shoved him in a taxi just after you'd left.

DANIEL. Poor old queen! Boring as fuck, but you can't help feeling for him. Oh Juanita, what are we to do? Guy of all people! Jesus fucking Christ! Give us a fag.

JOHN. You don't smoke.

DANIEL. What the fuck!

> DANIEL *starts looking through the records as* JOHN *finds a cigarette. He lights it and hands it to* DANIEL.

> Thanks, pet. I tell you, the Heath was so muddy, it was like an ice rink. I was doing Sonja Henie impersonations all over the shop. And I lost a lens! I walked into at least half-a-dozen trees. Tried to go down on one of them. But you know how you get – sort of cock crazy. It was like Harrods' sale. You've no idea! Well, maybe more British Home Stores, but who cares? There were plenty of bargains in plenty of basements. And beautiful! Even though it was pissing down. I was moved to do a snatch of Titania at one point until an overweight biker insisted on chewing my nipples off. There was even an encampment of the homeless sitting round a pile of sodden twigs. It was like Act Three of *Carmen*. (*Taking out a record.*) This is the one.

> *He puts it on the turntable.*

> Breakfast disco!

> *He puts the stylus on the record: 'Starman' by David Bowie.* JOHN *laughs.* DANIEL *takes hold of him and they start dancing.* DANIEL *sings along with it. Eventually* JOHN *does too. Then they quieten down, stop dancing and split up.* JOHN *wanders over to the conservatory and looks out.* DANIEL *notices the pile of photographs and sombrely looks through them. Then he puts them down and takes off the record before the song's finished. Pause.*

> So what will you do?

JOHN. I haven't begun to think.

DANIEL. It's mad. The best-laid plans, etcetera. Mind you, you've never made any.

JOHN. What about you? Will you stay on at the flat?

DANIEL. No. I've stuck it for two years, but whatever I do,
I can't get rid of him. Not that I want to, in one sense, but
trivial reminders are somehow the most melancholic and
I don't want to be sad. Why should I be? We had a great
time together.

Beat.

This place, though. You could keep it. After all, it doesn't
hold any memories particularly and you want to sell
Holland Park, so why not?

JOHN. As I say, I haven't given it a thought yet.

DANIEL. What a wonderful thing to do! You know he was
mad about you?

JOHN. Why didn't you tell me?

DANIEL. I don't think I believed it and you'd have run a mile.

JOHN. I wouldn't have.

DANIEL. John!

JOHN. We could've talked about it, sorted it out somehow. I
don't know –

DANIEL. Did you know Bernie had slept with Reg?

Beat.

JOHN. No.

DANIEL. He told me last night when he was drunk. Bernie of
all people! It was the last thing I needed to hear. It's opened
up a whole fucking can of worms, I tell you!

Beat.

John?

JOHN. What?

DANIEL. There's something I've been meaning to ask you.

JOHN. Yeah?

DANIEL. Yes. You remember Guy's flatwarming?

JOHN. Yeah.

DANIEL. And you said that you'd bumped into Reg the night before at that film?

Beat.

JOHN. Yeah?

DANIEL. I've always wondered . . . I shouldn't say this . . . oh, fuck it! . . . Well, it seemed such a coincidence and I've always wondered whether you spent the night together. Did you? It wouldn't matter if you had – well, it would, but . . . I've always been curious. Shit, I don't know what I'm going on about! I mean, what's a night between friends? But did you? Did you spend that night with Reg?

Beat.

JOHN. A night with Reg?

DANIEL. Mm.

JOHN. The night before the flatwarming?

DANIEL. Yes.

JOHN. That was ages ago.

DANIEL. That's not the point. You'd still remember.

JOHN. No – I mean, why would you ask that now?

DANIEL. You did, didn't you?

JOHN. Daniel –

DANIEL. Didn't you?

Pause.

JOHN. No. Of course I didn't.

Pause. He tentatively embraces DANIEL. *After a while,* DANIEL *succumbs to the embrace.*

DANIEL. I'm sorry . . .

JOHN. No, no . . .

DANIEL. Oh . . .

By now, the drizzle's stopped. A bird starts singing.

I'm losing the people I can talk to.

JOHN. You can talk to me.

DANIEL. We've got to keep in touch.

JOHN. Yes.

DANIEL. No – this time, we've got to. I needed you when Guy was ill. I nearly didn't find you in time. So we will, won't we?

JOHN. Yes, we will.

Beat. They kiss affectionately, then break the embrace.

DANIEL. I think I'll go. I'm suddenly very tired. Apologise to Eric, will you?

JOHN. Yes.

DANIEL goes to the door.

Dan?

DANIEL stops and turns. They look at each other. A couple of other birds have joined in the singing.

DANIEL. Yes?

Beat.

JOHN. I'm pretty tired, too. I haven't been sleeping too well lately.

Beat.

DANIEL. We'll speak later.

He goes out. The birdsong continues. JOHN lights a cigarette. Enter ERIC with a tray of coffee.

ERIC. Has he gone?

JOHN. He said sorry. He was a bit knackered.

ERIC looks at him. JOHN looks away. ERIC puts the tray down.

ERIC. How would you like it?

JOHN. Black. Thanks.

ERIC pours a cup and gives it to JOHN. Then he pours himself a cup. He looks again at JOHN, who's concentrating on his coffee. The birdsong continues.

ERIC. Noisy little buggers, aren't they?

No response. ERIC *sips his coffee.*

Want to watch telly?

No response. ERIC *searches out a TV magazine and looks through it.*

There's a pop show, game show, film . . .

JOHN. Which one?

ERIC. Some French thing . . . No . . . Sounds dead boring.

He puts it aside and looks at JOHN *yet again, who still doesn't return the look. Then he goes to the conservatory entrance and looks out.*

It might be sunny today. You could come round the pub for lunch. Sit outside.

JOHN. Yes, I might.

ERIC (*casting his eye over the conservatory*). This needs doing. The garden's a mess an' all. You've got to have them done. Guy'd be furious otherwise.

He looks across at JOHN. *Eventually,* JOHN *looks at him. The birds continue singing. The lights fade.*

End.

THE DAY I STOOD STILL

For my father

Kenneth Lee
(1911-1974)

and my godchildren

Rosanna Michell
and
Alice May Wilkinson

And still I return like a line to the centre,
Like fire to the sun and the stream to the sea.

Monteverdi, *L'Incoronazione di Poppea*
Act 1, Scene i. Libretto: Busenello

The Day I Stood Still was first performed in the Cottesloe
auditorium of the National Theatre, London, on 22 January
1998. The cast was as follows:

HORACE	Adrian Scarborough / Callum Dixon
JUDY	Catherine Russell / Daisy Beaumont
GUY	Geoffrey Church
TERENCE	Jake Wood / Joseph Swash
JIMI / JERRY	Oliver Milburn

Director Ian Rickson
Designer Mark Thompson
Lighting Designer Hugh Vanstone
Sound Designer Simon Baker
Composer Stephen Warbeck
Musicians Bernie Lafontaine (clarinet), Graeme Taylor (guitar)

Characters

HORACE

JUDY

GUY

TERENCE

JIMI

JERRY

Setting

The sitting room of an upper-storey apartment in a North London mansion block. There is a small balcony with a railing and outside shutters. The furniture includes a late Georgian dining-chair and a Victorian upright piano.

Casting

Horace, Judy and Terence should each be played by two actors. Jimi and Jerry should be played by one actor.

SCENE ONE

Early evening. JUDY *is embracing* HORACE. HORACE *wears glasses.* GUY *looks on with a carrier bag.* JUDY *breaks the embrace.*

HORACE. The thing is –

JUDY. Have you lost weight?

HORACE. No –

She embraces him again.

JUDY. It's so gorgeous to see you. Just gorgeous.

GUY. Gorgeous.

She breaks the embrace.

HORACE. You must be Guy.

GUY (*French*). Guy.

JUDY. Clarified butter, not Bonfire Night.

GUY. Enchanté, Horace.

HORACE (*extending a hand*). Pleased to meet you –

GUY *ignores the hand and kisses him twice.*

JUDY. Oh, Horry!

HORACE. I'm completely lost for words.

JUDY. Is this a bad time?

HORACE. No, no. It's just that –

JUDY. We got in yesterday, we're off again tomorrow, and I thought I must see Horace. So here we are!

HORACE. Here we are, indeed! Gosh! I haven't got a thing in, I'm afraid.

JUDY. We can't stop.

HORACE. Just some Ryvita and . . . you see, the thing is –

JUDY. I hope you don't mind, but Guy's brought a little snack.

GUY. A little snack.

HORACE. Has he?

JUDY. And something lovely to wash it down with. Instant celebration!

HORACE. That's very kind of you, but Judy –

JUDY. Do you mind if I give the nanny a quick call?

HORACE. Of course not. Help yourself.

JUDY. Only she's new, and Puerto Rican. (*Dialling*.) It's so gorgeous to see you.

HORACE. How is Jimi?

GUY. The kitchen is . . . ?

HORACE. Oh yes. It's . . .

He leads GUY *out, surreptitiously checking his watch.*

JUDY (*on the phone*). Elvira, how is he? . . . Where is he? . . . What's he doing? . . . Well, make sure he doesn't sit on it . . . We won't be long.

She replaces the receiver as HORACE *comes back in.*

We took her on just before we left. Guy's rather fond of her. I'm not so sure. Apparently, she's worked for the Claptons.

HORACE. He says he's okay in there, but I feel a bit –

JUDY. Oh, he'll be fine. He's happiest in a kitchen.

HORACE. If you're sure.

JUDY. I'm sure.

HORACE. It's just rather odd having –

JUDY. You don't mind?

HORACE. No. I hope he doesn't. It's a bit of a mess, actually.

JUDY. Don't worry. He'll be fine.

HORACE. Good. So Jimi's alright, is he?

JUDY. Oh, adorable.

HORACE. It'd be nice to see him.

JUDY. I know, I know. Maybe on our way back.

HORACE. Only I'd like to make a good fist of being a
godparent rather than just –

JUDY. Of course, yes, and I want that too. It's just so tight this
time, but as I say, coming back, maybe there'll be –

HORACE. I was so touched – that I was asked.

JUDY. You look really well.

HORACE. Judy, the thing is –

Enter GUY.

GUY. Oil?

HORACE. Pardon?

GUY. Oil.

HORACE. Oil. Oh yes. On the windowsill.

GUY. Window . . . ?

JUDY. Le rebord.

GUY. Ah, bon.

He's gone.

HORACE. Why does he want oil?

JUDY. For the mayonnaise.

HORACE. Mayonnaise!

JUDY. For the asparagus.

HORACE. I thought it was a snack.

JUDY. It is a snack. He's unbelievable.

HORACE. He must be. Mayonnaise is quite hard, isn't it?

JUDY. He saw this asparagus and just couldn't resist it. That
little greengrocer down the road . . .

HORACE. Oh yes.

JUDY. There's something about him, isn't there?

HORACE. The greengrocer?

JUDY. Guy.

HORACE. Oh, (*English.*) Guy . . . (*French.*) Guy. Yes, he
    seems nice.

JUDY. My first taste of the older man. He's not exactly
    Belmondo, but he makes up for it in other ways. He's an
    angel. An angel. I didn't know what the hell to do – should
    I stay, come back? I hadn't a clue. Then Guy appeared and
    everything fell into place.

HORACE. So you'll be staying there?

JUDY. Oh yes. I'm moving into his apartment. It's a much
    better location than – where I am now. It's the block next to
    Woody Allen's.

HORACE. Really?

JUDY. He's got a cow on the roof – Woody Allen, that is – it's
    not real – and Lilian Gish is on the other side.

HORACE. Well!

JUDY. You must come and visit.

HORACE. I've never been.

JUDY. Oh, you absolutely must.

HORACE. Maybe I will.

JUDY. It's the best place in the world.

HORACE. I'm not that keen on travel, you know. I like
    watching travel programmes and I find that kind of enough.
    Going's always a let-down, don't you think?

JUDY. God, I couldn't survive without travelling.

HORACE. It's a real shock to see you.

JUDY. A shock?

HORACE. A nice shock. But when I opened the door –

JUDY. I couldn't resist dropping in. You don't mind?

HORACE. No, only when I opened the door, I thought –

JUDY. God, this is strange.

HORACE. Is it?

JUDY. Being here.

HORACE. Yes. I'm thinking of doing something with it. I still
see Mum and Dad everywhere.

JUDY. Like what?

HORACE. What?

JUDY. What were you thinking of doing with it?

HORACE. I don't know. Maybe making the balcony bigger.

JUDY. How would you do that?

HORACE. I don't know. Or knocking a wall down or
something. It's nice, though, isn't it?

JUDY. You'll take root.

HORACE. It's not that long.

JUDY. I've lost count of the places I've lived. You should
move.

HORACE. It's nice.

JUDY. Don't you feel it's time?

HORACE. No.

   Enter GUY.

GUY. Do you have a . . . ?

   He does a mime.

HORACE. Pepper-mill?

   The mime continues.

   Screwdriver?

GUY (*still miming*). For the . . . ?

JUDY. Qu'est-ce que tu veux, dindon?

GUY. Un pilon et mortier.

JUDY. Pestle and mortar.

HORACE. Sorry.

GUY. Okay.

He's gone.

HORACE. A pestle and mortar? Why does he want that?

JUDY. I don't know. Garlic, herbs . . .

HORACE. For what?

JUDY. He's such a sweetheart. He just doesn't get English
     at all.

HORACE. How does he get by?

JUDY. Fine, fine.

HORACE. But doesn't he need to understand what people are
     talking about as a psychotherapist?

JUDY. Oh, but he does understand. He does. Language isn't
     everything, Horace.

HORACE. Right.

JUDY. And lots of his clients don't speak English anyway.
     What are you doing at the moment?

HORACE. I'm still at the museum.

JUDY. Still?

HORACE. Yes.

JUDY. You'll ossify if you're not careful.

HORACE. I like my job. When I don't, I'll change.

JUDY. But you're in your prime. Any minute now, you'll start
     slipping into middle age.

HORACE. Not yet.

JUDY. Not long. You should be doing things and going places.

HORACE. I don't want to. I'm fine as I am. I like this place,
     and I've got my music, my books, a friend or two. Honestly,
     Jude, I'm okay. I'm fairly happy.

JUDY. Do you still write?

HORACE. Well, you know . . . Judy, the thing is –

JUDY. What?

HORACE. Someone's coming.

JUDY. We're not stopping.

HORACE. No, but he might be here (*Checking watch.*) fairly soon.

JUDY. Would that be a problem?

HORACE. No, but I thought I ought to warn you. In fact, I'll just . . .

HORACE *goes to the balcony and looks down.* JUDY *notices the piano. He re-enters.*

I'm sorry, would you like a drink or something?

JUDY. We can go, if you'd prefer.

HORACE. Honestly, that's not what I mean. I just thought I ought to – let you know. That's all.

JUDY. Did you ever try getting your novel published again?

HORACE. You give up after a while. I thought I should try another one, something new.

JUDY. Good.

HORACE. Yes.

JUDY. And are you?

HORACE. Yes. Well . . . you know. I sometimes wonder how many ideas a person has in a lifetime – good ones, that is. One or two, if you're lucky.

JUDY. I'd have thought a few more than that.

HORACE. I mean, most of us don't have anything to say, do we, that really needs saying, or anything to do that's that important, and most of the time we're thinking about nothing in particular, aren't we?

JUDY. I've never had time to think about it.

HORACE. Maybe it's just me.

JUDY. What if you've already had the couple of ideas you're going to have in your life?

HORACE. Now there's a thought.

Enter GUY with three glasses of wine, which he passes round.

GUY. In ten minutes, we have a gorgeous snack.

JUDY. You darling! Horry, I can't tell you how lucky I am! He's so good at it.

GUY. Ma petite figue –

JUDY. And he can cook. (*Toasting.*) À la vôtre!

GUY. À la vôtre!

HORACE. À la – cheers . . .

They drink.

GUY. You like chocolate?

HORACE. Yes. Yes, I do, actually.

GUY. Because in the kitchen I find a drawer full of Mars bars.

HORACE. Ah –

JUDY. Horry!

HORACE. They were on special offer.

JUDY (*to GUY*). You shouldn't be going through people's drawers.

He embraces her.

Well, maybe some people's . . . Dindon . . .

He fondles her.

Ooh, dindon . . . (*Gently breaking the embrace.*) Non. So have you got anyone?

HORACE. In what sense?

JUDY. You know exactly what I mean. (*To GUY.*) He's always been a bit of a dark horse, even as a boy.

GUY. A black stallion.

JUDY. Yes, I didn't quite mean that.

GUY *wanders onto the balcony.*

HORACE. That was practically the last time you saw me.

JUDY. When?

HORACE. As a boy.

JUDY. Nonsense. We've met loads of times since then.

HORACE. Not loads, Jude. A handful, maybe.

JUDY. It's hard keeping up. Time vanishes, doesn't it?

HORACE. I know. It just happens like that. I know.

JUDY. So have you?

HORACE. Pardon?

JUDY. Met anyone.

HORACE. Well, to tell you the truth, the someone I'm expecting is –

JUDY. Horry!

HORACE. Yes. That's why it's all a bit –

JUDY. How long have you been seeing him?

HORACE. Oh, er –

JUDY. You little bugger! I can't wait! We can all have nibbles together.

HORACE. Judy –

JUDY. And then we'll leave you to it, don't worry!

GUY. The view is fantastic.

HORACE. When it's clear, you can see the Downs.

GUY. Ah, the Downs!

HORACE. Yes.

GUY. What are the Downs?

HORACE. Sort of hills.

JUDY. Collines.

GUY. Ah! Les collines!

HORACE. Yes.

GUY. A beautiful apartment.

HORACE. Thank you. There are one or two little drawbacks,
but –

GUY. Drawbacks?

HORACE. Problems.

GUY. Ah, oui.

HORACE. Well, one problem, really –

*A church clock starts to strike the hour. Its proximity makes
it alarmingly loud.*

JUDY. Jesus Christ!

HORACE (*checking his watch*). It'll be –

Stroke two.

– over soon.

JUDY. How the hell – ?

Stroke three.

How the hell do you live with that?

Stroke four.

HORACE. It's a case of having to, really. You kind of –

Stroke five.

Anyway, you've heard it before.

JUDY. Have I?

Stroke six.

It was never that loud, surely.

HORACE. It's never changed.

Stroke seven. Silence.

GUY. So.

HORACE. So.

GUY. So what is the problem?

HORACE. That was it.

GUY. Ah, bon.

JUDY (*indicating hallway*). Darling . . . I can't quite remember –

HORACE. It's at the end of the passage.

JUDY. Bless you.

She exits.

GUY. There's someone down there.

HORACE *darts onto the balcony.*

HORACE. Where?

GUY. Oh! Disparu!

HORACE. Where did he go?

GUY. Je ne sais pas.

HORACE. Was he just standing there?

GUY. He look up and then – disparu.

HORACE. Oh.

GUY. Perhaps he go into the trees.

HORACE. Yes. Anyway . . .

GUY. She is so beautiful.

HORACE. Judy?

GUY. So beautiful and good.

HORACE. Mm.

GUY. Me, I am surprised, the age I am, that she would join with me.

HORACE. You're not very old. And she seems happy enough.

GUY. I hope. You, she like very much.

HORACE. Does she? We hardly see each other.

GUY. You are old friends.

HORACE. In that we met a long time ago, yes. She sort of pops into my life now and again.

GUY. But you are a godparent?

HORACE. Yes, although I rather think that might have had
more to do with Jerry. Did you meet him?

GUY. No, unfortunately.

HORACE. He was another old friend I hardly ever saw. In fact,
I didn't hear that he'd died until after the funeral. I suppose
Judy had so much on her plate and, apparently, it was all
very low-key.

GUY. Do you want kids?

HORACE. No. No, I don't think so.

GUY. You don't like them?

HORACE. From when they're about fifteen I do. No, no, I
didn't mean that. Yes, I like kids. Sort of. I'd like to see
more of Jimi. I've only met him the once, at the christening.
They came over here for that, what with family and things. I
was really touched when I was asked to be a godfather. It
came completely out of the blue. I mean, we hadn't been in
contact for ages. I'd like to see Jimi grow up and do
whatever children do, but as you live in New York – well, I
won't get the chance, I suppose. C'est la vie!

GUY. Ah, oui. C'est vrai.

HORACE. Oui.

   They drink.

GUY. I hate New York.

HORACE. Do you?

GUY. A terrible place, and for children . . . You know
something, Doris –

HORACE. Horace.

GUY. I want to live again in France – and Jimi, so beautiful for
him. Don't say nothing, but I hope that Judy, when she see
my family and the place we live, I hope she think, 'Ah, yes,
I would love to live here!'

HORACE. Mm. She's quite strong-willed, though, isn't she?
And what with her career –

GUY. But la France – paradis! You know it?

HORACE. When I was a boy, I went to Calais to stay with a penfriend, but we didn't really hit it off.

GUY. You must go back.

HORACE. To Calais?

GUY. To France.

HORACE. Yes, maybe. Perhaps.

GUY. You understand me?

HORACE. Yes: you think I should go back to France.

GUY. No, no – my accent, is it very strong?

HORACE. Well, it's – there, but then again, you're French.

GUY. But you understand what I say?

HORACE. Oh yes. We've all got accents, I suppose.

GUY. You have an accent?

HORACE. I've probably got a bit of something or other, and Judy used to have an accent, apparently, when she was a girl.

GUY. Judy?

HORACE. Yes. She comes from Birmingham originally. Now, that's a very strange accent.

GUY. She still has it?

HORACE. No. She'd lost it by the time I met her. But I remember that, if you took her unawares, like waking her up or something, she'd lurch into Brummie without thinking about it and then get very cross.

GUY. Brummie?

Enter JUDY.

JUDY. Are you telling him all my secrets?

HORACE. I don't know your secrets.

JUDY (*embracing him*). Oh, Guy, Guy!

They kiss.

Do you know, Horace, when he combs his hair, he can make sparks fly?

HORACE. Gosh.

JUDY. You can actually hear it crackle.

GUY. Mes cheveux, oui. Electric.

HORACE. Gosh.

JUDY. I think you should check les asperges. They're getting a bit jumpy.

GUY. Ah, bon.

He exits.

JUDY. Could I just give Elvira a quick tinkle?

HORACE. Yes, yes.

JUDY (*dialling*). The poor baby won't know which continent he's on . . . Elvira, how is he? . . . Let me speak to him . . . Jimjams, sweetie! . . . It's Mummy, silly . . . Are you being a good Jimjams? . . . You darling sweetie heart! . . . (*Handing him the phone.*) Say hello.

HORACE. What?

JUDY. Speak to him.

HORACE. What should I say?

JUDY. Anything you like. He's four; he can talk.

HORACE. Jimi . . . Jimi . . .

JUDY. What's he say?

HORACE. He's breathing heavily.

JUDY. The flight's left him blocked.

HORACE. Jimi . . . (*Taking phone from ear.*) Ow!

JUDY. What?

HORACE. He blew a raspberry.

JUDY. Funny little thing! (*Into the phone.*) Funny little darling, aren't you? (*To* HORACE.) Carry on. He'll probably recognise your voice.

HORACE. Judy, the only time we've met, he was being dangled over a font. We've hardly bonded.

JUDY. Say something.

HORACE. Jimi . . . It's Horace . . .

Beat.

JUDY. What's he say?

HORACE. Nothing . . . Jimi! Hello! (*To* JUDY.) He said hello.

JUDY. Ah!

HORACE. Yes? . . . Yes . . .

JUDY. What did he say?

HORACE. He said, would I give him a shiny new pound.

JUDY. Oh, the darling darling! (*Taking the phone.*) My little treasure, of course Horrid Horace will give you a shiny new pound . . . Now you be a good boy . . . Bye bye, my darling . . . Bye bye, darling . . . Bye bye . . . Bye . . .

She puts down the phone.

Ohh! He said, (*Imitating* JIMI.) 'The fairy come to see me.'

HORACE. The fairy?

JUDY. Yes, the honey. He thinks a fairy watches over him at night. Isn't that sweet? He does make me laugh. He's just getting into the pooh-willy-bum phase. Mind you, that can get a little tiresome.

HORACE. How long does that last?

JUDY. From the men I know, the rest of his life. Oh God, I do hope not! When I see him playing with his willy and other boys' willies, I wonder will he ever take silk or do something clever in the City.

HORACE. Or follow in his father's footsteps.

JUDY. He's not musical.

HORACE. He's four.

JUDY. I do adore him so.

HORACE. What do I actually do as a godparent?

JUDY. I'm not sure.

HORACE. I mean, if you dropped down dead, would one of us take over? Isn't that the sort of thing a godparent does?

JUDY. I've already made arrangements for that eventuality.

HORACE. Oh.

JUDY. Flossie and Caulfield would take him in.

HORACE. Flossie and who?

JUDY. Caulfield, Flossie's other half. She's my best mate. They live in The Dakota. Fabulous apartment.

HORACE. But what if they died?

JUDY. Well, I don't know. I suppose my mother would look after him.

HORACE. And what if she died?

JUDY. It'd be fucking bad luck!

HORACE. I was just wondering.

JUDY. Dying's not part of my game plan.

HORACE. Does Jimi still have that (*Touching his forehead.*) – ?

JUDY. No, he doesn't.

HORACE. Oh. Did you – ?

JUDY. It went.

HORACE. Oh.

GUY *comes into the room with the open bottle of wine and tops everyone up.*

So where are you actually en route to?

GUY. En route! Ah, oui!

JUDY. He's taking us to meet la famille, aren't you, my love?

GUY. Ah, ma famille, ma famille . . .

JUDY. They're just above the Camargue, a tiny village called Vieille –

GUY. Vergervieux.

JUDY. Vergervieux, that's it, and apparently they have a fantastic house called Le Chardonneret. Lovely name, isn't it?

GUY. Beautiful in pie.

HORACE. Isn't it a wine?

JUDY. A finch, darling.

GUY. A bird.

JUDY. That's what I said.

GUY. Very beautiful.

JUDY. A goldfinch, I think. Fabulous colours.

GUY. En croute. (*He kisses his fingers.*)

JUDY. Guy, darling, you can't eat them.

GUY. Tourte au chardonneret – fantastic!

JUDY. They're pretty little fluffy things. You wouldn't want to put one in your mouth.

GUY. Fluffy?

JUDY. And they've also got use of a pool which they share with a couple of gîtes.

GUY. I cook for you.

JUDY. No, dindon, pas de chardonneret, jamais!

GUY. Judy –

JUDY. Okay?

GUY. Okay.

Beat.

HORACE. I wouldn't know one bird from another.

GUY. I get the snack.

He goes out.

HORACE. I just need to check . . .

He goes onto the balcony and looks down. JUDY *looks at the piano, then touches it.* HORACE *comes back in.*

JUDY. Is this the one . . . ?

HORACE. The one that Jerry played, yes.

JUDY. It was so long ago.

HORACE. Some things stay in your mind.

JUDY. Yes.

HORACE. It was a nice time.

JUDY. I can only remember bits. I know I'm rather naughty
about keeping in touch.

HORACE. It takes two. And you've got a lot on.

JUDY. Well, yes. I simply can't afford to slouch.

HORACE. I'm sure you can't.

JUDY. You know I'm associate editor now.

HORACE. No. That's great, Jude.

JUDY. Yes. It was so strange how we . . . how Jerry and I kept
coming back together. Little asteroids colliding. Just when I
thought, well, that's it, that's over, we'd meet by chance, or
really like it was always meant to be, and when I had Jimi
and we finally tried living together like people do . . . He
wasn't easy, Horace. I know you had a soft spot for him,
but . . . when you actually live with someone . . . It wasn't
easy. What a waste! He was the most gifted person. He
could have been a great pianist.

HORACE. Yes.

JUDY. A great pianist. Lots of people think this. But he
wouldn't play the game. He had it all and, for some God-
forsaken reason, he didn't want to know. And now: nothing!
It makes me so fucking angry.

HORACE. Yes, but if he didn't want to –

JUDY. If you have the gifts, it's your duty to use them.
Otherwise, what the hell's the point?

She produces a cigarette case and takes out a small joint.

Do you mind?

HORACE. No.

JUDY. A relaxant from Hawaii.

She lights it and inhales loudly and deeply. She passes it to HORACE, *who inspects it.*

There's this woman, she hangs round our neighbourhood, a sort of bag-lady, and she thinks she's in a queue. She takes a step forward, then stops, and waits, then she takes another step and waits again. Darling, it doesn't do anything for you if you just look at it.

HORACE. Sorry.

He takes a small puff.

JUDY. I can't bear to see her. She makes me want to scream.

She takes the joint from HORACE *and proceeds to smoke it voraciously as she speaks, down to the last millimetres.*

I keep hoping she'll drop down dead or get run over – but no. When we left for the airport yesterday, she was outside our apartment block, still in her queue.

HORACE. She's probably English.

JUDY. Jerry was drinking like a fish. Did you know that?

HORACE. How would I?

JUDY. And God knows what else he was on!

HORACE. He was always a bit of a rebel.

JUDY. Most people grow out of it.

HORACE. Well, maybe.

JUDY. He didn't understand me. I'm not sure he wanted to. I wonder if two people can ever understand each other, their deepest feelings and thoughts? Physically, we were – well, obscenely intimate, but we remained apart. The more intimate we were, the more isolated I felt.

HORACE. And Guy?

JUDY. Guy's an angel – affectionate, considerate. He might kill me with kindness.

HORACE. How's Jimi taking it all?

JUDY. He seems to like Guy, and Guy's very good with him.

HORACE. I meant Jerry. Does he understand?

JUDY. He keeps asking, 'Where's Daddy? Where's Daddy?'
He gets hysterical and I don't know how to comfort him.

Pause.

What was that thing Jerry used to play?

HORACE. He played lots of things.

JUDY. It was a part of something . . . I can't remember.

HORACE. It was fun, though, wasn't it?

JUDY. What?

HORACE. That first summer.

JUDY. Was it? I'm not so sure. To be honest, it all seemed
rather desperate. At least, it was for me.

HORACE. I thought we all had fun.

JUDY. It's too long ago.

She covers her face.

Jerry . . .

*He looks at her, glances towards the kitchen, then at his
watch.*

HORACE. Can I get you anything?

*She shakes her head and sits on the upright chair. It
collapses beneath her.*

Shit!

She cries like a child.

(*Helping her up.*) I'm so sorry.

GUY *enters with a platter of asparagus.*

GUY. The snack! Judy!

He rushes to her.

JUDY. I'm alright, alright . . .

HORACE. I've got to have that done.

GUY. Ma chérie!

JUDY. Shit!

She's quickly recovering her composure.

HORACE. I keep forgetting. Are you hurt?

JUDY. No, no, I'm alright.

HORACE. I keep meaning to –

JUDY. You've got to move, darling. This whole place is falling apart.

GUY. Ma petite.

HORACE. You're sure you're not hurt?

JUDY. I am not hurt, just slightly humiliated. Give me a drink.

HORACE does the honours as GUY comforts her.

GUY. I know what you want.

JUDY. What do I want?

GUY. A snack.

JUDY (*giggling*). You silly thing!

GUY takes an asparagus spear, dips the tip in mayonnaise and holds it by JUDY's mouth.

GUY. Just for you.

JUDY. Merci, monsieur.

Looking into GUY's eyes, she lets the spear slide into her mouth. HORACE checks his watch. She bites the spear and eats.

Mm. Now, that's what I call a snack.

The doorbell rings.

HORACE. Ah.

JUDY. Your friend.

HORACE. Excuse me.

He exits. GUY licks JUDY's lips clean.

GUY. Judy.

From the hallway, subdued voices.

JUDY. Dindon.

Enter HORACE *and* TERENCE.

Hello.

HORACE. This is . . .

TERENCE. Tebbit. Terence Tebbit.

JUDY. Terence.

She extends her hand.

Hello.

He shakes it.

I'm Judy and this is Guy.

TERENCE. Who?

GUY. Guy.

TERENCE. What's that, then?

HORACE. His name.

GUY (*shaking hands*). Enchanté.

TERENCE. Yeah.

GUY. You like a snack?

TERENCE. No. I'm alright, thanks.

HORACE. A glass of wine?

TERENCE. I'm alright.

GUY (*offering asparagus*). Horace, Judy . . .

HORACE (*taking a spear*). Thank you.

GUY (*raising glass*). À la vôtre!

JUDY. À la vôtre!

HORACE. À la –

TERENCE. Yeah.

They drink.

JUDY. So have you been together long?

HORACE. No. It's . . .

TERENCE. Not long.

HORACE. No.

JUDY. Well, I must say, Terence, you're frightfully well put together. You must work out an awful lot.

TERENCE. I try and keep my hand in.

JUDY. I bet you do. So where did you meet? Surely not at a gym. I can't imagine Horace in a gym.

HORACE. Well, we –

TERENCE. No, we didn't meet at a gym.

HORACE. No.

JUDY. I thought not.

TERENCE. No.

Beat.

HORACE (*to* TERENCE). So you . . . (*He doesn't know how to continue and takes a big glug of wine.*)

JUDY. It's so important, isn't it?

TERENCE. What's that?

JUDY. Keeping trim.

The phone rings. HORACE *goes to it.*

I work out five times a week –

HORACE (*answering phone*). Hello? . . .

JUDY. – and I feel great.

HORACE. Oh dear . . .

JUDY. So much more energy –

HORACE. Dear me . . .

JUDY. – and so much less stress.

HORACE (*offering her the phone*). It's Elvira.

JUDY. Jesus Christ!

She grabs it.

Yes? . . . What is it? . . . What? . . . Run away? Dear God in heaven, what am I paying you for, woman?!

She slams down the phone.

I knew I shouldn't have hired an Hispanic. We've got to go. Guy, on y va. (*To* TERENCE.) It's my little boy. He's a bit of a . . . (*Kissing* HORACE.) I'm sorry, darling.

HORACE. Don't worry.

JUDY. This is a complete disaster. Maybe on the way back from France we might find a spare twenty minutes –

HORACE. That'd be nice.

JUDY. – or whatever. We've really got to –

HORACE. You go. It's fine. We'll speak.

JUDY. Allons-y!

GUY. Je viens.

JUDY. I'll phone you tonight or –

HORACE. Yes.

JUDY (*to* TERENCE). It would have been so nice to have had a bit longer –

TERENCE. Yeah.

JUDY. Guy!

GUY. Okay, okay!

She's gone.

(*Grabbing a piece of asparagus. To* TERENCE.) Goodbye.

He goes.

HORACE. I'll . . .

HORACE *follows.* TERENCE *breathes a sigh of relief. He looks around. He goes onto the balcony and looks over. He comes back in as* HORACE *re-enters.*

I'm so sorry about that.

TERENCE. 'S'alright.

HORACE. I had no idea they were coming. They took me completely by surprise. In fact, when the door went, I thought it was you. Thanks for not . . . you know . . .

TERENCE. 'S'alright.

HORACE. I just thought it would be easier if . . . She's an old friend, you see. She lives in New York and that's her new – partner. I haven't seen her for years. Well, a few years – ago was the last time. I mean, I don't see her because I never go to – I never go over there. We met at school – not the same school, but we both knew – we had a mutual chum. Sorry, you don't need to know any of this.

TERENCE. 'S'alright.

HORACE. And they had a baby – the mutual chum and her – and I'm a godparent, so . . . I do hope Jimi'll be alright. Sorry, can I get you something? A drink, or – ?

TERENCE. No.

HORACE. Right.

Beat.

Funny how people can pop in and sort of . . . funny, isn't it?

TERENCE. This place . . .

HORACE. What?

TERENCE. Something about it.

HORACE. I've lived here a good many years. It belonged to my parents.

TERENCE. Something familiar.

HORACE. Really?

TERENCE. French, was he?

HORACE. Who?

TERENCE. That geezer.

HORACE. Yes, he was – is.

TERENCE. Fucking Frogs. No disrespect.

HORACE. No.

TERENCE. We used to call them tampons.

HORACE. Why?

TERENCE. Stuck-up cunts, aren't they?

HORACE. Oh yes, I see.

TERENCE. Yeah. Anyway, where do you want to do it?

HORACE. Could we wait just a minute?

TERENCE *(checking his watch)*. If you like.

HORACE. I've – I've never done this before. Would you like to sit down?

> HORACE *moves the broken chair out of the way.*

Bit of an accident. Georgian. Late, I think.

> TERENCE *sits on the sofa.* HORACE *hovers.* TERENCE *indicates for him to sit next to him.* HORACE *does so.*

Would you like some music?

TERENCE. No.

Beat.

HORACE. Do I pay you before or – ?

TERENCE. Later. I might do a runner if you give me the dosh now.

HORACE (*amused*). Yes.

TERENCE. No, I might.

Beat.

HORACE. So your name's Terence.

TERENCE. Yeah.

HORACE. Right.

Beat.

Not Bronco.

TERENCE. That's my trading name.

HORACE. I see.

TERENCE. When I came in just now with them two here, I kind of – forgot myself, know what I mean?

HORACE. Yes, yes, I do. You carried it off enormously well. Thank you.

TERENCE. 'S'alright.

Beat.

HORACE. What should I call you?

TERENCE. You don't have to call me nothing.

HORACE. Right. I'm Horace, by the way, should you want to . . . call me something.

TERENCE. Yeah.

Beat.

HORACE. So have you been at it long?

TERENCE. About a year. Since I left the marines.

HORACE. You were a marine, were you?

TERENCE. Yeah.

HORACE. The agency said you'd been in uniform, but I didn't pursue it. The marines. Gosh! How was that?

TERENCE. What?

HORACE. Well, being a marine.

TERENCE. 'S'alright. Made some good mates.

HORACE. Right.

TERENCE. Yeah.

HORACE. Why did you leave?

TERENCE. I finished my contract.

HORACE. Right. So did you go straight into . . . ?

TERENCE. Just about.

HORACE. Right.

TERENCE. And when I'm not shagging for a living, I do a bit of bouncing.

HORACE. Bouncing?

TERENCE. Yeah.

HORACE. Right. (*Penny dropping.*) Oh, as in 'bouncer'!

TERENCE. Yeah.

HORACE. So you manage to keep the wolf from the door?

TERENCE. I manage to keep him fucking miles from the door.

HORACE. Yes. Good.

TERENCE. Yeah. So what do you like?

HORACE. Ah, well –

TERENCE. I don't take it up the arse, right?

HORACE. Right.

TERENCE. And rimming's extra.

HORACE. Right.

Beat.

If we were to – get round to that, about – how much do you think – approximately?

TERENCE. Negotiable.

HORACE. Right.

TERENCE. Anything else, help yourself.

HORACE. Yes. Thank you.

TERENCE. You ever tried lenses?

HORACE. What's that?

TERENCE. Contact lenses.

HORACE. Oh, lenses! Yes, I have, as it happens, but I've got greasy tear ducts. You think I should?

TERENCE. It's up to you, mate. I've seen you before.

HORACE. I don't think you have. Anyway, maybe –

TERENCE *puts his hand on* HORACE*'s knee.*

TERENCE. You alright?

HORACE. Yes, yes. It's just that . . . it's been quite a while.

TERENCE. Why's that?

HORACE. I don't know, really. I think about it, and occasionally get quite close to doing it, and it's – kind of worked out once or twice, but . . . To be honest, I'm not that experienced – at all.

TERENCE. What's so special about tonight, then?

HORACE. How do you mean?

TERENCE. Well, if you don't shag much, why've you suddenly decided to pay for it?

HORACE. Do you know, I don't know. Every now and again, I think I should do something about it, so I suppose that's what this is. I'm not the most adventurous person, but once in a while, I feel I ought to push the boat out.

TERENCE. There's nothing wrong with you, is there?

HORACE. No.

TERENCE. I'm not going to pull your knickers down and find you got a cunt and nine bollocks or nothing.

HORACE. No, no. I'm perfectly – you know.

TERENCE. That's weird.

HORACE. What is?

TERENCE. Not doing it much.

HORACE. Weird? Oh Christ, do you think I'm weird?

TERENCE. I don't know.

HORACE. Maybe I am. Maybe everyone thinks I'm weird. It's never crossed my mind before. Well, that's not strictly true.

TERENCE. Look, mate, no one's saying you're weird. I'm just saying that not shagging much is weird, in that I have not met any geezer who has said that before. Right?

HORACE. Right.

TERENCE. Fucking hell!

HORACE. Sorry.

Beat.

Well, to be honest, I suppose there is a reason. It's because of someone else. I suppose I'm in love – in a manner of speaking.

TERENCE. You don't sound very sure.

HORACE. No, no, I am.

TERENCE. I mean, either you are or you're not, know what I mean?

HORACE. You're right, yes, and I am.

TERENCE. So why don't you shag him?

HORACE. He's dead.

TERENCE. Oh.

HORACE. He died about a year ago.

TERENCE. Oh.

HORACE. Blood poisoning. Extraordinary, really. He cut himself – just a nick, a tiny nick – on one of those things that you – stick in paper – well, through paper that's got holes in it – do you know what I mean?

TERENCE. Yeah.

HORACE. – And it keeps it all together. A sort of – long silvery thing with two prongs on it –

TERENCE. I know what you mean –

HORACE. – that you put through another silvery thing –

TERENCE. Yeah, I know.

HORACE. – and the prongs kind of flatten out when you –

TERENCE. Yes, I do know what you mean.

HORACE. Yes. Well, he nicked himself on one of those and got blood poisoning and died . . . so quickly.

TERENCE. Probably rust.

HORACE. Yes. Extraordinary.

Beat.

Unfortunately, the silvery thing was holding together a manuscript of a novel I'd written. I so wanted him to read it, but he never got round to it because I gather that, when he took it out of the envelope – that's when he . . .

TERENCE. Nicked himself.

HORACE. Yes.

TERENCE. You a writer, then?

HORACE. No. Well, yes, but I don't earn a living from it. In fact, I don't earn anything from it. In fact, that novel's the only thing I've written – so far. And you, do you do it much – outside office hours, so to speak?

TERENCE. I haven't got anyone, if that's what you mean. So this dead bloke, knew him long, did you?

HORACE. Yes. We were at school together. He was the mutual chum I mentioned – of me and Judy.

TERENCE. You started early.

HORACE. Do you think so?

TERENCE. The first sex I had, outside the family, I was twenty-three.

HORACE. Ah no, I don't mean we –

TERENCE. What?

HORACE. Like – did anything, really – to speak of . . .

Beat.

Funny, isn't it?

TERENCE. Is it?

HORACE. Meeting like this.

TERENCE. We've met before.

HORACE. I don't think so.

TERENCE. We have, mate. I'm sure of it. What sort of guy do you like, then?

HORACE. Well, I suppose all sorts, really. I like you.

TERENCE. What was the bloke from school like?

HORACE. Jerry? Oh. He was . . .

TERENCE. You haven't forgotten, have you?

HORACE. No. Jerry was . . . I don't know. What sort of guy do you like?

TERENCE. Young.

HORACE. Young, yes, I like that, too. You're young, for goodness sake, and I'm not that old.

TERENCE. I mean, young.

HORACE. Uh-huh.

TERENCE. Really young.

HORACE. What, you mean . . . ?

TERENCE. Not toddlers, but – kids, you know.

HORACE. Uh-huh. That must be quite difficult.

TERENCE. You can always get one for a packet of fags, a couple of quid. No problem.

HORACE. Right.

TERENCE *picks up an asparagus spear and takes a bite.*

TERENCE (*throwing it down*). Ugh! Fucking horrible!

HORACE. Are you sure you wouldn't like a drink?

TERENCE. That what they eat in France, is it?

HORACE. Why don't I put on some music?

TERENCE. Whatever you like, mate.

He goes onto the balcony as HORACE *chooses a record and puts it on: Beethoven's Fourth Piano Concerto, First Movement. As the music starts, he hovers by the hi-fi.*

HORACE. Maybe not.

He takes it off. He looks at TERENCE, *then takes off his glasses and pockets them. He goes on to the balcony and stands next to* TERENCE, *who's looking at the view. They don't touch.*

TERENCE. I lived near here as a kid.

HORACE. Really?

TERENCE (*pointing*). Yeah, over there. Still looks the fucking same.

HORACE. The thing is – I'm really pleased to meet you. As I say, I haven't done it for a while, and I really feel I'd like to – with you.

HORACE *tentatively takes hold of* TERENCE*'s hand. Beat. He rests his head on his shoulder.* TERENCE *pats* HORACE*'s head.*

TERENCE. Fuck it.

He comes back into the room. HORACE *follows.*

HORACE. Sorry, have I – ?

TERENCE. It's not you, mate. I was just thinking . . . a mate of mine. We was on duty once. Belfast. One minute, we was talking, next minute, he's dead. Sniper. Don't even hear it. Dead. Fuck it.

HORACE. I'm sorry.

TERENCE. It's what you're paid for.

HORACE. I suppose it is.

TERENCE. That's the way it goes, isn't it? You're shat into the world, find there's a load of other poor cunts who didn't ask to be here, work your bollocks off trying to get on with them, then realise you're on your tod. Fucking joke, isn't it?

HORACE. Was your mate – was he . . . ?

TERENCE. We was good mates.

HORACE. Right.

TERENCE *shows him a chain he's wearing around his neck.*

TERENCE. This was his. We swapped chains after we'd been there for a bit. He gave me this and I gave him mine, one I'd had a good few years. It was sort of to mark the fact that

we'd both survived the first five months. He didn't survive
the sixth.

HORACE. It's funny, that guy I was telling you about, my
friend from school, he gave me a chain.

TERENCE. Have you still got it?

HORACE. No, unfortunately. I misplaced it or something.
Anyway . . .

TERENCE. Tell you what, let's call it a night.

HORACE. Oh.

TERENCE. I've lost it, know what I mean?

HORACE. Yes. Shame.

TERENCE. Sorry, mate. I won't charge you or nothing.

HORACE. No, it's not that – and I think you should. After all,
you've made the effort to come here.

TERENCE. It's okay.

HORACE. Let me give you something at least.

He hands him a note.

TERENCE. Ta, mate. That's very decent of you.

HORACE. Perhaps we might make another date.

TERENCE. Yeah. You got the agency's number.

HORACE. Yes.

TERENCE (*patting* HORACE*'s shoulder*). Cheers, mate. I'll
see myself out.

HORACE. Cheers.

TERENCE *leaves.* HORACE *is still. The front door is
opened and shut. Pause. He goes to a drawer and takes out
a Mars bar. He starts eating it. The phone rings. He
swallows a mouthful and answers it.*

Hello? . . . Ah, yes. Hello . . . They left about a quarter of
an hour ago . . . You've found him! Thank God for that! . . .
On top of the wardrobe? . . . Oh dear. Well, you must

keep your eye on him. They'll be back any minute now . . .
Yes . . . Yes . . . Goodbye . . . Oh, er – adios – yes . . .

He puts down the phone and takes another bite. He thinks
for a second, then puts the same piece of Beethoven back
on: the opening of the Fourth Piano Concerto. He listens
and takes another bite as the lights fade.

SCENE TWO

Evening. The music continues. The doors onto the balcony are
closed. A CD player has been added to the hi-fi. The broken
chair is mended. HORACE, in an old shabby dressing gown,
is sprawled on the sofa, a glass of vodka in his hand, listening
to the music, engrossed, his eyes closed. His glasses are on a
side table. The room is dark, lit by a single lamp. The door to
the hall is closed. Light from the hall glows round the edge of
the door. As the music reaches bar 50, the hall door slowly
swings open, spreading light across the room. Silhouetted in
the doorway is a YOUNG MAN. HORACE *is oblivious.*
Pause.

YOUNG MAN. Excuse me.

No response.

Excuse me.

HORACE *suddenly comes to with a yell and leaps to his feet.*

HORACE. What the fuck – ?

YOUNG MAN. Sorry.

HORACE. What the fuck are you – ?

YOUNG MAN. Sorry.

HORACE. Who the fuck are you?

YOUNG MAN. I rang the bell.

HORACE (*grabbing his glasses and putting them on*). Get out.

YOUNG MAN. I'm sorry.

HORACE. Get out.

He stumbles to the CD player and turns off the music.

I'll call the police.

YOUNG MAN. No, don't.

HORACE (*picking up the receiver*). I will.

YOUNG MAN. Please don't.

HORACE. Then get the fuck out.

YOUNG MAN. Okay.

HORACE. Out!

YOUNG MAN. I'm going, alright?

HORACE. Now!

YOUNG MAN. Alright?

He doesn't move. HORACE *suddenly freezes. He struggles to see the* YOUNG MAN's *face because the light's behind him. They stare at each other. Pause.*

Are you Horace?

Beat. HORACE *nods. He puts the phone down. He slowly approaches the* YOUNG MAN. *He switches on another lamp. We see the* YOUNG MAN *more clearly. He's seventeen, in school uniform, with a small rucksack on his shoulder.* HORACE *quietly gasps. Pause.*

I'm Jimi.

Pause as they stare at each other.

I rang the bell a few times, then gave the door a push and it opened, so I came in. I didn't know what else to do. I'm sorry.

Beat.

I'll go, if you want.

Beat. JIMI *holds out his hand to* HORACE. *For a moment* HORACE *can't move, then tentatively takes the outstretched*

hand. They don't shake, but keep hold of each other's hands
for several seconds, eyes fixed on each other. Then:

Pleased to meet you.

HORACE. Jimi . . . (*Then he lets go of* JIMI*'s hand, pulling*
himself together.) I'm always forgetting to push the snib
down. One day, someone'll just walk in and . . . I was
floating away with the music. It was rather loud, I'm afraid,
but I don't see the point of listening to Beethoven unless
it's absolutely deafening. Oh God, everything's a terrible
mess. Would you like a drink? I have to own up to being a
bit pissed, actually. I'm trying to unlock the imagination.
Vodka or – ?

JIMI. Thanks.

HORACE. How do you take it?

JIMI. However you take it.

HORACE. The last time I saw you – how old are you now?

JIMI. Seventeen.

HORACE. Seventeen. Shit! The last time I saw you, you were
a little baby . . . a little baby . . .

He starts fixing the drinks.

Make yourself at home, please. Sit down, whatever. I'm
sorry I wasn't more welcoming. How's your mother?

JIMI. She'll be alright.

HORACE. Where is she?

JIMI. I never know. Somewhere in Australia, I guess.

HORACE. Don't you live there now?

JIMI. She's based in Brisbane for a few years. I pop over in the
holidays.

HORACE. So you're at school here?

JIMI. She thought I should do A-levels in England, so she's
had me transported to some dump in Hampshire. It's like
Dotheboys Hall.

HORACE. Oh dear.

He hands him a drink.

JIMI. Thanks.

HORACE. Cheers.

JIMI. Cheers.

They drink.

HORACE. Would you like any food or – ?

JIMI. No, thank you.

HORACE. A bath or – I'm not saying you need one. I just mean, feel at home.

JIMI. Thanks. I'm fine.

HORACE. How long have you been here?

JIMI. Eighteen months.

HORACE. Gosh! Judy told me you were moving to Australia, but she didn't say you were coming here to school. Maybe it hadn't been sorted out. What a shame! We could have made contact before. Never mind. Why are you here?

JIMI. You're not angry, are you?

HORACE. Of course I'm not. I just want to know.

JIMI. I thought it was time we met. That's all.

Beat.

HORACE. Yes. Yes, good idea! So do you have – one of those things – oh, what are they called? – an exeat? That's it: exeat! God, I haven't used that word for a quarter of a century!

JIMI. Not exactly.

HORACE. You haven't run away, have you?

JIMI. Kind of.

HORACE. Oh.

JIMI. Sort of AWOL, for a bit.

HORACE. Oh.

They sip their vodka.

Jerry was – your dad was always in trouble. It was ridiculous. I never was, of course. I was boringly well-behaved, but Jerry! My God!

JIMI. That school, it's a waste of time, I tell you. But there's no arguing with Mummy.

HORACE. She's always been a bit like that.

JIMI. She thinks I'm not motivated, that there's nothing driving me. She's scared I'll end up drifting.

HORACE. She's your mother. She's bound to worry, even if there isn't anything to worry about. You're her sort of masterpiece. Isn't that right?

JIMI. Bloody hell!

HORACE. Mothers are like that.

JIMI. 'The world belongs to those who know where they're going,' that's what she says.

HORACE. There might be something in that.

JIMI. Do you know where you're going?

HORACE. Oh no. I never go anywhere.

Beat.

I'm a bit thrown, actually, you being here like this. You know you're quite like your father, don't you?

JIMI. Yes. I've seen photographs. I've seen one of you.

HORACE. Really?

JIMI. Well, I think it's you. There's dad as a teenager and this other guy in glasses.

HORACE. Have you still got it?

JIMI. Yes. Mum was having a clear-out before we moved to Oz, and I noticed it and kept it.

HORACE. You haven't got it with you, have you?

JIMI. No, but it's safe.

HORACE. Good.

JIMI *looks at the balcony.*

JIMI (*dawning realisation*). That's it, isn't it?

HORACE. What?

JIMI (*going to the balcony*). Where the photograph was taken.

He opens the doors and walks out.

You were standing here with that view behind you.

HORACE. Well, it wouldn't be exactly the same view –

JIMI. Incredible!

HORACE. I can't quite remember –

JIMI. You've been living here all this time?

HORACE. Yes.

JIMI. Christ! (*Re. the view.*) Oh, this is great. London, just lying there! Imagine, taking off and swooping across to Canary Wharf! Fantastic!

HORACE. It's a bit chilly, isn't it? I think you should come in. You'll catch cold.

JIMI *steps inside.* HORACE *shuts the doors.*

JIMI. Have you still got the beads?

HORACE. Beads?

JIMI. That you were wearing in the photograph.

HORACE. I was wearing beads?

JIMI. You looked pretty weird.

HORACE. Oh dear.

JIMI. Still, I suppose that was the fashion.

HORACE. Was your dad wearing beads?

JIMI. No. He was wearing a chain.

HORACE. Of course he was. God, that chain! He gave it me, you know.

JIMI. Did he? Have you still got it?

HORACE. No. It disappeared. One minute I had it, the next minute it had gone. I can't tell you how upset I was.

Beat.

What was the name of . . . ? Guy, that's it! What happened
to Guy?

JIMI. Who?

HORACE. Your mum had a French friend called Guy.

JIMI. I don't know who you're talking about.

HORACE. You all lived together for a while. Don't you
remember? In New York.

JIMI. Oh, hang on a minute, yes. He cooked a lot or
something.

HORACE. That sounds like Guy.

JIMI. And she found him having it off with some foreign bird
in the kitchen.

HORACE. Oh dear.

JIMI. I guess that was the end of him. Mum enjoys her
independence, but doesn't much enjoy anybody else's. He
died not long after that. Apparently he choked on something
he'd cooked.

HORACE. My God!

JIMI. Got a feather stuck in his throat, I think Mum said.

HORACE. Poor Guy.

JIMI. She didn't seem too bothered.

HORACE. You're being a bit hard on her.

JIMI. It's the truth. Mum's got through a few blokes in her
time. They pass through so quickly, it's hardly worth getting
to know them.

HORACE. Now, come on.

JIMI. She gets bored, that's all.

HORACE. Why are you here?

JIMI. I've told you.

HORACE. Tell me again.

JIMI. I wanted to meet you. You're my godfather. You knew my dad.

HORACE. But why have you gone to all this trouble? You could have got my number, we could have arranged to meet.

Beat.

JIMI. I had a dream last night. I was in a garden – something like a garden – and it felt like home. I was looking around, and then Dad was there standing next to me. He asked if I was alright and I said yes, and I asked if he was alright and he said yes, and he gave me a smile, and then I woke up. I tried to go back to sleep and pick up where I left off, but that never works, does it? I wanted to meet you, the guy my dad had his arm round in that picture, the two of you looking like cats that got the cream.

HORACE. What did your dad look like in the dream?

JIMI. Like that. Like the photo.

Beat.

HORACE. Would you like another?

JIMI *nods.* HORACE *takes his glass and fixes two more drinks.* JIMI *takes out a pack of cigarettes.*

JIMI. Do you mind?

HORACE. No.

JIMI. Do you want one?

HORACE. Why not?

JIMI *offers him one.*

Thanks.

JIMI *lights their cigarettes.* HORACE *hands him his drink.*

JIMI. So what was he like?

HORACE. Who?

JIMI. My dad.

HORACE. Your dad was . . . he was great.

JIMI. You met at school?

HORACE. Yes. We became aware of each other when we were about sixteen. He'd mixed with other boys before that, a different crowd than what I used to hang out with. Actually, we'd come into contact a few years before in a school play, one of those mystery things – The Creation. He was The Serpent.

JIMI. What were you?

HORACE. Eve.

JIMI. How did you manage that?

HORACE. I was in a flesh-coloured body-stocking with a fig-leaf. But we didn't really have that much to do with each other. I think he thought I was a bit – a bit of a poof. In fact, I know he did, because he used to say things like, 'You're a bit of a poof, aren't you?' But I didn't really mind because he was at that age when boys can be like that, but a few years later . . . he'd changed. It was probably all to do with puberty and everything, but he was – really nice to me and we became mates. It was music, really. He was a very good musician.

JIMI. I know.

HORACE. Truly gifted. He arranged a concert once. Lots of people were involved and he played some fantastic stuff. But I'll always remember, he got a couple of trebles, really quite young, to sing this duet by Monteverdi. It was most inappropriate, lyrics-wise, but that was Jerry for you: always chancing his arm.

JIMI. Why was it inappropriate?

HORACE. They were declaring undying love to each other, and they were eleven. Still, there were no complaints, probably because it was in Italian. It was the most exquisite moment. These pure voices, with Jerry accompanying them on piano. It was the only time I saw him lost for words.

Beat. JIMI *goes out onto the balcony.* HORACE *hovers, then steps out next to him.*

JIMI. Don't you ever feel you could raise yourself even a few inches off the ground, and glide, glide away?

HORACE. To be honest, no.

The nearby church clock starts striking the hour very loudly.

JIMI. Jesus!

HORACE. Sorry.

Stroke two.

I've had to live with this for years –

Stroke three.

You kind of get used to it.

Stroke four.

JIMI. Jesus!

HORACE. It is a bit loud, I know, but –

Stroke five.

– but it'll be over in a second or two.

Stroke six.

It's strange, but after a while –

Stroke seven.

– you sort of don't hear it.

JIMI. I've run away.

Stroke eight.

HORACE. What? What did you say?

JIMI. I've run away.

He comes back in as the clock strikes for the ninth and final time. HORACE *steps inside and shuts the balcony doors.* JIMI *starts pacing restlessly.*

HORACE. You said.

JIMI. What?

HORACE. You've already told me you've run away.

JIMI. Yeah.

HORACE. For a bit.

JIMI. That's right, yeah.

HORACE. Yes. Are you alright?

JIMI. Yeah.

HORACE. God, it's cold out there!

JIMI. Did you and Dad ever take drugs?

HORACE. No.

JIMI. Didn't you?

HORACE. Not that I remember.

JIMI. You look like you did.

HORACE. What do you mean?

JIMI. In the picture.

HORACE. Oh. Well, we might have had a – little something or other.

JIMI. Would you like a little something or other now?

HORACE. What are you talking about?

JIMI (*taking out a little packet*). Would you like a little something now?

HORACE. I'm really not sure whether –

JIMI. This guy at school, he's always got a little something or other. He's one of Lord Charlecote's sons. (*Undoing the packet.*) Would you like some?

HORACE. You shouldn't be taking that. What is it?

JIMI. Coke.

HORACE. Well, you shouldn't be taking it. You shouldn't be taking anything. You shouldn't be smoking, for goodness sake!

JIMI. Would you like some?

HORACE. And are you sure you need any? You've been a bit jumpy all evening.

JIMI. Would you?

HORACE (*with a barely discernible nod*). Mm.

JIMI *starts organising the coke.* HORACE *hovers.*

It's so nice seeing you without a lump on your head – God, I'm sorry!

JIMI. What?

HORACE. You used to have one as a baby, (*Indicating the middle of the forehead.*) right there. You didn't know, did you?

JIMI. No.

HORACE. God, I am sorry. Jerry thought you were from another planet. He said it was an implanted radio to receive messages from your mother-ship.

JIMI. I don't think I've seen any photographs of me as a baby.

HORACE. Sorry.

JIMI. What happened to it?

HORACE. It went, apparently, of its own accord. It seems these things come and go. I didn't mean to . . . I'm sorry.

JIMI. No problem.

JIMI *chopping the coke,* HORACE *watching.*

HORACE. That was the last time I saw Jerry.

JIMI. When?

HORACE. Your christening, which was the first time I saw you. We had a great time, your dad and me. Not at the christening. Well, it was alright, as christenings go – not that I've been to many – any, really – oh, well, one or two. But when we were younger – your dad – your dad was every-thing that was – happy and good then – at that time in my life, and which has gone now – like him. There was one day, one day we had – when I met your mother, actually – which was sort of complete. One of those moments in life when you realise, 'Ah, that's what it's like to be happy.' I hoped there'd be more days like that, but there weren't. Not quite like that, anyway. When I'm dying, it's that moment that'll make me think it was all worthwhile. My life crystallised in the memory of a moment. It was like we were outside time.

JIMI. How long's a moment?

HORACE. It's not a minute or a second. It's a mystery. A moment is part of the mystery of life.

JIMI. You're not dying, are you?

HORACE. No.

JIMI. Are you?

HORACE. I'm perfectly well.

JIMI. You're not ill?

HORACE. No. I'm perfectly well. Why do you ask?

JIMI. Have you got a note?

HORACE. What?

JIMI. I've only got a scrunched-up fiver.

HORACE. Right. (*Looking through his wallet.*) Do you need some? I mean, apart from –

JIMI. No.

HORACE. Sure?

JIMI. Well, I suppose the odd spare quid always comes in handy.

HORACE *takes out a £50 note and hands it to* JIMI.

HORACE. Keep it.

JIMI. No, no –

HORACE. It's yours.

JIMI. Brilliant!

JIMI *rolls up the note.*

HORACE. Actually, I have had this before – once – in the museum basement – with an Egyptologist.

JIMI. Did you like it?

HORACE. I liked the Egyptologist.

JIMI *offers him the rolled note.* HORACE *looks at the coke.*

JIMI. A quatrain of cocaine.

HORACE. What do you mean?

JIMI. Four lines.

HORACE. Very good.

He snorts.

(*Passing the note to* JIMI.) Thank you.

JIMI *snorts a line.*

I've always wondered what it was like to be a godparent. So.

JIMI. So, Horace. You don't mind me calling you that, do you?

HORACE. It's my name.

JIMI (*giggling*). I know.

He goes out onto the balcony.

HORACE. Oh dear. Not again.

JIMI. Oh, Horace!

HORACE (*following him out*). Isn't it too cold for this?

JIMI (*holding out his arms to the view*). Horace, Horace, wouldn't it be great to fly?

HORACE. Not too loud, Jimi.

JIMI. To take off and fucking fly!

HORACE. Is this the coke talking?

JIMI. No, I've always wanted to fly. Look at the moon, Horace!

HORACE. Yes.

JIMI. What a fucking lovely moon!

HORACE. Jimi, you must keep your voice down.

JIMI. The mooniest fucking moon I ever did see!

HORACE (*momentarily thrown*). What did you say?

JIMI. Wow! This is great, Horace. Let's have another drink.

HORACE. You really mustn't catch cold.

He comes back in and starts fixing drinks.

JIMI. I want to be a planet, Horace –

HORACE. Oh, God!

JIMI. I want to be part of the planetary system.

HORACE. Jimi –

JIMI. I want to be a part of history!

HORACE (*to himself*). Horace, why are you tense? Why are
    you feeling so tense? Oh, fuck it!

He takes the glasses and vodka bottle onto the balcony.

Help yourself.

JIMI. I want something to fight for.

HORACE. Want, want, want.

JIMI. Don't you, Horace? Don't you want something to fight
    for, Horace?

HORACE. You don't have to keep saying my name.

JIMI. Something to believe in. That'd be great, wouldn't it,
    Horace? And to have somebody – have somebody to believe
    in. That's the thing! To have someone to grow strong with. I
    mean, not everyone lets you down, do they?

HORACE. Let's go in.

JIMI. Have you got anyone, Horace?

HORACE. It's cold, Jimi.

JIMI. Have you?

HORACE. Let's go in.

He waits for JIMI *to step past him, then comes in himself
and shuts the doors.*

Are you sure you're not hungry?

JIMI. Yeah, yeah, I'm fine.

He's rolling up the note again.

HORACE. Do you think you should?

JIMI. Horace, we've hardly started. Enjoy yourself.

He hands HORACE *the note.*

HORACE. Yes. Yes, maybe you're right.

He snorts, then hands the note back to JIMI.

Thank you.

JIMI *snorts.*

JIMI. I've done a bit of writing, you know.

HORACE. Good.

JIMI. You have, too, haven't you?

HORACE. No.

JIMI. I thought you'd written a novel.

HORACE. Ah, the novel, yes. That was years ago.

JIMI. What was it about?

HORACE. This and that.

JIMI. What?

HORACE. Obsessive desire. Bleeding humanity. The tragic inexplicability of existence. The usual.

JIMI. Can I read it?

HORACE. Yes, yes, you can. I'll dig out a copy for you. Actually, Judy's probably got one, or maybe it didn't survive the clear-out. No, I'll get you one.

JIMI (*toasting with the vodka*). Cheers.

HORACE. Cheers.

They drink.

Jimi.

JIMI. Yes?

HORACE. Why did you tell me you'd run away?

JIMI. Cos I have.

HORACE. I mean, why did you tell me again?

JIMI. I don't know.

He downs the rest of his vodka.

It's hard, though, isn't it, writing?

HORACE. It is.

JIMI. I wonder what the secret is?

HORACE. If there is a secret, I don't know it. Having ideas and expressing them, that's writing for you. I'm the last person to ask.

Beat.

I read somewhere that you must always remember that no two things are the same, exactly the same: no two roses, no two worms, no two apples or birds or grains of sand, no two things are ever exactly alike, and you must be able to distinguish each clearly and accurately. I read that some-where or other. Does that help? No two hairs or cells of skin are ever indistinguishable. No two hands, fingers, thumbs or nails, chins, eyebrows, ears . . . You are so like him.

JIMI. What?

HORACE. Your hair, your eyes, your nose – lips . . . When I saw you, for a second, I thought you were him.

Pause.

It's wearing me out.

Pause. JIMI *goes over to the piano and sits on the stool. Music is open on the stand. He starts sightreading, with great difficulty, the opening of Beethoven's Fourth Piano Concerto.* HORACE *is taken aback. As* JIMI *struggles with the music,* HORACE *goes over and stands behind him.* JIMI *stops playing for a moment, then continues. Eventually* HORACE *raises a hand, intending to touch* JIMI's *hair. Before contact is made,* JIMI *stops playing again.* HORACE *takes his hand away as* JIMI *takes his hands from the keys.* HORACE *freezes.* JIMI *suddenly throws his arms around* HORACE's *waist and buries his face in his belly.*

Jimi . . . Jimi . . .

It seems JIMI*'s crying.*

Jimi, what's wrong? What is it? What's wrong?

JIMI *suddenly gets up and starts pacing in an effort to keep control.*

What is it?

JIMI *paces himself to a standstill, his hands covering his face.*

Tell me, Jimi. Please.

JIMI. He told me . . .

HORACE. Yes?

JIMI. He told me this morning . . .

HORACE. Yes?

JIMI. . . . before prayers that . . .

HORACE. What?

JIMI. That that's it.

HORACE. Oh.

JIMI. It's over.

HORACE. Who told you this?

JIMI. Poppy.

HORACE. Who's Poppy?

JIMI. The cunt I've fallen in love with.

HORACE. Poppy?

JIMI. It's a nickname. We've all got them.

HORACE. Right.

JIMI. I'm sorry. Forget it. I didn't mean to –

HORACE. There's nothing to be sorry about. Tell me about him. Tell me about Poppy.

JIMI. Well – he appeared about – six months ago – exactly six months ago – and we hit it off, just like that. I'd played around, as you do, even had a few girlfriends, but Poppy – well . . .

Beat.

It was him who started it all. He made the first move. We were doing a cross-country run, jogging along together, having a bit of a chat, and he suddenly stopped and said, 'Why don't you kiss me?', so I did, and from that moment to – to this morning, we haven't stopped.

Beat.

He's kind of completely taken me over. It's been incredible; the best – the very best time of my life, and now . . .

HORACE. You've no idea why he'd say that that's it?

JIMI. No, no, I don't. It doesn't make sense. When he spoke to me today, there was nothing – nothing in his eyes – nothing to acknowledge what we'd . . . He's the only thing, Horace, that's meant anything. If that is it, then I don't see the point.

HORACE. I'm sorry. That's a terrible thing to –

JIMI. People always let you down, don't they?

HORACE. Well –

JIMI. Give up on you, die on you, always fucking let you down.

HORACE. I'm not sure that's always –

JIMI. What the fuck am I going to do?

The phone rings. Neither of them moves. It continues ringing. HORACE *picks up the receiver.*

HORACE. Hello? . . . Judy! What a surprise! . . .

JIMI *frantically indicates that he doesn't want her to know he's there.*

Is everything alright? . . . What's happened? . . . Yes? . . . He's at school here? . . . I didn't know that . . . Run away? . . . No, he's not here. Why on earth would he be? . . . Well, I think that's a bit extreme . . . Look, boys of his age, you know what they're like. He'll probably turn up in next to no time . . . Yes. I think the headmaster's right: leave it till morning and see what happens . . . Where are you? . . . Yes, Brisbane'd be nice . . . I'll think about it . . . Yes,

I'll phone a few travel agents . . . Okay . . . Lovely to hear from you . . . Bye.

He puts the phone down. JIMI*'s started pacing round the room.*

JIMI. Wouldn't you bloody know it?

HORACE. She phoned the school, just to say hello, I think, and the headmaster obviously had to tell her you weren't there.

JIMI. Wouldn't you just bloody know it?

HORACE. He sounds like a decent bloke because she was saying he ought to call the police and he thought it wasn't necessary – yet. So I reckon if you turn up sometime tomorrow or – whenever . . . Would you like something to eat?

JIMI, *still pacing, doesn't seem to hear.* HORACE *goes to a drawer and takes out two Mars bars. He offers one to* JIMI.

JIMI. Thanks.

They unwrap their bars and start eating them. JIMI *paces intermittently.* HORACE *starts to as well.*

So what do you think, Horace? It's a joke, isn't it?

HORACE. Well, it's . . .

Beat.

It's very difficult.

JIMI. I know that.

HORACE. I think it's fair to say that I do understand how important – Poppy is to you and how – awful it must be for you at the moment, but I think it's also fair to say that, in time, the chances are that you'll meet someone else who could mean as much, if not more to you than Poppy does now.

Beat.

So maybe the best thing would be to – would be to forget him.

Pause.

But then again . . .

Beat.

JIMI. There won't be anyone else. I don't want anyone else. I want him. Do you understand that?

HORACE. Yes.

JIMI. I want him.

JIMI's foot goes through a floorboard. He yells in pain.

HORACE (*rushing to him*). Jesus!

JIMI. Fuck!

HORACE. Are you alright?

JIMI. Fuck in fucking hell!

HORACE (*trying to release his foot*). Does it hurt?

JIMI. Of course it fucking hurts!

HORACE. Gently does it . . .

HORACE very carefully releases his foot.

There we go.

JIMI. Fuck!

HORACE. There's a bit of blood. Let's sit you over here and I'll put something on it.

He helps JIMI to the upright chair and carefully sits him down. The chair collapses beneath him and he falls to the floor.

Oh, God! What the fuck am I doing?

JIMI bursts out laughing.

Jimi, I'm so sorry. I've been meaning to get that bloody chair done for –

JIMI gets hysterical. He starts to roll around the floor. HORACE watches and smiles.

Do you know – your mum – your mum sat on that years ago and it – it did the same thing!

JIMI (*clutching his crutch*). Shit, I've wet myself!

  HORACE *starts to giggle.*

  I've fucking wet myself!

HORACE. I could get you a change of – if you'd like –

JIMI. Eh, Horace – Horace –

HORACE. What?

JIMI. I've really put my foot in it this time, haven't I?

  This finishes him off. HORACE *looks at him, then glances at the hole in the floorboard. He freezes, staring at the hole.*

  You'll have to move, Horace – only thing for it.

  HORACE *reaches into the hole and takes out a gold chain. He holds it up and looks at it, amazed.* JIMI *eventually notices this. He crawls to* HORACE *and also looks at the chain.*

  Dad's?

  HORACE *nods.* JIMI *delicately touches the chain.*

  Dad . . .

  Pause. Then HORACE *kneels behind* JIMI *and fastens the chain around his neck. He retrieves his Mars bar and resumes eating it.* JIMI *gets up and looks in a mirror. He touches the chain. He goes over to* HORACE *and stands above him. Beat.* JIMI *very tentatively places a hand on* HORACE*'s head, then gently strokes his hair. Beat.* HORACE *very gently lets his head rest against* JIMI*'s thigh. The lights fade.*

SCENE THREE

It's a summer afternoon. The balcony doors are open. A fair can be heard in the distance. Some of the furniture is stacked against walls. A tea-chest remains unpacked. The floor is bare. There's a dansette and a stack of records. An acoustic guitar leans against the piano. HORACE, *aged 17, is looking in a mirror putting on a string of beads. He's wearing gold-rimmed National Health spectacles and a few bracelets and badges, including a military medal on a ribbon. He studies himself. He decides to take off the beads. He dashes onto the balcony and looks out. Beat. He dashes back in. He checks himself in the mirror again. The beads go back on. He puts the stylus on a record already on the turntable: 'Strange Orchestras' by Tyrannosaurus Rex. He starts moving to it and then tries to sing along. The door is pushed open revealing* JERRY, *aged 17.* HORACE *hasn't noticed him.* JERRY *stands watching for a while, then:*

JERRY (*singing with the record*). 'Then they giggle and they wiggle through the door in the big dark oak tree.'

   HORACE *spins round, covered in confusion.*

HORACE. Hi.

JERRY. Hi.

   HORACE *takes the record off.*

Steve Peregrine Took on pixiephone.

HORACE. Yeah. Hi.

JERRY. Hi. The door was open.

HORACE. Oh, right. I must remember to push the snib down. Mum and Dad'll kill me. You found it alright, then.

JERRY. Yeah. It's cool.

HORACE. Yeah. I'll show you round, shall I?

JERRY. Yeah, yeah, later.

HORACE. Yeah.

JERRY (*going onto the balcony*). Great view! That's amazing!

HORACE. Yeah.

JERRY. Amazing! It makes a change from Edmonton, I bet.

HORACE. Yeah, although I quite liked Edmonton. I'd have been happy to stay there.

JERRY. But you've got the whole of London at your feet!

HORACE. Yes. It is nice, I must say.

JERRY. It's great.

HORACE. Yeah.

Beat.

Mum and Dad are away. They needed a break after the move. They're not coming back till tomorrow, so we've got the whole place to ourselves, if we want.

JERRY. Great!

HORACE. Yeah.

JERRY. We could go to the fair.

HORACE. Yeah, yeah, we could.

JERRY (*coming back in*). And a piano! Fantastic!

He plays a ten-second boogie.

Great!

HORACE. Yeah. Do you want anything?

JERRY. What have you got?

HORACE. I've got some pop.

JERRY. What sort?

HORACE. Dandelion and burdock.

JERRY. I'll wait.

HORACE. Right. Oh, by the way, I've finished with your *Hobbit*, if you want it back.

JERRY. Have you read it?

HORACE. Mm.

JERRY. What do you think?

HORACE. It's good, yeah.

JERRY. You didn't like it, did you?

HORACE. I did.

JERRY. You didn't. I can tell.

HORACE. I did.

JERRY. You didn't, Horace.

HORACE. Well, I didn't get it, really.

JERRY. It's easy.

HORACE. I don't mean like that. I mean, like, I don't get
gnomes and things.

JERRY. It's not just gnomes, mate.

HORACE. Isn't it?

JERRY. No.

HORACE. Well, I'm afraid I couldn't see beyond the gnomes.
That's all I got: gnomes.

JERRY. And anyway, they're not gnomes; they're dwarves.

HORACE. Are they?

JERRY. Yeah. Read it again.

HORACE. Again?

JERRY. Give it another go.

HORACE. You think I should?

JERRY. Yeah, cos once you get into it – wow!

HORACE. Right. I'll hang on to it, then, shall I?

JERRY. Yeah.

HORACE. Right.

He takes a slightly bent, untipped cigarette from his pocket.

Look.

JERRY. Great!

HORACE. Park Drive. I nicked it from Dad.

JERRY takes out a packet of ten No. 6.

JERRY. Nicked from the newsagent down the road.

HORACE. Great! So we're alright for fags.

JERRY. Yeah, and Jude rolls her own, so we're well in.

HORACE. Who?

JERRY. Jude. Judy.

HORACE. Who's Judy?

JERRY. She's this girl I met a week or so ago from the girls' school. Her family's just moved down from the Midlands. She's incredible.

HORACE. You never said.

JERRY. It's only just happened.

HORACE. And she's coming here?

JERRY. Yeah, any minute now. It's alright, isn't it? She's really cool. You'll love her.

HORACE. Will I?

JERRY. Yeah, she's fantastic.

HORACE. Great!

JERRY. I'll tell you something, Horry, she can't get enough of it.

HORACE. Can't she?

JERRY. No.

HORACE. Enough of what?

JERRY. You know . . .

HORACE. You've done it with her?

JERRY. Yeah. On our first date.

HORACE. Gosh.

JERRY. And I'll tell you something else: (*Confidentially*.) she sucks like a dream.

HORACE. Does she?

JERRY. Yeah. She can get the whole thing into her mouth.

HORACE. Gosh.

JERRY. Right up to the pubes, and she says next time she's going to try and get my balls in as well. Can you imagine?

HORACE. She must have a big mouth, then.

JERRY. You've got to give it a go, Horace.

HORACE. What, you mean . . . you want me . . . you want
me to – ?

JERRY. A bit of mutual's okay, but sinking your prick into
pussy – fuck!

HORACE. Oh. Right.

JERRY. You've just got to do it.

HORACE. Yes. I'll think about it.

JERRY. Absolutely definitely, old mate. Take it from me.
(*Noticing guitar*). Fantastic!

> JERRY *picks up the guitar and starts tuning it.* HORACE
> *hovers, then wanders onto the balcony. Out of* JERRY*'s
> eyeline, he mouths 'Fuck, fuck, fuck', full of angst.* JERRY,
> *oblivious, starts strumming, then sings a slow version of
> 'To Love Somebody'.* HORACE *is breathing deeply in an
> effort to calm himself. He turns to look at* JERRY *and
> becomes entranced.*

(*Singing*.) 'There's a light, a certain kind of light,
That never shone on me.
I want my life to be
Lived with you, lived with you.
There's a way, everybody say,
To do each and every little thing.
But what does it bring,
If I ain't got you, ain't got you . . .

> *Unnoticed by either,* JUDY, *aged 16, has appeared in the
> doorway with a shoulder-bag. She can't see* HORACE. *She
> stands watching* JERRY. *Eventually, he spots her. He
> doesn't stop singing and performs for her.*

'Hey baby, you don't know what it's like,
Baby, you don't know what it's like
To love somebody, to love somebody,
The way I love you.'

> *At first,* HORACE *can't work out what's going on, then
> steps inside and notices her.* JERRY *breaks off.*

JERRY (*to* JUDY). Hi.

JUDY (*to* JERRY). Hi.

HORACE. Hi.

JERRY. This is Horace.

JUDY. Hi.

HORACE. Hi.

JERRY. Judy.

HORACE. Right.

JUDY. Yeah. Hi.

HORACE. Hi.

JUDY. You can call me Jude.

HORACE. Right.

JUDY. Yeah. Got anything to drink?

HORACE. Dandelion and burdock.

JUDY. Fuck. I've just had some Dimyril, see, and I'm a bit –

The church clock starts striking the hour loudly.

JERRY. Fuck me!

HORACE. Yeah. They didn't tell us about this –

Stroke two.

– when we came to view it.

JUDY. Wow!

Stroke three.

This fucking Dimyril, man! I can hear a sort of –

Stroke four – the last.

Wow! (*Subsiding into* JERRY *and closing her eyes.*) Mmm
. . . baby, baby . . .

JERRY. Where is it?

*Eyes still closed, she fumbles in her bag and takes out a
medicine bottle.* JERRY *takes it from her.*

HORACE. What's Dimyril?

JERRY. An expectorant.

HORACE. Has she got a cough?

JERRY (*unscrewing the cap*). Not after half a bottle.

He takes a swig and offers it to HORACE. *He takes the bottle and eyes it suspiciously as* JUDY *lifts her open mouth to* JERRY's. *They kiss with great passion.* HORACE *takes a swig. It tastes disgusting. He watches them kissing for a while, then takes another swig. He starts looking through his records and puts on the title track of the LP 'Are You Experienced?' by Jimi Hendrix.*

JUDY (*breaking from the kiss*). Oh, yeah! Jimi, Jimi . . .

JERRY. Got a roll-up?

She hands him her bag, grooving to the music. HORACE *starts grooving in a minor way.*

JUDY. Oh, Jimi . . . I saw his trousers split in Coventry. Amazing!

JERRY's *taken out a small tin.*

There's some grass in there if you want.

JERRY. Yeah. Beautiful.

He starts rolling a joint.

Hey, Horry, what about that bastard Eccleston, eh? I mean, what a bastard!

HORACE. I don't have that much to do with him.

JERRY. He had the cheek to say to me – listen to this – the barefaced cheek to say that, without a doubt, the best riff The Stones have ever done is 'Mother's Little Helper'. 'Mother's Little Helper'! I said, 'That's not a proper riff, Eccleston, let alone a good one.' I said, 'You wouldn't know a decent riff if it came up and bit you on your fat arse.'

HORACE. I quite like 'Mother's Little Helper'.

JERRY. The song's not at issue; it's the riff.

JUDY's started half-squatting up and down, slowly, arms half-raised, in time to the music.

JUDY. Every time I hear The Stones, I just – well up, you know? Beautiful Brian, dead as fuck. I loved Brian . . . Harry.

JERRY. Horry.

JUDY. Yeah, I really loved him. I reckon he's floating around, floating around up there, being beautiful just for us.

HORACE. So which one do you think's best?

JERRY. Obvious: 'Jumpin' Jack Flash'.

HORACE. Yeah, I suppose so. I like 'Have You Seen Your Mother, Baby'.

JERRY. I'm not talking about songs; I'm talking about riffs.

HORACE. Good, though, isn't it?

JERRY. Jude, what are you doing?

JUDY (*half-squatting dreamily*). I'm leaping with Armstrong . . . moondancing with Jimi . . . fantastic . . .

JERRY licks the paper and seals the joint.

JERRY. Got a light?

HORACE. Yeah.

He hands him the matches. JERRY *lights up and inhales.*

JERRY. Mmm. Beautiful . . .

He hands it to HORACE, *who takes a drag.* JERRY *lies on the floor and puts his legs up against a wall at a right-angle, his arms behind his head.* HORACE *passes the joint to* JUDY, *then goes to the record player. He takes off the LP and puts on a single: 'The Wind Cries Mary'.*

JUDY (*on hearing the intro*). Yeah . . .

She lies on her stomach, her face next to JERRY's. *Their position evokes a still of James Dean and Natalie Wood in* Rebel Without a Cause. *She holds the joint for him to drag on. He does so. Then she has another drag, puts her lips over his and blows the smoke into his mouth.* HORACE *stands watching.*

HORACE. That's what they did in *Pierrot le Fou*.

JERRY. What?

HORACE. Smoke like that.

JUDY. No, they didn't.

HORACE. They did.

JERRY. You're on dodgy ground, Horry. This girl is in love with Belmondo.

JUDY. And you, baby . . . (*Kissing him.*)

HORACE. I'm sure they did.

JUDY. Jean-Paul, Jean-Paul . . .

She kisses him again.

HORACE. I'm right, aren't I, Jerry?

JERRY. Ah, mon petit potiron.

JUDY (*feeling his crotch*). Oh, monsieur, qu'est-ce que c'est?

JERRY. La plume de ma tante.

HORACE. Aren't I?

JUDY. Ooh la la!

They kiss again, HORACE *watching.* JERRY *clocks him over her shoulder.*

JERRY. So who do you like, Horry?

HORACE. In what way?

JERRY. Film stars. Which ones flick your switch?

HORACE. I don't know. No one, really.

JERRY. There must be someone.

HORACE. Well, there are people I like watching. Rita Tushingham – she can be good, Albert Finney, Hayley Mills –

JERRY. Hayley Mills?

HORACE. Yes.

JERRY. Hayley fucking Mills?

JUDY. Who the fuck's Hayley Mills?

JERRY. 'Let's get together, yeah, yeah, yeah . . . '

HORACE. I know she's a bit passé –

JERRY. A bit? She must be over twenty by now!

HORACE. But something like *Whistle Down the Wind* –
I really rate that, and she was great. I reckon that film'll
survive us all.

JERRY. What are you talking about?

HORACE. Really stand the test of time, you know?

JERRY starts giggling.

What is it?

JERRY. It's just dawned on me.

JUDY. What, baby?

JERRY. If you sucked off Belmondo, you'd have a frog in your
throat.

He carries on giggling. Then JUDY *gets it and starts
giggling too.*

A frog in your throat.

They get hysterical. HORACE *doesn't.*

Then you'd really need your Dimyril.

Ongoing hysteria. HORACE *goes over to them.*

HORACE. Can I have some more, please?

They haven't heard. HORACE *takes the joint from* JUDY
and smokes it. Their hysteria subsides into a snog. JERRY
starts undoing her jeans. She helps him. HORACE *watches,
dragging on the joint.* JERRY *puts his hand down the front
of her jeans.*

JERRY. Mmm . . . yeah . . . my favourite hobbit-hole.

They kiss.

You're not going to believe this, but I know somebody who
doesn't get *The Hobbit*.

JUDY. What?

JERRY. Thinks it's about gnomes.

They kiss.

JUDY. It is about gnomes.

JERRY rolls on top of her. He puts his hands up her top and fondles her breasts. She moans. HORACE watches in increasing discomfort. JERRY works down her body, kissing her navel, then licking beneath it. As he starts to inch her jeans down, she snores. He looks up at her face. She's out for the count. He smiles at HORACE. HORACE doesn't return the smile and goes onto the balcony. By now, 'The Wind Cries Mary' has finished. JERRY gets to his feet. He wanders onto the balcony.

JERRY. She's crazy. She's something else.

Beat.

What's wrong?

HORACE. Nothing.

JERRY. Have I said something?

HORACE shakes his head.

It's not about *The Hobbit*, is it?

HORACE. No.

Beat.

JERRY. We should go to the fair.

HORACE. Yeah.

JERRY. Horace, tell me. Come on. Don't get sad. It's a nice day. We're having a nice day.

A luxurious snore from JUDY.

HORACE. I just think . . .

JERRY. What?

HORACE. That you could've told me – about Judy.

JERRY. I didn't know she was coming till the last minute.

HORACE. I didn't mean that – although, to be honest, I was looking forward to – just us two.

JERRY. Sorry.

HORACE. No, you shouldn't be sorry.

JERRY. Anyway, the state she's in, it is just us two. So what did you mean?

HORACE. I don't know.

JERRY. What could I have told you?

HORACE. That you'd met her, that's what you could've told me.

JERRY. But I have told you.

HORACE. Like, you could've told me earlier. It's important. If she's important to you, then it's important. I need to know.

JERRY. It's only been going on for a week or so.

HORACE. She is important to you, isn't she?

JERRY. Yes, I suppose she is.

HORACE. I don't know what I'm saying.

JERRY. Anyway, you do know now.

HORACE. Yes. Right. I do know.

JERRY. They've got some mean dodgems.

HORACE. You're important to me, Jerry.

JERRY. Yeah, and you are to me.

HORACE. Like, I see our friendship as – special, not like any other friendship I've got.

JERRY. Yeah.

HORACE. And with you having done A-levels early and pissing off to university –

JERRY. I might not've got the grades.

HORACE. Of course you'll get the grades. I'll miss you, and with another year at school and you not being there, I'll miss you, Jerry.

JERRY. We'll keep in touch.

HORACE. It won't be the same. That's what I want.

JERRY. There's vacations and things.

HORACE. Yes, I know, I know.

JERRY. And you'll make other friends.

HORACE. Well, I might do, but that doesn't change what I'm saying. I'm talking about you.

Beat.

It's going to be brilliant for you.

JERRY. Bollocks!

HORACE. It is, Jerry. You'll go right to the top.

JERRY. There's nothing stopping any of us from doing that.

HORACE. Believe me, you will.

JERRY. You'll go right to the top.

HORACE. Doing what?

JERRY. I don't know. Writing, that's it!

HORACE. I can't write.

JERRY. You can.

HORACE. Nothing special.

JERRY. You might. You could write a novel.

HORACE. A novel!

JERRY. Yes, that's it: write a novel.

HORACE. I'll never write a novel.

JERRY. Of course you will.

HORACE. What would I write a novel about?

JERRY. I don't know. Love, death, murder, passion –

HORACE. I don't have anyone to be passionate about, do I?

JERRY. That's no excuse. Beethoven wrote the Appassionata and he had no one to be passionate about. Just imagine,

Horry, in a few years time, we could both be doing our thing, and we'll bump into each other somewhere exciting, like we'll both be passing through Paris or Peking, and I'll have some gorgeous girl in tow – I know: Julie Christie! By then, I'll have Julie Christie on my arm.

HORACE. And who will I have on my arm?

JERRY. I don't know – Hayley Mills, and I'll say, 'Hi! How's things?' and you'll say, 'Fine. I've just finished my first novel,' and I'll say, 'Great! Send me a copy,' and when I get it, I'll think about us up here and how it all began.

JUDY snores.

She's worse than my dad.

HORACE. So you don't mind?

JERRY. What?

HORACE. What I've said about us.

JERRY. Why should I mind?

He takes a squashed Mars bar out of his pocket and unwraps it.

The munchies.

HORACE. Right.

JERRY. Courtesy of your local newsagent.

HORACE. Oh. Right.

JERRY bites the bar.

JERRY. I love Mars bars, don't you?

HORACE. I don't eat that much chocolate.

JERRY (*proffering the bar*). Give it a try.

He holds it while HORACE *takes a mouthful.*

What do you think?

HORACE. Mm. Quite nice. I sort of see what you mean.

JERRY has another bite.

Jerry?

JERRY. Mm?

HORACE. You know what you said about a bit of mutual?

JERRY. Yeah.

HORACE. You've done that, have you?

JERRY. Course. Haven't you?

HORACE. Sort of. There was this little kid next door in Edmonton. We used to do things in the shed. (*Re. the Mars.*) Do you think I could . . . ?

JERRY. Help yourself.

HORACE has another bite.

So – is that it?

HORACE. What?

JERRY. Things in the shed – that's all you've done?

HORACE. Kind of.

JERRY. Shit, Horace, all the more reason, mate. Go with a girl. It'll change your life.

HORACE (*coping with Mars in the mouth*). But I don't want to! You must know that! I want to do it . . . I want to do it with you. Sorry.

Beat.

JERRY. You'll meet loads of people.

HORACE. Yes, I might –

JERRY. Loads.

HORACE. But that wouldn't change – doesn't change – what I feel.

JERRY. There'll be someone else.

HORACE. No, I don't think there will.

They look at each other, face to face. Pause. For a second, they seem to get fractionally closer.

JUDY (*coming round, in a strong Birmingham accent*). Fucking beautiful!

HORACE *and* JERRY*'s moment is broken.*

I fucking love you, Jimi! (*Singing, still with an accent.*)
'After all the jacks are in their boxes . . . '

HORACE. Why's she talking like that?

JERRY. She does when she's just woken up.

JUDY (*singing*). 'The traffic lights, they turn on blue
tomorrow . . . '

JERRY. Birmingham.

HORACE. Right.

JERRY. She's lost her accent, but it comes back when she's not
thinking, like when we're doing it.

JUDY (*with the accent*). I love you, Jimi! And Brian, I love
you, too!

JERRY. The first time, I thought I was bringing Beryl Reid to
orgasm.

He steps into the room. HORACE *follows.*

Hey, Jude!

JUDY. Mm?

JERRY. How you doing?

JUDY (*without the accent*). Oh. Hi, babe.

JERRY. Hi.

JUDY. Have I been asleep?

JERRY. Yep.

JUDY. Oh, Christ!

She struggles to her feet. JERRY *puts what's left of the
Mars bar on the floor and helps her.*

JERRY. Alright?

JUDY (*on the verge of vomiting*). Oh, fuck . . . .

HORACE. Hold on. It's only down the corridor.

JERRY. Hold on, babe!

HORACE *hurriedly leads her out.* JERRY *lights a cigarette. He sits at the piano. He casually starts playing 'Pur Ti Miro' from Monteverdi's* L'Incoronazione di Poppea, *whistling quietly to himself.* HORACE *comes back in. After a while,* JERRY *stops playing.*

Did she make it?

HORACE. Just.

JERRY. She's overdone it a bit.

HORACE. Yeah.

JERRY *starts playing the opening of Beethoven's Fourth Piano Concerto with great aplomb.* HORACE *hovers, then gradually sidles closer to the piano ending up behind him. Pause. With great difficulty, he raises his hand intending to stroke* JERRY's *hair. Before he makes contact,* JERRY *breaks off playing.* HORACE *takes his hand away.* JERRY *stands. They look at each other.* HORACE *awkwardly removes his glasses. Beat.* JERRY *ruffles* HORACE's *hair affectionately and meanders over to the balcony.* HORACE *is left stranded.* JERRY *leans against the jamb of one of the balcony doors, holds his face up to the sun and closes his eyes.*

JERRY. Mmm, Horry, feel that sun . . . So warm. The sunniest fucking sun I ever did see!

HORACE *looks across at him.*

(*Sliding slowly down the jamb until he's sitting on the floor*). Oh yeah . . .

His back is against the jamb, his face still upturned and his eyes still closed. HORACE *continues to watch. For a while, all that can be heard are the distant sounds of the fair. Then* HORACE *goes over to the dansette and takes off the record. Some pebbles land on the balcony unnoticed. As* HORACE *replaces the record in its sleeve, some more pebbles land, this time jolting* JERRY *from his reverie.*

What the fuck . . . ?

BOY (*from down in the street*). Oi, poofter!

JERRY *leaps to his feet and looks over the balcony railing as* HORACE *dashes out.*

JERRY. Come up here and say that, you little sod!

HORACE. Ignore him.

BOY (*off*). I fucking will, mate, if you're not fucking careful.

JERRY. It'd make my fucking day, you little bastard.

HORACE. Oh, God, the neighbours! Keep it down, please!

BOY (*off*). Fuck you, shitface!

HORACE. Oh, Jesus!

> *Enter* JUDY *looking the worse for wear, with streaked make-up etc.*

JUDY. What's going on?

> *She goes out onto the balcony.*

JERRY. Some arsehole getting a bit lippy.

HORACE. Let's go back in.

JUDY. He's a kid.

JERRY. He's an arsehole.

BOY (*off*). Fucking lesbian!

JUDY. Cheeky little fucker! Fuck off, you little bastard!

HORACE. Oh, God! Please!

BOY (*off*). You fucking wait!

JERRY. We're waiting, arsewipe.

HORACE. Please! Look, he's going, okay? Let's leave it, alright?

JERRY. Little sod.

HORACE. We'll go back inside.

JUDY. No, hang on. I've had an idea.

> *She comes into the room and looks in her bag.*

HORACE (*in the balcony doorway*). How are you feeling?

JUDY. A bit better, thanks.

HORACE. It helps sometimes, doesn't it?

JUDY. What?

HORACE. Throwing up.

JUDY. Oh, yeah, yeah. Don't really think about it.

She takes out a Brownie camera and goes back onto the balcony.

Right. (*To* HORACE). . . . Oh, fuck, what's your name?

JERRY. Horace.

JUDY. Fucking weird. Look, you stand next to Jerry.

HORACE does so. She looks through the camera.

Yeah. Move across a bit – get a bit of the view.

They do so.

Yeah. Great. Right, now, do something.

JERRY. What?

JUDY. I don't know.

JERRY puts his arm around HORACE's shoulders.

JERRY. How's that?

JUDY. Great! Now, smile!

JERRY and HORACE smile. She clicks the camera.

Fantastic! That'll be fantastic! (*To* HORACE.) You take me and Jerry.

She gives him the camera, goes to JERRY and embraces him. HORACE looks through the camera.

HORACE. If you move a little bit further apart –

They do so.

Very good. That's very good.

He tries to click it, but nothing happens.

JUDY. What's wrong?

He checks the camera.

HORACE. Run out of film.

JUDY. No!

JERRY. Never mind.

HORACE. That was the last one.

JUDY. Oh no!

JERRY. We'll get another one.

JUDY. But I wanted us out here.

JERRY. We'll take some later.

JUDY. Like this.

HORACE. Sorry.

JUDY. Like we are now.

JERRY (*putting an arm round her*). Come on, Jude, it's not that bad.

JUDY. It is.

JERRY. Tell you what, I'll take you on the Ghost Train.

JUDY. What?

JERRY. And the dodgems.

JUDY. We're going to the fair?

JERRY. And the Tunnel of Love, and the Wall of Death.

JUDY. Fantastic! I love fairs!

She gives JERRY *a kiss.*

I need a piss.

She darts into the room, picks up her bag and goes out.

JERRY. Are you coming?

HORACE. Yeah. Unless you'd rather –

JERRY. What? No, come.

HORACE. Right.

Beat. JERRY *takes off the gold chain from round his neck. He lightly touches it with his lips, then offers it to* HORACE.

I couldn't. No, I couldn't.

JERRY. Go on.

HORACE. No.

JERRY. Go on.

HORACE *takes the chain.*

Better not wear it yet.

Pause.

HORACE. Thank you.

JERRY. One day, you might look at that and think, 'Now, what was his name? Ah, yes: Jerry, that was it. I wonder what he's up to?'

HORACE *smiles.*

I'd better see if Janis Joplin's alright.

HORACE. Jerry.

JERRY. Yeah?

HORACE *takes off his medal and offers it to* JERRY. JERRY *takes it.*

Thanks. (*As he puts it in his pocket:*) Ow!

He's pricked a finger on the pin.

Shit!

HORACE. You alright?

JERRY. Fuck it!

He sucks the blood.

HORACE. Sorry.

JERRY. It's my own stupid fault.

HORACE. Let's have a look.

HORACE *takes his hand and looks at the finger.*

JERRY. It's nothing.

JUDY (*off. Singing*). 'Do you, don't you want me to love you . . . '

HORACE *continues to hold his hand.*

'I'm coming down fast but I'm miles above you . . . '

JERRY. It's gone all over you now.

He withdraws his hand and licks his finger again.

JUDY (*off*). Jerry!

Beat. JERRY *goes out.* HORACE *looks at the blood on his hand. He raises it to his mouth and licks it.*

JERRY (*from hall*). You coming, Horace?

HORACE. I'll join you later.

JERRY (*off*). Don't be long.

HORACE. The dodgems. Twenty minutes.

JERRY (*off*). See you.

JUDY (*off*). À bientôt.

The front door being closed. He looks at the chain, then goes to the mirror. He gently kisses it and puts it round his neck. Meanwhile, a pair of hands come into view, grasping the railings on the balcony. Then a BOY *pulls himself up so that his head and shoulders are visible through the railings. He checks the coast is clear and manages to haul himself up and over the railings. He's about 13 and has a fading black eye. The* BOY *spots him and creeps into the room, warily looking about him whilst taking something out of his pocket. He comes up behind* HORACE. *In a flash, he simultaneously pulls* HORACE'*s head back by the hair and holds a knife against* HORACE'*s throat.*

BOY (*sotto voce*). Where are your mates?

HORACE *is paralysed.*

(*Pressing the knife harder.*) Where the fuck are they?

HORACE. Gone.

BOY. Sure?

HORACE (*nodding*). Just now.

BOY. Where?

HORACE. The fair.

BOY. All by yourself, are you?

HORACE *nods.*

Little queer all by himself?

No response.

(*Yanking his head.*) Yeah?

HORACE *nods.*

You tell your mates that, if I ever see them, I'm going to cut their fucking throats out, cos I don't like fucking queers shouting at me. You got that?

HORACE *nods.*

(*Pressing the knife harder.*) I didn't hear.

HORACE. Yes.

BOY. Good.

He spots the discarded Mars bar. Keeping the knife at HORACE's *throat, he reaches for it.* HORACE *takes advantage of this: he grabs the* BOY's *wrist and bends it back in an attempt to make him drop the knife.*

Ow!

HORACE. Let go of it!

BOY. That fucking hurts!

HORACE. Go on! Let it go!

The BOY *lets the knife go.*

BOY (*rubbing his wrist*). There's no need to be like that.

HORACE *picks up the knife and examines it, as the* BOY *picks up the Mars bar and takes a bite.*

HORACE. It's rubber.

BOY. 'S'good, innit? Won it at the fair.

HORACE. What the fuck are you playing at?

BOY. Your mates pissed me off.

HORACE. You can't just come into people's homes.

BOY. I was like fucking Spiderman, straight up the drainpipe. Fucking amazing!

HORACE. And you shouldn't be climbing up buildings. It's dangerous. And anyway, what the hell are you doing being so unpleasant!

BOY. Unpleasant? I was fucking terrifying!

HORACE. No, you weren't.

BOY. I scared the shit out of you.

HORACE. Of course you didn't.

BOY. Course I did. Come on, own up, I was good, were'n' I? I saw one of my brothers do that to a darkie. He really did shit himself. Mind you, the knife was real.

HORACE. Look, fuck off, you little bastard, (*Re. the Mars.*) and that's not yours to eat, anyway! (*The* BOY *puts the last bit of Mars in his mouth.*)

BOY. He got Borstal for that.

HORACE. I'm pleased to hear it.

BOY. Second time round. He's fucking great. (*Looking round the room.*) Movin' out, are you?

HORACE. Moving in, and it's none of your business.

BOY. We live round here.

HORACE. Oh, Christ!

BOY. My name's Terence. What are you called?

HORACE. I'm not telling you.

TERENCE. I just thought, when we bump into each other –

HORACE. We won't.

TERENCE. Be like that! Anyway, we live in that new council block down the hill. You can see it from up here. It's in a terrible fucking state already. The council don't give a toss. You smash a window and they don't do nothing about it. It freezes your bollocks off in winter.

HORACE. If you didn't smash the windows in the first place –

TERENCE. You getting smart?

HORACE. I think you should go.

TERENCE. Why?

HORACE. You shouldn't be here. I don't want you here. I don't like you, for Christ's sake!

TERENCE. Got any money?

HORACE. No.

TERENCE. Come on! My brothers have fucked off and left me. They've gone on the heath with the slag from the chip-shop and I ain't got a penny. Go on. Give us something.

HORACE. I said, no.

TERENCE. Tell you what, you can wank me for a quid.

HORACE. I beg your pardon?

TERENCE (*rubbing his crotch*). Go on, have a feel. It's nice.

HORACE. Absolutely not!

TERENCE. 'Absolutely', is it?

HORACE. I wouldn't pay for you if you were the last person on earth. Anyway, I don't need to pay for it, you cheeky bastard.

TERENCE. You should be so fucking choosy!

HORACE. Piss off!

TERENCE. Alright. If you give me that chain.

HORACE *instinctively raises his hand to his neck.*

HORACE. No.

TERENCE. I'll go if you do.

HORACE. You'll go anyway.

TERENCE (*snatching at it*). Come on, give it here.

HORACE. No!

He starts undoing it, backing off from TERENCE.

TERENCE (*stalking him*). Give it!

> *He snatches at it again, but* HORACE *manages to pocket it.*

HORACE. Just piss off!

> TERENCE *leaps at* HORACE. *They fall to the floor,
> scrapping,* TERENCE *trying to get the chain from*
> HORACE*'s pocket.*

TERENCE. I want that fucking chain!

HORACE. Get the fuck off!

> HORACE *manages to scramble to his feet and move away.*
> TERENCE *leaps at him again and they crash into an
> upright chair. It collapses and they fall to the floor.*

Oh my God! They'll kill me! Aunty Pauline's antique chair!
Look what you've done!

TERENCE. I didn't do nothing!

HORACE. Jesus Christ!

> TERENCE *leaps on him again and manages to get his hand
> in his pocket.* HORACE *struggles to get him off.*

TERENCE. Where's it gone?

HORACE. Get off me!

TERENCE. It's not here.

> *He desists.* HORACE *feels in his pocket.*

HORACE. You've nicked it.

TERENCE. I ain't.

HORACE. Give it back!

TERENCE. I ain't got it!

> *This time,* HORACE *leaps on him, putting his hands around
> his neck.*

HORACE. Give it back!

> TERENCE *starts choking.*

Give it me!

TERENCE (*struggling to speak*). I ain't got it!

HORACE *lets him go and starts crawling round the floor, desperately looking.*

(*Holding his neck, tearful.*) You could've killed me! I'll get my brothers round here, you wait!

HORACE. Please, please, tell me if you've got it! Please!

TERENCE. I ain't fucking got it! It must have dropped out.

HORACE. Jesus Christ!

TERENCE. It's only a fucking chain.

HORACE (*jumping to his feet and confronting* TERENCE). It is not just a fucking chain! Now, get out!

TERENCE. You wait, mate!

HORACE. Get out!

He grabs him and propels him through the door.

TERENCE (*off*). You ain't seen the back of me!

HORACE (*off*). Out!

A door slam. HORACE *re-enters and frantically resumes searching.*

It's got to be here, got be here . . . (*Looking everywhere.*) Jesus, Jesus, Jesus . . .

The search becomes more frenzied. He ransacks the tea-chest, then starts moving furniture to look underneath, upturning various pieces.

It'll turn up . . . It's got to . . . It can't just disappear . . . Oh, Christ! . . . It'll turn up . . . It will turn up . . . Jerry . . . Jerry . . .

He starts to slow down and eventually stops, exhausted. The room is in chaos. He takes several deep breaths and finally calms himself. Pause. He closes the outside shutters, then shuts the balcony doors, darkening the room. He closes the door to the rest of the flat. He looks at the piano. Pause. Very slowly, he goes over to it and stands behind the stool. He raises his hand, then places it on the head of an imaginary person sitting on the stool. He gently strokes the 'hair', then bends to kiss the 'head'. He straightens up, his arms at his side, and stands motionless. 'Pur Ti Miro' from L'Incoronazione di Poppea *starts playing sung by two trebles with piano accompaniment. He closes his eyes. The lights fade and reach blackout as the music finishes.*

End.

MOUTH TO MOUTH

For my mother

The whole art of living is to make use
of the individuals through whom we suffer.

Proust

Mouth to Mouth was first performed at the Royal Court
Theatre, London, on 1 February 2001. The cast was as follows:

FRANK	Michael Maloney
LAURA	Lindsay Duncan
GOMPERTZ	Adam Godley
DENNIS	Peter Wight
PHILLIP	Andrew McKay
CORNELIA	Lucy Whybrow
ROGER	Barnaby Kay

Director Ian Rickson
Designer Mark Thompson
Lighting Designer Hugh Vanstone
Sound Designer Paul Arditti
Choreographer Quinny Sacks
Composer Stephen Warbeck
Musician Sabbo

The production transferred to the Albery Theatre, London,
produced by Royal Court Theatre Productions, Ambassador
Theatre Group and Bill Kenwright in association with Karl
Sydow, on 17 May 2001, with the following cast changes:

GOMPERTZ	Ian Gelder
ROGER	Ray Stevenson

Characters

FRANK, *forty-six*

LAURA, *forty-five*

GOMPERTZ, *thirty-five*

DENNIS, *forty-three*

PHILLIP, *fifteen*

CORNELIA, *twenty-eight*

ROGER, *thirty-four*

Setting

The action takes place in a house and a restaurant.

A tango. Lights up on:

The Kitchen

FRANK *and* LAURA *sit by the open French windows which look out onto the garden. Adjoining the kitchen is a pantry, also in view. Sunlight streams in.* FRANK *has a huge bandage over his left eye.* LAURA*'s wearing sunglasses. She's smoking. The tango music cross-fades with the sounds of summer gardens: the steady rhythm of a sprinkler system, an intermittent distant strimmer, children playing and birdsong. Also, from another part of the house, we hear a piano: a faltering rendition of the Aria from Bach's Goldberg Variations.*

FRANK. . . . so I'm – I'm having it off tomorrow.

Beat.

They said it should do the trick, but I might have to have another put in; depends if I keep taking the tablets. We'll see. It's so lovely here.

He lifts his face to the sun.

You could almost forget you're in Balham.

For a moment he's distracted by something in the garden. LAURA *looks at him. He returns his attention.*

It was odd, I must say, walking into the operating theatre. I mean, you don't usually do that, do you? Usually you're wheeled in totally out of it, but I just walked in totally *compos mentis.* Of course, once it had started, I didn't have a clue what was going on. She asked if I was okay, but I was concentrating so hard on not panicking, I don't think I answered, and the only time she told me what was happening was when she put it in and stitched it up, then it was over. Incredible, isn't it? You drop in after breakfast and you're home by lunchtime. (*Re. the garden*). I'm sure someone . . .

Beat.

What I can't work out is whether or not she popped the eyeball out of its socket. The thought of lying there with one of my eyes dangling on my cheek . . . It's no good, you know. I was given the impression it was going to be alright, but I can tell by the way they are with me that it's not quite going according to plan.

LAURA *squeezes his hand.*

Funny how things turn out, isn't it? We thought it was just going to fall into our laps.

Beat.

Laura . . .

She looks at him. Beat. He kisses her hand. They gaze out at the garden.

God, I need this break and if it doesn't work out, well . . .

Beat.

I had dinner with my doctor last night. It's quite nice really how we've sort of meandered into a friendship. He thinks I'm mad. He says it's just a blip. I mean, I'd put up with it all if I was sure it was working: the bad dreams, the way I look – but no, I've had enough. Tantamount to suicide according to Doctor Gompertz, but I look at it as a way of taking control.

LAURA *lights another cigarette from the one she's smoking.*

You'll miss this place, won't you? Anyway . . .

Beat.

He does go on. He lost his partner ages ago now, but he always comes back to it. Gets himself into such a state, especially when he's had a few, and I never got round to talking about –

Pause.

Well, there was something – that I particularly wanted to talk about which is why I'd arranged to meet him in the first place, and I – I never got round to it.

He's distracted again by something in the garden.

Look, down the bottom there, I'm sure . . . Probably just a shadow. I thought – for a second, I thought it was –

The kitchen table suddenly shifts about a foot. He leaps to his feet and stares at it. LAURA *tenses.*

Jesus!

Pause.

Better be off.

She looks at him.

. . . In a bit.

He sits down again.

Laura, there's something –

The sound of a motorbike approaching. They freeze. The piano stops. The bike gets closer. LAURA *starts to remove her glasses. Blackout as the bike gets louder. It cuts out as the lights snap up on:*

A Restaurant

FRANK *and* GOMPERTZ *at a table. They have drinks and menus.* FRANK *has the dressing over his left eye.* GOMPERTZ *has his face in his napkin. He lets out an involuntary sob.* FRANK *is acutely embarrassed.*

GOMPERTZ. Sorry . . .

FRANK. No, no, it's . . .

GOMPERTZ. Sorry . . .

FRANK. No . . .

   GOMPERTZ *wipes his eyes and face with the napkin, then takes a slug of his drink.*

GOMPERTZ. See, people don't have time to remember, don't even care to remember, but I do. I still can't believe it. The

blink of an eyelid and life's changed forever. What's the
fucking point! Sorry, you were saying . . .

He lights a cigarette.

FRANK. About the bad dreams. Last night, for example, I
dreamt Alan Rickman was being fried for charity.

GOMPERTZ. He was in here last week.

FRANK. And a few nights ago I turned over in bed and Dennis
Nilsen was lying next to me; a dream, but nonetheless –

GOMPERTZ. The truth is, when it comes down to it, I just
don't trust people. I don't believe a word they say. When I
think of his memorial, all the speeches, the pieces and
poems, the commiserations and the promises to keep in
touch – all crap, isn't it? Self, self, fucking self! (*Re. menu.*)
Ooh, Cuttlefish Mousse. Mind you, there've been so many
sodding memorials these past years –

FRANK. Isn't that what you feed budgies?

GOMPERTZ. It's a joke. Unknown at birth, forgotten when
you're dead, and a load of bollocks in between. Life's a
cunt and no mistake. Baryshnikov.

FRANK. What?

GOMPERTZ *nods in the appropriate direction.*

Oh yes.

GOMPERTZ. Forever alone, that's our lot, and try as we
might, we can't change it. We hitch up with someone, fool
ourselves we've cracked it, give life to other desolate
beings, but we're still alone.

FRANK. This is a real treat. Thanks ever so much.

GOMPERTZ. I mean, look at us: conglomerations of meat and
juices tarted up in Armani. And where do we all end up? In
a mass of stinking putrefaction. (*Winking and smiling at
someone.*) Hi.

FRANK. So tell me, what was it that attracted you to
medicine?

GOMPERTZ. The laughs. How's the eye?

FRANK. Fine.

He sips his drink, but misses his mouth.

GOMPERTZ. And the glamour.

FRANK (*wiping the spilt drink with his napkin*). Peter, would she actually have taken my eye out of its socket? I mean, would it have just been hanging on my cheek?

GOMPERTZ. And that sense of being in control.

FRANK. Control. Yes, that's kind of what I wanted to talk to you about.

GOMPERTZ (*indicating with a nod*). Pinter.

FRANK (*looking round*). Oh yes.

GOMPERTZ. And look who he's with. Intriguing. Carry on.

FRANK. What?

GOMPERTZ. Your dreams.

FRANK. Oh, right. The dreams. Well, I suppose I could just about cope with those, but it's everything else: the diarrhoea, the nausea, headaches, the incessant pill-taking and needles, and most of all, the way my body's changing shape. I used to have quite a decent body, but now I'm like something out of *The Bridge on the River Kwai*: my limbs are like twigs, my neck's like a turkey's, and my bum hangs from my back like a pair of old curtains in a caravan. It's getting me down. I can't bear to look in the mirror any more. (*Indicating his eye bandage.*) And if this can happen when I'm on medication –

GOMPERTZ. It's a blip, I've told you, just a blip.

FRANK. And it's not just the medication. I need to get away. I need a change of routine.

GOMPERTZ. Kipper Soufflé with Cornichon and Sun-blush Tomato Salsa . . .

FRANK. And I really want to get on with my writing. You know, sometimes I think that's more important to me than my health. Does that sound crazy?

GOMPERTZ (*indicating with a nod*). See that busboy?

FRANK. What?

GOMPERTZ. Lets you snort a line off his stiffy in the lav.

FRANK. Gosh.

GOMPERTZ. Not too pricey either, dirty bitch.

FRANK. Anyway the point is –

GOMPERTZ *suddenly lets out a sob.*

Oh dear.

GOMPERTZ. Sorry . . .

FRANK. No, no . . .

GOMPERTZ. It's just – the busboy, as in – walking under one.

FRANK. Ah.

GOMPERTZ. Bloody typical! He didn't even die of the fucking thing that was meant to kill him. (*Taking something from his pocket.*) Run down by a 134 –

FRANK. I know –

GOMPERTZ. – and such a poetic soul!

It's a cocaine inhaler. He takes a discreet snort.

FRANK. Yes –

GOMPERTZ. Sorry, what were you saying?

FRANK. I've got a bit lost.

GOMPERTZ. Something about writing.

FRANK. Oh yes. Well, you know I've been blocked for God knows how long.

GOMPERTZ. What a way to go!

FRANK. The point is, I think at last I might have an idea, which in a roundabout way is also what I wanted to talk to you about.

GOMPERTZ *passes the inhaler to* FRANK.

Oh. Thank you.

He awkwardly attempts a snort.

GOMPERTZ. Sardine Saltimbocca and Dwarf Corn Mulch? Battered Boudin on Sweet Cicely Coulis? Chef must be shooting up again. Suppose I'll go for the shank of sodding lamb.

He takes another slug of his drink.

All that struggle and angst, worries about money, arguing about whether to go to Polynesia or New England, wondering what colour to paint the gazebo, then nothing. And we were getting on so well. No sex, of course – we went outside the relationship for that. And the mash, I suppose. I'm always having the fucking mash. I think it's best, don't you? –

FRANK. I like a nice mash –

GOMPERTZ. – Not having sex with your partner. It makes things so much easier. Of course, we had sex at the beginning, but when you start falling asleep in the middle of it, time to call it a day, eh?

FRANK (*handing back the inhaler*). I suppose so. Peter, there's something –

GOMPERTZ. How the fuck can you not see a bus? He wasn't wearing his glasses, of course – vain little queen – but a bright red double-decker!

He snorts.

He wasn't that blind. God, I miss him! Sometimes, you know, and it's usually when I'm sober, I'm convinced he's around. Like I can smell his scent, follow it across a room, or just sense him at my shoulder. It's nice . . . You've never lived with anyone, have you?

FRANK. Not in a romantic way. But funnily enough that's also sort of tied up with what I wanted to talk to you about.

GOMPERTZ. Do you think we should have a shag?

FRANK. No.

GOMPERTZ. Best not. You were saying . . .

He lights another cigarette.

FRANK. I saved someone's life, you know –

He suddenly winces and holds his stomach.

GOMPERTZ. Alright?

After a moment:

FRANK. Mm.

GOMPERTZ. Of course, there's still a combination you haven't tried.

FRANK. There probably is, but what I'm trying to tell you – one of the things I'm trying to tell you – is that I've had enough, and so I've decided – after careful consideration, I have decided . . .

GOMPERTZ. Yes?

FRANK. . . . to stop my medication.

GOMPERTZ *is suddenly still; for the first time* FRANK *has his full attention.*

You have to understand, it wears you down after a while. You try something, it works, then it doesn't and your test results go pear-shaped. You try something else, it may work, it may not, and so it goes on. And before each check-up, wondering if your tests are alright, and if they're not, then what? I want to be free of all this, at least for a while, and also give my body a rest from all the poison I've been pumping into it.

GOMPERTZ *hands him the inhaler.*

Thank you.

He takes a discreet snort, GOMPERTZ *watching him.*

So . . . what do you think?

GOMPERTZ. What would you like me to think?

FRANK. You must have an opinion.

GOMPERTZ. Why?

FRANK. You're a doctor.

GOMPERTZ. It's your choice.

FRANK. Peter –

GOMPERTZ. If that's what you want . . . I must say, I'm
surprised. We've monitored you with the greatest care for
the past several years, prescribed the best and latest
treatments. I wouldn't be so crass as to mention what that's
cost, but the good thing is that, after all this time, you're
still here to tell me you want to give it all up and, as I say,
it's your choice.

FRANK. Look –

GOMPERTZ. It's strange because you've always been so co-
operative. I expect this from younger guys, but not from
people your age. You can remember what it was like, and
putting up with a bit of discomfort –

FRANK. A bit!

GOMPERTZ. – is surely preferable to falling off your fucking
perch, but if you've developed a death wish, fine. As I say,
it's your choice.

FRANK. I can always start up again if things get dodgy.

GOMPERTZ. It doesn't work like that and you know it.
Now let me tell *you* something: there was this guy I was
treating, about your age, and one day he said exactly what
you've just said and, try as I might, I could not make him
see sense –

FRANK. Peter, there's something else –

GOMPERTZ. – so he went ahead, gave up all his medication,
even wrote an article in one of those mindless radical rags
about how the doctors were poisoning their patients –

FRANK. There's something else –

GOMPERTZ. – and within a matter of months he was back on
the ward with dementia, and in no time at all –

FRANK. Peter, will you please listen!

Beat.

Sorry. The thing is, there's something else – on my mind. In
fact it's driving me mad and I haven't been able to talk to
anyone about it.

Beat.

About a year ago, almost to the day, something happened, a dreadful thing, and I don't know for sure whether or not it was my fault. In fact I don't think I'll ever know, and I feel so guilty, I can't bear it any more, which is one of the reasons why – well, why I need a bit of a break.

GOMPERTZ. We all have our secrets.

FRANK. You see, I've got this friend – Laura – and she . . .

GOMPERTZ. Yes?

FRANK. She had a do – about a year ago, as I said, and –

The bleep of a pager.

GOMPERTZ. Arseholes!

He takes a pager out of his pocket and reads the message.

Wouldn't you know it!

As he gets out his mobile and dials:

Just when we were getting to the interesting bit.

FRANK. Anyway . . .

GOMPERTZ. Sorry. (*Into his mobile.*) Hi, Crippen here . . . Yes . . . Mm . . .

The tango strikes up as the lights fade. Lights up on:

The Sitting Room

The music fades. LAURA *is putting out nibbles, plumping cushions and generally tidying,* DENNIS *is putting on a tie and* FRANK *is having a drink. He isn't wearing an eye bandage.*

LAURA. How could you do this? It's Phillip's night and you have to invite them.

DENNIS. I didn't exactly invite them –

LAURA. Typical of Roger; he has you round his little finger.

DENNIS. They're passing through – what could I do?

LAURA. You could've said no and suggested another night.

DENNIS. This is the only night they're free.

LAURA. And this is a night we're not free.

DENNIS. I thought you might be quite pleased to see them –

LAURA. I'm sure Frank doesn't want to hear you going on and on about this. (*To* FRANK.) How's your drink?

FRANK. It's –

LAURA. Have an olive. They're Sicilian. (*To* DENNIS.) Why you didn't leave the machine on –

DENNIS. He's my brother. I haven't seen him for five years.

LAURA. And if you don't phone Abdullah's soon, they won't be able to get us all in. (*Re. the tie.*) You're not wearing that, are you?

DENNIS. Roger and Cornelia sent it me last Christmas.

LAURA. I am not going out with you with boomerangs hanging from your throat.

DENNIS *glances at* FRANK, *eyes to heaven. As he goes out:*

(*To* FRANK.) Don't you adore this?

She opens a fan with a flick of her wrist.

Phillip bought it for me in Madrid. I think I'll take it to the restaurant; it can get awfully sweaty on a Friday night.

FRANK. Where is Phillip?

LAURA. He's supposed to be in the shower, but he's probably still asleep. He looked like shit when I picked him up from the airport. (*Calling through a door.*) Darling, they'll be here in a sec.

A grunt from a distant part of the house.

God knows what he's been up to! Little Sanchez – that's his penfriend – is such a gentle, mousey thing, not Phillip's style at all. In fact when he stayed here, he was so nice, he

bored me to death. But I'm sure they've been up to
something. Every time I phoned him, they seemed to have
been to the Prado. I know it's big, but please! The good
thing is that Señor Morales – that's Sanchez's father – said
his Spanish had improved no end. Almost as good as his
French, thanks to you.

FRANK. He's a bright boy.

LAURA. I don't know who he gets it from. I was never that
hot academically.

FRANK. Maybe he gets it from his dad.

She snorts.

LAURA (*taking his glass*). Top up?

FRANK. So tell me about Cornelia.

LAURA. She's utterly irritating. I can't stand her. I suppose
she's quite pretty in a predictable sort of way, which is why
Roger hitched up with her no doubt, but if you didn't know
otherwise, you'd think she probably worked on the bread
counter at Kwik Save. The fact that she's a rather hot
interior designer wouldn't enter your head. Apparently she
picked up loads of commissions while they were in
Australia.

FRANK. I thought she did something academic.

LAURA. She's taken up Anglo-Saxon as a hobby. Can you
imagine? It makes me quite nauseous. And now she's
pregnant after many years of trying, so brace yourself for a
lot of expectant-mother chat. And Roger! Well, I just want
to slap him, he's so puerile. Obviously got away with
murder as the baby of the family. He makes Phillip seem
quite mature.

FRANK. Ah well, Phillip –

LAURA. What do you mean, 'Ah well, Phillip'?

FRANK. Well, I mean . . . well –

LAURA. I am not saying that he's a paragon, but when one
looks at the male influences in his life –

FRANK. Thank you!

LAURA. I don't mean you, and you know it. God above, if it weren't for you . . . !

She gives him a quick hug and kiss.

No, I am referring to the other men in his life.

FRANK. You're very hard on Dennis.

LAURA. He can be hard on me; he's just quieter about it. I'm so pleased Phillip's back. When it's just the two of us, we seem to row more. It's a miracle we don't kill each other.

FRANK. You can't row all the time.

LAURA. When we're not sulking we are, but the sulking doesn't last because we have to get on to the next row. You're better off single, I tell you. Oh, God!

She's suddenly still.

I hate the way I sound sometimes. When I think of how I've let things slip! I'm forty-five and what have I got to show for it? I've done nothing that I meant to do. I haven't even started. I'm just a mother, and that's about it.

FRANK. That's important.

LAURA. It's not enough.

FRANK. Anyway, you're always doing things. You never seem to stop.

LAURA. I know, I know. I have my classes, the choir, the garden, this committee, that committee, but what's it amount to? It doesn't make me feel any better. Oh, I'm sorry, going on and on, as if you haven't got enough on your plate. Tell me about you. Are you well? You look well. And your writing. Tell me about that.

FRANK. Well, it isn't quite coming together at the moment –

LAURA. Have I always been like this? Maybe I have. What an awful thought! No, I don't think so. I think I've changed, haven't I? Or maybe I haven't. No, I'm sure I used to be happy. Or maybe I wasn't. I don't know. Do you think I've changed? If it weren't for Phillip, I'd go mad. Sorry, you were saying . . .

FRANK. It doesn't matter.

LAURA. Yes, it does. Your writing. Tell me.

FRANK. I'm finding it pretty difficult, to be honest. I can't put my finger on why exactly –

LAURA. No ideas.

FRANK. That could be it. But no, I'm having quite a hard time. I'm always being accused of writing about the same thing.

LAURA. And what would that be?

FRANK. Well, me, as it happens, which simply isn't true. They say it's a sign of creative bankruptcy.

LAURA. I'd have thought personal experience was the only thing worth writing about.

FRANK. But my life isn't that interesting, and if it were, I wouldn't have the time to write about it.

LAURA. Oh, I do wish tonight weren't happening!

FRANK. Yes, well . . . Nice olives.

LAURA. You're right, you know: I am hard on Dennis. Perhaps we're just too used to each other.

FRANK. Could be.

LAURA. I'm lucky to have him, I suppose – in a way. He's a kind man, don't you think?

FRANK. He is.

LAURA. And he's been quite good to me, hasn't he?

FRANK. Yes, he has.

LAURA. Always there to – fall back on. Comfy, somehow – like a beanbag. (*She flicks open the fan.*) This is the loveliest . . . I'm going to leave him, you know.

FRANK. You've been saying that for years.

LAURA. But this time I mean it. When Phillip's finished A-levels . . .

PHILLIP *has appeared in the doorway, dishevelled and shirtless.*

Darling! You're not going out like that, are you?

PHILLIP. I'm knackered.

LAURA. Come here and give your mother a big hug.

He ambles over and she embraces him.

Ah! My angel! Have you missed me?

PHILLIP. Yeah.

LAURA. You horror! I bet you didn't think of me once.

FRANK. Hello, Phillip.

PHILLIP. Hi.

FRANK. Had a good time?

PHILLIP. Yeah.

LAURA. You've grown so much. (*To* FRANK.) Don't you think he's grown?

PHILLIP. I've only been gone a few weeks.

LAURA. You're not my little boy any more.

PHILLIP. Mum!

The sound of a motorbike approaching.

LAURA. I bet that's them.

PHILLIP. Has Roger got a motorbike?

LAURA. Apparently.

PHILLIP. Brilliant!

LAURA. He probably fancies himself as Brando or James Dean. It's absolutely pathetic.

The bike gets closer.

Darling, clothes.

And closer.

Dennis!

Blackout as the bike gets ever louder. It cuts out as the lights snap up on:

The Sitting Room

LAURA, DENNIS, PHILLIP, FRANK, ROGER *and* CORNELIA, *three months gone, with drinks and nibbles.* CORNELIA *has a carrier bag at her feet.* PHILLIP *has a packet of photographs.*

CORNELIA. 'What is the point,' I said, 'of having tulipwood shelving around your bath if you're going to deface it with bottles of Asda shampoo and conditioner?' Toiletries tell you so much about a person, don't you think, Laura?

LAURA. Do they?

CORNELIA. Oh yes.

LAURA. Well, there you go.

DENNIS. So you'll be in Edinburgh for the birth.

CORNELIA. Yes. Our own little bairn. I'm so excited.

ROGER. Finally hit the bull's eye.

LAURA. There's a small Moroccan round the corner.

ROGER. Hear that, Frank?

LAURA. You all like couscous, don't you?

CORNELIA. Oh yes, we love it, don't we, Roger?

ROGER (*to* FRANK). You knew Laura when she was a girl, did you?

FRANK. Not quite that far back.

ROGER. Pity. I was hoping you'd give me a blow-by-blow of what she looked like in a gymslip and navy blue knickers. Do you know, Phil, I was only a year older than you are now when I first met your Mum?

PHILLIP. Oh.

ROGER. Yeah. A succulent seventeen-year-old, barely out of short trousers, never been kissed.

DENNIS. Never been kissed!

CORNELIA (*getting something from the carrier bag*). So I'd only have been eleven when you got married, Laura. Just imagine!

LAURA. Yes.

CORNELIA (*handing* LAURA *an oddly shaped parcel*). This is for you.

LAURA. Oh. Thank you.

CORNELIA. Well, for all of you really. A little Australian memento.

LAURA *unwraps it. It's an abstract wood carving.*

LAURA. It's . . .

CORNELIA. Aboriginal.

LAURA. Yes.

CORNELIA. We think it might be Gumbaingari, but we're not sure. And we think it's called 'The Kiss', but we're not sure of that either.

LAURA. Well, it's . . . nice, whatever.

She hands it to DENNIS.

CORNELIA. The Aborigines are so fascinating, aren't they, Roger? And they do these wonderful paintings and things about animals and this and that and Dreamtime and what-have-you.

PHILLIP. We've got an Aussie teacher at school.

CORNELIA. Oh.

LAURA. Surprisingly charming.

PHILLIP. He told us all about Dreamtime.

CORNELIA. And did it fascinate you?

PHILLIP. Yeah. I'm kind of interested in all that.

LAURA (*to* DENNIS). Has Marigold told you all about Dreamtime?

ROGER. Who's Marigold?

LAURA. His new dental nurse from Darwin.

CORNELIA. We never got up that far.

LAURA. Very talented, apparently.

DENNIS. She is.

LAURA. And quite sweet.

DENNIS. You've hardly met her.

LAURA. Even though there is something of the marsupial about her.

PHILLIP. Big tits.

LAURA. Phillip!

ROGER. I could do with a filling.

CORNELIA. Do you know anything about Dreamtime, Laura?

LAURA. No.

PHILLIP. Of course, there is a theory that time doesn't exist, not as we generally perceive it, anyhow. It's like each of our lives is already set up just waiting for us to step into. It's all out there, all decided for us. We kid ourselves we have a say in the matter, but in truth we don't have any choice at all.

ROGER. Bollocks! Course we do. Look, here's my finger, here's my nose, and I'm now choosing to stick it up there.

LAURA. Australia hasn't done you any favours, has it?

PHILLIP. But how do you know that wasn't already planned?

ROGER. Give us a break, Phil. This is education for you. Fills your head with bollocks.

LAURA. It obviously filled your head with bollocks, Roger, but some people know how to benefit from it.

ROGER. Forget about A-levels. Go out into the real world. Get a job. Much healthier.

LAURA. That is such an irresponsible thing to say.

ROGER. All this academic nonsense does your head in.

CORNELIA. I'm an academic now, so watch what you say.

DENNIS. Ignore him, Phil. My little brother was a star pupil in spite of himself. He got the best grades of his year.

PHILLIP. You didn't go to university, though, did you?

DENNIS. That's because Daddy made him an offer he couldn't refuse.

ROGER. And I've never looked back since.

CORNELIA. What do you do, Frank?

FRANK. I'm a writer.

CORNELIA. A writer! What do you write?

FRANK. Plays.

CORNELIA. Plays! I say! Would I have seen any?

FRANK. No, I don't think so.

CORNELIA. You never know. Come on, try me.

LAURA. Phillip, what about your photos?

PHILLIP. Oh yeah.

CORNELIA. Go on, Frank. Throw a few titles at me.

LAURA. Then we really ought to go, alright, Dennis?

DENNIS. Alright.

CORNELIA. I love theatre. I wish Roger liked it more, (*To* ROGER.) but it just doesn't do anything for you, does it, popsy?

ROGER. I prefer the pub.

CORNELIA. Do you like theatre, Phillip?

LAURA. He's a very good actor, actually.

PHILLIP. Mum!

LAURA. He played Mercutio in *Romeo and Juliet*. He was fantastic.

PHILLIP. Mum!

DENNIS. You were good, Phil.

LAURA. I was so proud of you. I thought, 'My God, I've bred another Brad Pitt!'

CORNELIA. Ooh, I'd like to breed a Brad Pitt.

ROGER. I'd like you to breed a Pamela Anderson.

CORNELIA. Honestly! Now, Frank –

LAURA. Phillip, your photos.

CORNELIA. I wish you'd tell me. It's not every day I meet a playwright.

FRANK. Well, the last thing I wrote – a few years ago now – was something called *A Piece of Cake.*

CORNELIA. Where was it on?

FRANK. The Palladian.

CORNELIA. The Palladium! Did you hear that, Roger?

FRANK. The Palladian. It's a pub. In Enfield.

CORNELIA. Oh.

ROGER. Sounds like my kind of theatre.

CORNELIA. *A Piece of Cake.* What was it about?

FRANK. Proust, basically. A fictitious meeting between Proust and – and myself, actually.

LAURA. It was very good, wasn't it, Dennis?

DENNIS. Yes.

ROGER. Fucking Proust.

CORNELIA. Roger!

ROGER. Boring as batshit. Sorry, Frank, but –

FRANK. He's not everyone's cup of tea.

ROGER. You're not kidding. We did him in French. Someone should have shoved that madeleine right up his fucking arse.

LAURA. Roger, will you please watch your language?

CORNELIA. He's always like this on red wine.

ROGER. One of his sentences was so long, I'd grown half an inch by the time I reached the end of it.

LAURA. Phillip, if you don't show us your photos now –

ROGER. Talk about ego! Jesus Christ! Always writing about himself. I mean, who gives a toss if a whiff of his Aunt Léonie's old knickers sent him off into a four-volume reverie?

LAURA. You've made your point.

ROGER. Pampered, bedridden mummy's boy! I'd have given him a smack in the mouth. Fucked-up little snob!

DENNIS. Roger –

ROGER. Mind you, if you think about it, we're all fucked up, aren't we?

CORNELIA. Roger!

ROGER. Give us a drink, Den.

LAURA. Honestly!

   DENNIS *obliges.*

ROGER. You see, the problem is, we've got nothing to fight for any more.

LAURA. Oh my God . . .

ROGER. That's the problem. I mean, look at us: classless snobs. (*Re.* DENNIS.) The Dentist. (*Re.* CORNELIA.) The Designer. (*Re.* FRANK.) The Writer. (*Re. himself.*) The Wine Dealer. (*Re.* LAURA.) The . . . Anyway, we're floating around, not knowing our arses from our elbows, cos we've turned our backs on our real selves and now don't know who the fuck we are. Still, what's it matter? I tell you, Phil, the only thing you need to learn is that, when it comes down to it, you're on your own, and if you understand that, you'll be alright. Do you know, Laura, you're looking sexy as fuck?

   He has a glug of wine, then a mouthful of crisps. Pause.

CORNELIA. Have you read *Beowulf*?

FRANK. No.

CORNELIA.

> 'Ðaem eafera wæs æfter cenned
> geong in geardum, þone God sende
> folce tō frōfre.'

Isn't that wonderful? I studied it at night school in Sydney on my Anglo-Saxon course. It's fascinating. If you ever get the chance.

FRANK. Yes.

CORNELIA. I'm going to carry on up in Edinburgh. I don't want to let it go. Have you been to night school, Laura?

LAURA. I don't have the time.

CORNELIA. Have you, Dennis?

DENNIS. No.

CORNELIA. Have you, Frank?

FRANK. . . . Yes.

CORNELIA. Oh! What did you do?

FRANK. Playwriting Skills.

CORNELIA. Oh.

FRANK. I still go, as it happens.

LAURA. Phillip, photos.

CORNELIA. It must be quite hard to make a living as a writer.

FRANK. Yes, it is. I do some teaching to make –

CORNELIA. Oh! What do you teach?

FRANK. English.

CORNELIA. Oh!

FRANK. To foreign students.

CORNELIA. Oh.

LAURA. Phillip!

PHILLIP. Yeah. Right.

He sorts through his photos.

CORNELIA. I love photos.

FRANK. Have you been to Madrid?

CORNELIA. No, I don't like bullfighting.

DENNIS. That shouldn't stop you going.

CORNELIA. I just don't like the idea of being near it. The thought that I might be looking at a Velasquez or having a paella a few streets away from a bull being murdered . . . (*Shuddering.*) Ooh . . .

FRANK. Murdered?

LAURA. You've just spent several years in a country where they kill kangaroos.

CORNELIA. Yes, but they don't put on tight trousers and do it in rings.

PHILLIP. It's fantastic.

LAURA. What is?

PHILLIP. Bullfighting.

CORNELIA. Phillip, you didn't go to a bullfight, did you?

PHILLIP. Yeah. It's incredible.

CORNELIA (*upset*). Oh . . .

LAURA. You didn't mention it.

PHILLIP. It was just part of the holiday. We did loads of things.

LAURA. You went just the once?

PHILLIP. Once or twice.

CORNELIA (*more upset*). Oh . . .

PHILLIP. Sanchez's family are aficionados. They taught me all about it.

LAURA. But Sanchez is such a mousey little thing. I wouldn't have thought it'd be his bag at all.

PHILLIP. He's a big fan. Took me through it step by step. It's amazing.

CORNELIA. Those poor bulls . . .

PHILLIP. It gets you right in the gut, like nothing I've ever seen.

ROGER. That's right.

CORNELIA. How do you know?

ROGER *shrugs*.

You haven't been to one, have you?

ROGER. Just the once.

CORNELIA. When?

ROGER. On a school trip to Spain.

DENNIS. Oh, I remember you going on that trip. You bought Mum a fan –

CORNELIA. The school took you to a bullfight?

ROGER. No.

DENNIS. And Dad a chorizo.

ROGER. A few of us snuck off to see what it was all about.

DENNIS. And me bugger all, I seem to remember.

CORNELIA. Oh, Roger!

ROGER. I didn't kill the bull myself.

LAURA. Let's see the photos.

CORNELIA. Not if they're of bullfighting, thank you very much!

PHILLIP *hands* LAURA *a photo*.

PHILLIP. That's Sanchez outside – somewhere or other.

LAURA (*passing it on, as she does with each one*). You see, he is mousey.

PHILLIP. And this is Sanchez outside . . . Anyway, it's Sanchez.

LAURA. Are there any of you?

PHILLIP. Yeah. This is Sanchez, and there's me, and we're in that big square thing.

LAURA. What big square thing?

PHILLIP. A sort of square, y'know.

DENNIS. Plaza Mayor.

PHILLIP. Yeah. No, another one.

LAURA. Who took it?

PHILLIP. His sister.

LAURA. I thought she was away.

PHILLIP. Yeah. She's studying in Buenos Aires, but she was home for the summer. That's me in a market.

LAURA. Did Sanchez take that?

PHILLIP. Er . . . yeah –

LAURA. No, he couldn't have. He's there in the background looking at the puppies.

CORNELIA. Puppies! Let me see.

LAURA *passes her the photo.*

LAURA. So who did take it?

PHILLIP. Dunno. And this is –

CORNELIA. Oh no!

ROGER. What's wrong?

CORNELIA. The puppies! They're all in cages, squashed together like sardines. Poor little things! What do they do to them?

PHILLIP. Eat them.

CORNELIA (*appalled*). Oh!

DENNIS. Phillip!

PHILLIP. They sell them. They sell birds and monkeys too. It's unbelievable, this market.

CORNELIA. Monkeys!

PHILLIP. This is me having a coffee.

LAURA. Where's Sanchez?

PHILLIP. . . . He stayed in that day, that's right.

LAURA. Stayed in?

PHILLIP. Yeah. Got the runs.

LAURA. So who took it?

PHILLIP. His sister.

LAURA. What's that?

PHILLIP. Where?

LAURA. On the table.

PHILLIP. 'T's a cup of coffee.

LAURA. In the ashtray.

PHILLIP. Oh. That's a cigarette.

LAURA. Your cigarette?

PHILLIP. No. His sister's. And this is –

> LAURA *takes it from him.*

. . . at a pool. It's me.

LAURA. Yes, I can see that.

PHILLIP. Sunbathing.

LAURA. Who took it?

PHILLIP. His sister. (*Re. the next photo.*) And this one's –

LAURA (*still on the pool photo*). I suppose that packet of cigarettes is hers too.

PHILLIP. Yeah, it is.

ROGER. Bet you're glad you got these out, eh, Phil?

CORNELIA. Do you smoke, Frank?

FRANK. I used to.

PHILLIP (*re. next photo*). Anyway, this is –

CORNELIA. Do you, Dennis?

DENNIS. No.

CORNELIA. Do you, Laura?

LAURA (*studying the pool photo intently*). What?

CORNELIA. Smoke.

LAURA. No.

CORNELIA. Well, that's the thing, you see. Interesting, isn't it?

LAURA (*re. the pool photo*). What is that?

PHILLIP. What?

LAURA (*pointing*). That.

PHILLIP. A smudge.

LAURA. It doesn't look like a smudge to me.

ROGER. Let's have a look.

LAURA (*not letting him*). What is it?

PHILLIP. Dunno.

LAURA. Phillip.

PHILLIP. What?

LAURA. There's something at the top of your leg on the inside of your thigh and I want to know what it is.

PHILLIP. 'T's a birthmark.

LAURA. Phillip!

> DENNIS *takes it off her.*

What is it?

Beat.

PHILLIP (*muttering*). Tattoo.

LAURA. Excuse me?

PHILLIP. It's a tattoo.

LAURA. A tattoo?

> PHILLIP *nods.*

What does it say?

PHILLIP. Adelaida.

LAURA. And who is Adelaida?

Pause.

PHILLIP. His sister.

LAURA. Jesus Christ!

ROGER. Let's see.

DENNIS *gives it to him.*

PHILLIP. It's only a couple of centimetres.

LAURA. The length is not the point.

ROGER. Some people think so.

LAURA. How could you think of doing such a thing, disfiguring yourself like that?

DENNIS. Come on –

LAURA. What do you mean, 'Come on'?

PHILLIP. It's only a tattoo.

ROGER. I've got one.

LAURA. What's that got to do with it?

ROGER. I had it done in Sydney.

CORNELIA. Isn't that a coincidence?

ROGER. A little koala.

CORNELIA. On his bottom.

ROGER (*indicating*). Just there.

CORNELIA. So sweet. He's chewing a eucalyptus leaf.

FRANK. Did it hurt?

ROGER (*enthusiastically*). Yeah!

CORNELIA. We call him Colin.

LAURA. Will you shut up for a minute!

DENNIS. Laura.

LAURA. I'm going to phone Sanchez's father.

PHILLIP. No, Mum.

LAURA. This is an absolute outrage. How could he allow it to happen?

PHILLIP. He didn't know anything about it. It was all my idea. It was a joke. It's got nothing to do with Señor Morales.

LAURA. His daughter's a grown woman!

PHILLIP. She's only twenty-two.

LAURA. And she's given free rein to mess about with my son.

PHILLIP. It wasn't like that.

LAURA (*to* DENNIS). Haven't you got anything to say?

DENNIS. Well –

LAURA. I can't believe this is happening.

PHILLIP. We didn't do anything. She just – joined in from time to time.

LAURA. So why is her name emblazoned across your crotch?

PHILLIP. It was a joke. That's all.

LAURA. I am so disappointed in you.

She walks out. We hear her going upstairs and slamming a door.

PHILLIP. Anyway, it'll come off – won't it?

ROGER. Yeah. They do it with lasers.

PHILLIP. It's only a fucking tattoo.

He walks out. We hear him stamping upstairs and slamming a door. Pause.

ROGER. Want to see the bike?

DENNIS *nods and follows* ROGER *out.*

CORNELIA. Do you live around here, Frank?

FRANK. No. The other side of town.

CORNELIA. Oh. Whereabouts?

FRANK. Snaresbrook.

CORNELIA (*pityingly*). Ah.

Beat.

Do you have a partner?

FRANK. No.

CORNELIA (*again pityingly*). Don't you?

FRANK. It's not a problem.

CORNELIA. That's good.

Beat.

Is Frank short for anything?

FRANK. No.

CORNELIA. It's nice being called by your full name, isn't it?

FRANK. I've never thought about it.

CORNELIA. Lots of people call Roger, Rog, but I don't. His name's Roger and that's what I call him. And our child, whatever he or she might be called, will be what he or she is called. Australians tend to shorten everything, you know.

FRANK. Do they?

CORNELIA. Yes. Breakfast's brekky, chicken's chook, this afternoon's this arvo, and Roger was always Rog. I was Corny.

FRANK. Really.

CORNELIA. And sometimes Cor. Silly, isn't it? And then there are some words that they make longer, but I can't remember what they are.

The sound of the bike being revved.

People think I'm stupid, you know.

FRANK. Do they?

CORNELIA. Because I'm female and I've got a funny voice, but it doesn't bother me because I know I'm not.

FRANK. Obviously you're not.

CORNELIA. And if they got to know me, they'd realise it. Who's to say what an interior designer, fluent in Anglo-Saxon, should sound like?

FRANK. You're probably more intelligent than the whole lot of us.

She helps herself to a mouthful from one of the bowls.

That's pot pourri.

She spits it out.

CORNELIA. Ugh!

She rinses her mouth with her drink.

FRANK. Are you alright?

CORNELIA. Yes, yes.

FRANK. Would you like some water?

CORNELIA. No, I'm fine, thank you. They look just like those funny crisps, don't they?

More revving from outside.

Roger understands me. That's why I love him so much. I can't tell you, Frank, how happy I am that we're having a baby. You can't imagine the joy of having a part of Roger inside me.

More revving.

Anyway . . .

Beat.

I've worked hard to get where I am. I expect you have too.

FRANK. Yes, except that I haven't really got anywhere. Not for want of trying.

Revving.

CORNELIA. He does love his bikes.

FRANK. Of course there are some people who don't seem to have to work at anything. Phillip, for example. He picks things up just like that, whereas I've always had to graft.

CORNELIA. Yes.

FRANK. I sometimes wonder why I bother. It takes years to get an idea, years to write the bloody thing, then you're lucky if it gets read, and then they'll say, 'It's not quite for us, but we'd be interested in reading your next one,' and you think, 'But it nearly killed me writing this one.' Of course it's not always like that; you might hit the jackpot and get twenty performances in some clapped-out dive in the suburbs. Still, no one's holding a gun to my head.

Beat.

I saved his life, you know.

CORNELIA. Phillip?

FRANK. Yes.

CORNELIA. No, I didn't know.

FRANK. We were swimming in the reservoir, a few months ago now, and suddenly he disappeared. I dived under and dragged him out and – well, gave him the kiss of life.

CORNELIA. That's amazing. Have you learnt First Aid?

FRANK. No, no. I just – put my mouth over his – instinctively. Anyone would've, I think.

CORNELIA. Well . . .

Beat.

Have you thought of trying contact ads?

LAURA *enters. She clocks the two of them.*

You know, Laura, I was thinking, if you put a door in that wall there, and another one in the next room, you'd have a bit of an enfilade. That'd be nice, wouldn't it? Anyway . . .

She goes out.

LAURA. Imagine living with that!

FRANK. She's alright.

LAURA. Enfilade, my arse! Oh, Frank, how could he do that to himself?

FRANK. He's young.

LAURA. We're all young at some stage, but we don't go around branding ourselves.

FRANK. He's impetuous, headstrong. It's the sort of thing he'd do.

LAURA. It's the sort of thing Roger would do, but Phillip! It's so stupid. That beautiful skin!

FRANK. And it's not that visible. You'd have to look to find it. I mean, not everyone's going to see it, are they? Admittedly some people will, but then – well –

LAURA. I knew he couldn't have been to the Prado that many times. Every phone call was, 'Oh, we went to the Prado again.' He was lying to me, Frank. And I bet he hardly saw poor little Sanchez. He and Adelaida probably sent him off with some nachos and a handful of pesetas while they got up to all sorts in the Ramblas – when they weren't watching bulls being slaughtered.

FRANK. Aren't nachos Mexican?

LAURA. Oh, whatever.

FRANK. And the Ramblas are in Barcelona.

LAURA. I don't care if they're in fucking Brixton! The point is that this Spanish harpy has seduced my son and left her trademark on his testicles.

FRANK. Not quite.

LAURA. Give or take an inch. The thought of some greasy old man pricking my son's thigh with needles, and that harlot leering in the background with a fag in her mouth – oh God! Needles! What if they were infected?

FRANK. For God's sake!

LAURA. I'm sorry, Frank, but needles in a backstreet in Madrid!

FRANK. Why should it be more dangerous in Madrid? Millions of people get tattooed and they don't catch anything. Look at Roger; he's alright.

LAURA. That's a matter of opinion. I feel so betrayed. How could he do this to me? He's the only person I can rely on, apart from you, and now look what he's gone and done!

FRANK. Laura, he's had a tattoo. He hasn't eaten a baby. Anyway, I think you can get rid of them now with lasers.

LAURA. They're inedible.

FRANK. Indelible.

LAURA. Indelible, whatever! We really must get to the restaurant.

FRANK. Don't let it spoil this evening. Listen, don't let it spoil anything. In the scheme of things, Laura, it's not important.

Beat.

LAURA. I suppose not. It's just so hard, letting go. And the awful thing is, this is just the beginning.

PHILLIP has entered. He's holding a CD. She clocks him and turns away. FRANK suddenly feels out of place. Pause.

PHILLIP. She taught me to tango as well.

LAURA. Oh, my God!

PHILLIP. Mum, she's just a girl. She's nice. Honestly.

Beat. He puts the CD on the hi-fi: a tango. He slowly walks over to LAURA. He tentatively touches her hand. She snatches it away. Beat. He tries again. This time she allows him to touch her. He gently pulls her round to face him. He puts an arm around her waist and very slowly moves to the music. She impassively follows his lead. He gradually gains confidence and guides her through a few steps. She picks them up with relative ease. FRANK looks on. Soon they're dancing quite well together, eye to eye. At one point LAURA suddenly takes the lead and executes a fairly extreme manoeuvre with him.

Blimey, where d'you learn that?

LAURA. Oh, I've tangoed in my time.

They laugh and proceed to throw themselves into it. DENNIS appears. He takes in the scene and, unnoticed, exits into the kitchen. FRANK watches them as they dance, their eyes still fixed on each other, and the lights fade. The music continues as the lights come up on:

The Kitchen

DENNIS *is sitting at the kitchen table, dead still, expressionless. The tango can be heard from the sitting room.* FRANK *enters and is surprised to see him. They silently acknowledge each other.* FRANK *is unsure whether to stay.*

DENNIS. So how are you?

FRANK. Oh. I'm well, thanks.

Beat.

DENNIS. It's going okay then?

FRANK. Fine.

DENNIS. Good. That's good.

Beat.

No side effects or . . . ?

FRANK. No. Not yet, anyway.

Beat.

It's a bit of a leap in the dark, of course. For everyone, really, doctors included. I suppose I could wake up one morning with no teeth or a hump on my back or an extra eye or something. But so far, so good.

DENNIS. Yes.

FRANK. Yes.

DENNIS. Do you know Primrose Hill?

FRANK. . . . I've been there – once or twice, but – no, not really.

DENNIS. I . . .

DENNIS *puts his hand to his mouth.*

FRANK. Are you alright?

DENNIS *nods. Beat. He takes his hand away.*

DENNIS. Sorry.

FRANK. There's no –

DENNIS. Sorry.

FRANK. – no problem.

    DENNIS *gets up and shuts the door. Beat.*

DENNIS. Madrid's a marvellous city.

FRANK. Yes.

DENNIS. Marvellous.

FRANK. Yes. Yes, I've heard it's marvellous.

DENNIS. Yes.

    Beat.

I haven't been since Franco, if truth were told, but I would imagine it's – it's still marvellous.

FRANK. Yes, I'm sure it is.

DENNIS. Yes.

    Beat.

You know, he'd never sleep – never sleep without her at his side. One couldn't blame him, of course. She's always doted on him and always will, no doubt. But if she wasn't there, he'd scream and scream for his mummy. I'd never have believed how lonely one could feel. It won't be too long before he's calling me 'the old man'.

FRANK. I'm sure he – he thinks as much of you as he does of Laura. I'm sure he does. It must be wonderful to have a son like him.

    Beat.

DENNIS. It's a funny business.

    Beat.

FRANK. Dennis, why did you mention Primrose Hill?

DENNIS. Mm. I think I'm losing her. Yes. I'm losing her.

    Pause.

One day, very shortly after we'd first met, in fact – that time I did some root-canal work for her . . . This particular day, an afternoon, we were sitting on top of Primrose Hill – it was the height of summer – and saw the most extraordinary thing: at the foot of the hill was a layer of snow, a vast expanse of thick white snow glistening in the sunlight. The middle of summer, it was, a hot July afternoon, and we were amazed. And I looked at her and thought, this is the most remarkable woman and I love her more than – more than . . . well . . . The snow – so strange. I thought we were blessed. I'm looking forward to my couscous.

FRANK. What was it? A freak snowstorm or – ?

DENNIS. A trick of the light. That's all it was. I'm having a relationship.

FRANK. Are you?

DENNIS. With Marigold.

FRANK. Oh.

DENNIS. She's a marvellous girl. Only nineteen. The best nurse I've had. She looks nothing like a marsupial. You won't tell Laura, will you?

FRANK. No, I won't tell her.

DENNIS. Thanks. So I'll be leaving her.

FRANK. Laura?

DENNIS. Yes. I love her to death, you know. One day she'll come round to loving me.

> PHILLIP *enters.*

PHILLIP. Mum said we ought to go.

DENNIS. Yes, we should. Right.

> *He leaves.* PHILLIP *takes a handful of crisps from an open bag on the kitchen table and stuffs them in his mouth. He goes to the fridge and takes out a bottle of beer.* FRANK *looks on.* PHILLIP *knocks off the bottle-top on the edge of the table. The froth oozes out. He swigs it. As he turns to* FRANK, *he suddenly finds himself in a clinch,* FRANK *kissing him passionately. He feverishly explores* PHILLIP's *body, then rubs his crotch. The kiss continues as they*

stagger back against the table, shifting it slightly. After a long time, FRANK *takes his mouth from* PHILLIP*'s and steps back.*

FRANK. Thanks for the postcard.

PHILLIP. 'T's okay.

He swigs his beer.

FRANK. It looked nice, the railway station.

PHILLIP. I couldn't remember the one you asked for.

FRANK. Antonello de Messina's 'The Dead Christ Held by an Angel.'

PHILLIP. Oh yeah.

FRANK. But it doesn't matter. It was nice you sent me one at all – what with everything that was going on.

PHILLIP. How are you?

FRANK. I'm fine.

PHILLIP. Drugs alright?

FRANK. Yes. So far.

He touches the wooden table-top. PHILLIP *flinches.*

I'm touching wood.

PHILLIP. Sorry. Better get ready.

FRANK. So will you be keeping in touch?

PHILLIP. Who with?

FRANK. Adelaida.

PHILLIP. Dunno.

FRANK. You will, won't you?

PHILLIP. Dunno. Maybe. You shouldn't have done that.

FRANK. You didn't seem to mind.

PHILLIP. You shouldn't have done it.

FRANK. You were getting a hard-on.

PHILLIP. I'm always getting a hard-on; I'm fifteen.

FRANK. Nearly sixteen.

PHILLIP. We've got to go.

FRANK. I've started dreaming about you.

PHILLIP. Jesus! I thought we said we'd forget about it.

FRANK. I'm afraid it's not that easy.

PHILLIP. I told you, it didn't mean anything. It doesn't mean anything.

FRANK. Well, that's gratitude for you.

PHILLIP. What are you talking about?

FRANK. You'd be dead if it weren't for me.

PHILLIP. No, I bloody wouldn't! I was fine and you know it, but you didn't give me a chance. You were attached to my face before I could say a word, like something out of *Alien*.

FRANK. You'd nearly drowned.

PHILLIP. I was winded, that's all.

FRANK. I saved your life. You know I did. You needed resuscitating.

PHILLIP. Since when did resuscitation involve a tongue down the throat?

FRANK. You're the one who started it with the tongues.

PHILLIP. Bollocks!

FRANK. You did.

PHILLIP. You'd got me pissed.

FRANK. Come off it!

PHILLIP. We've got to go.

They don't move.

Things have changed. It's different. I was younger then.

FRANK. It was two months ago!

PHILLIP. Yeah, but I feel older now cos of – y'know . . .

FRANK. Adelaida.

PHILLIP. Look, Frank, you're very nice. I really like you – I really, really like you – and I'm really grateful you helped me get through my French GCSE, but what happened at the reservoir – it was nothing. It was a mistake.

FRANK. You enjoyed it.

PHILLIP. There was nothing to enjoy. Nothing happened.

FRANK. You were all over me like a cheap suit.

PHILLIP. I'm at that sort of age. I'd shag a rat given half the chance.

FRANK. Thanks a lot.

PHILLIP. It's over, forgotten, okay?

FRANK. Life's not like that.

PHILLIP. We've got to go.

He turns to go. FRANK *stops him.*

FRANK. Phillip, just once – let's meet up – just one more time –

PHILLIP. For fuck's sake –

FRANK. Please –

PHILLIP. No.

FRANK. Just one more time. Please.

PHILLIP. No!

FRANK. Then let me see your tattoo.

PHILLIP. Frank –

FRANK. Go on.

PHILLIP. Stop it, please.

FRANK. Let me see it –

PHILLIP. We've got to go.

FRANK. – and that'll be it, I promise.

Once again, PHILLIP *starts to go and* FRANK *tries to stop him.*

PHILLIP (*roughly shaking him off*). No!

As PHILLIP's *about to walk out:*

FRANK. I'm not well, for fuck's sake!

PHILLIP *stops.*

PHILLIP. You said you were.

FRANK. Yes, but for how long? It isn't a cure, you know. I could build up a resistance and start getting infected all over again and then where would I be? There are only a limited amount of options left. The truth of the matter is, I'm probably not going to be around for that long. I have to make the most of everything. You do understand that, don't you, Phillip? You do, don't you?

PHILLIP (*muttering*). Yeah.

FRANK. I know I probably seem as if I'm coping, as if it's all okay, but believe me, I need support, I need comfort – I really do. At the reservoir, I know you were a bit drunk, and I know we probably shouldn't have, but it was alright, wasn't it?

Beat.

Wasn't it?

PHILLIP *shrugs.*

We're friends, that's all – I'm not suggesting we should be anything else – and I have been a good friend to you, I hope. Haven't I?

PHILLIP. Yeah.

FRANK. I've always tried to be there for you, like when things haven't been great with your mum and dad, and . . . well, you know.

Beat.

I only want to see your tattoo. That's not too much to ask, is it? Please.

PHILLIP. Someone might come in.

FRANK (*indicating the pantry*). We can go in there.

Beat.

PHILLIP. Just for a second, right?

FRANK. Right.

Businesslike, PHILLIP *goes into the pantry followed by* FRANK, *who shuts the door behind them.* PHILLIP *drops his trousers.*

PHILLIP. There you go.

FRANK *kneels to inspect it.*

FRANK. It's quite neat, isn't it?

PHILLIP. Okay?

FRANK. Let me just . . .

He gently touches it.

She's a lucky girl.

PHILLIP. We'd better –

FRANK *licks it.* LAURA *comes into the kitchen.*

LAURA. Phillip! Darling!

FRANK *and* PHILLIP *freeze.*

Where the hell . . . ? (*Going out.*) Phillip!

PHILLIP (*hurriedly pulling up and fastening his trousers*). That's it. Alright? Got that?

PHILLIP *rushes out of the pantry, across the kitchen, and disappears into the garden.*

FRANK (*rising panic*). Oh my God! What the fuck am I . . . ? Jesus . . . Jesus –

LAURA (*off*). Phillip!

FRANK *comes out of the pantry, shutting the door behind him.* LAURA *pops her head round the door.*

Do you know where Phillip is?

FRANK. No, I don't.

LAURA (*walking in*). We'll lose our table. Are you alright?

FRANK. Yes.

LAURA. What about the tango, eh?

FRANK. It was very good.

LAURA. You've got a bit of crisp on your mouth. (*Wiping it off.*) Mucky boy.

FRANK. Thanks.

LAURA. He's going to break a few hearts.

FRANK. Yes.

LAURA. The little devil! (*Calling.*) Phillip!

> *As she walks out, she does a little shimmy.*
>
> Phillip!
>
> *Fade. Lights up on:*

The Restaurant

FRANK and GOMPERTZ at the moment we left them. FRANK has the dressing over his left eye; GOMPERTZ is on his mobile.

GOMPERTZ. . . . Great . . . Ciao.

> *He puts his mobile away.*
>
> Thank God for that!

FRANK. Everything alright?

GOMPERTZ. I mislaid a little something, but the night sister's found it, bless her. The thought of a whole ward whizzed off its face! Sorry, you were saying . . .

FRANK. Where was I?

GOMPERTZ (*taking the inhaler from FRANK*). A dreadful do, or something or other.

FRANK. Yes. My friend Laura – this do she had . . . Have you ever done anything you were ashamed of?

GOMPERTZ. Oh yes. Yes. Just about everything.

He takes a snort from the inhaler.

FRANK. What you said – the blink of an eyelid and life's changed forever –

GOMPERTZ. There always seems to be that little surprise round the corner: the unrevealed secret –

FRANK. Yes.

GOMPERTZ. A double-decker bus –

FRANK. You see, at this do –

GOMPERTZ. We never seem to get beyond this point, do we?

FRANK. What happened – was just awful – unimaginably tragic. It's haunted me for a year. And the point is – I think it'd make quite a good play. You see, I'm coming round to the opinion that I have to use whatever's thrown at me.

GOMPERTZ *hands him the inhaler.*

Thank you.

He snorts.

GOMPERTZ. I might plump for the Corned Beef Hash.

FRANK. I'm right, aren't I?

GOMPERTZ. No, you're not. You're making a terrible mistake.

FRANK. I'm not talking about the medication.

GOMPERTZ. Look at the arse on that!

FRANK. It's no good, I've got to tell her. I've got to come clean about it. Tomorrow I'm going to go over there and I'm going to tell her.

GOMPERTZ. You still haven't told me what it was.

FRANK. No. Well, this do – a year ago –

His pager bleeps.

GOMPERTZ. Jesus Christ!

He checks it.

Sorry.

He dials a number on his mobile.

FRANK. It doesn't matter.

GOMPERTZ (*into his mobile*). Yeah? . . . Yes . . .

FRANK. Anyway . . .

GOMPERTZ (*into his mobile*). Fuck it! The silly queen hasn't
been taking his Septrin . . . (*Looking at his watch.*) Alright,
I'll be there in –

*Blackout as the sound of a motorbike cuts in, very loud. It
starts fading into the distance as the lights come up on:*

The Kitchen

LAURA *and* FRANK *at the moment we left them at the end
of the first scene, he with his eye bandage, she removing her
sunglasses. They listen as the bike fades into silence. Pause.
The piano starts up again from another part of the house: the
faltering rendition of the Aria from Bach's Goldberg Variations.
We become aware, as before, of the sounds of summer gardens:
the sprinkler system, a strimmer, children playing and
birdsong.*

LAURA. Phphillip . . . Phphillip . . . (*She has a stammer.*)
Exxactly a year ago . . . Phph . . . Phph . . .

FRANK *looks helplessly on.*

Every dday – mminute – I wonder if he mmeant to – or if
he wwas doing it jjust for the ththrill . . . or if ssomething
had upsset him and he'd chch-chchosen to – to . . . or was it
an accident wwaiting to happen? And I wwonder if, just ffor
a moment, as he was sspeeding along, I may have ccrossed
his mind. I hope it was for the ththrill of it. The ththought of
him being in ddespair . . . I wanted him to knnow that life
ccould be happy, but that sseems to be – the hardest lesson
to learn.

Beat.

FRANK. He was happy. I'm sure he was.

A drawer ejects itself from the kitchen table and smashes on the floor, scattering cutlery and making them jump out of their skin. The piano stops. They stare at the mess, then:

LAURA. (*shouting*). It's alright. Everyththing's alright.

Beat. The piano starts again.

FRANK. Shall I . . . ?

LAURA. Don't worry. I can ddo it. Honestly. I know you have to ggo.

FRANK. Laura.

LAURA. Yes?

FRANK. There's something I want to tell you –

ROGER *appears from the garden, taking them by surprise.*

ROGER. Morning.

FRANK. Roger.

ROGER. Hello, Marcel. (*Re. the bandage.*) Slipped with the eyeliner? Hello, Laura.

FRANK *suddenly winces and holds his stomach.*

FRANK. Sorry. Just need to . . .

ROGER. Touch of the tomtits?

He's gone. Beat. LAURA starts to pick up the cutlery. ROGER watches her.

LAURA. Wwhat brings you here?

ROGER. I was in town for a meeting, so I thought I'd pop in and say hello, so – hello. (*Re. the piano playing.*) Still got Liberace in the attic, then?

Beat.

I'll give you a hand.

He starts to help her.

LAURA. There's no need.

ROGER. I know.

Beat.

LAURA. How's Ccornelia?

ROGER. She's fine. Sends her love. She's – fine.

They continue in silence, then he stops and looks at her.

LAURA. Wwould you like a – ?

ROGER. No. (*Re. the ejected drawer.*) This, I presume –

LAURA. It's nothing. But the ssooner we leave this house, ththe better.

She stops too. Beat.

ROGER. Cornelia – she's changed, you know, since the miscarriage. Quite a bit. It's like she's gone into herself. She's not interested in work any more.

LAURA. That might be a phphase.

ROGER. Yeah. It might be. I try and do things to please her, but I don't always get it right. It's a drag sometimes, I tell you. I went with her to a piano recital a few weeks ago. The whole evening was devoted to a piece that was supposed to be an exact imitation of birdsong. It sounded nothing like bloody birds – well, no birds I've ever heard. Two fucking hours of plinkety-plonk, the sort of sound Cornelia makes when she's dusting the keyboard. It nearly drove me mad. I was twitching by the end.

LAURA. Pplease –

ROGER. It's true. I didn't stop till I went to bed. That's another thing, of course: she won't let me touch her any more.

LAURA. She nneeds time.

ROGER. Yeah. It's been months though.

LAURA. Then she needs mmore time.

ROGER. Yeah.

Beat. He looks at her, then turns away.

She's got a cat. Nice little thing. Sort of – furry. She calls it Smudge.

Beat.

Takes it everywhere.

LAURA. Not to the rrecital, I hope. Mmight have scared the birds.

They smile briefly. Unsure what to say, they look out at the garden. FRANK's appeared, unnoticed, in the kitchen doorway. He watches them.

ROGER. I'd love to have sat with my son, and have him tell me this and that, how much his mother pissed him off, or how he'd fallen for some girl and she was driving him mad and what should he do, and I'd have told him I was the last bloody person to ask . . . Still, it's not to be.

FRANK slips into the pantry to hide and listen.

If only I hadn't have left those fucking keys lying around!

Beat.

I'm sorry.

LAURA. No.

ROGER. I'm sorry.

Beat.

LAURA. On days like this he'd llie for hours, a hand across his eyes, ffloating away.

ROGER. You know, since we met, a day hasn't passed when I haven't thought about you.

LAURA (*nervously checking they're alone*). No . . . no –

ROGER. It's true.

LAURA. I don't wwant to hear –

ROGER. I promise you.

LAURA. Pplease –

ROGER. That day we made love –

LAURA (*putting her finger to his mouth*). Sh –

ROGER. Seventeen years ago –

LAURA. Roger, pplease –

ROGER. It was seventeen years ago.

LAURA. Yyyes.

ROGER. That's right.

LAURA. Ssseventeen.

ROGER. Yes.

Beat. FRANK *is riveted.*

I have spent years of my life with a woman who isn't even my type. And so little time with my boy.

Beat.

I'm right, aren't I?

She looks at him, is about to speak, then subsides against him. The piano and the other sounds fade as, from far in the distance, we hear the tango. Very gently they start to sway, LAURA *hanging limply in his arms.* FRANK *tentatively peers out of the pantry to see what's happening. The tango fades and they're still. In silence they look into each other's eyes.* FRANK *doesn't move a muscle. Then the Bach resumes on the piano. They part as* FRANK *darts out of sight.*

LAURA (*looking round*). Ffrank might –

ROGER. It's alright, 't's alright.

Beat.

I've got to go.

A moment as they look at each other.

LAURA. I'm sure Ddennis would like to ss –

ROGER. Next time, maybe.

He leaves through the garden. LAURA *watches him go as* FRANK *steps out of the pantry. The Bach resumes on the piano.*

FRANK (*pretending he's just come into the kitchen*). That's better. Suddenly hits you. I've had some near misses, I can tell you. Where's Roger?

LAURA. He had to ggo.

FRANK. I know the feeling. I haven't seen him since – well, since last year.

LAURA. He's in town for a mmeeting.

FRANK. Anyway, I suppose I ought to make a move.

LAURA. Wasn't there something you wwanted to tell me?

Beat.

FRANK. Yes, there was. I – I wanted to tell you . . .

Beat. He kisses her.

. . . that you're the best friend I've had.

She holds him tightly.

LAURA. Ththank you for coming. It means so much. I rreally hope ththings work out for you.

They part.

FRANK. I'll probably be back in no time.

He makes to go.

It's strange, you know: in the garden, when we were sitting here, I thought I saw, for a second –

LAURA. Yes – it was Rroger.

FRANK. I know.

LAURA. He always ccomes that way.

FRANK. Yes, but for a second, it was Phillip I thought I saw.

Pause.

LAURA. Then you were mmistaken.

Beat.

FRANK. Anyway, I must be off.

She closes the kitchen door. Beat.

LAURA. It was – just the once, and he was – just a kkid. One moment of – wwell . . . I thought, 'Oh, there'll be other ttimes like this,' and mmade myself fforget. But you know, there haven't been; ththat was it. And ttry as I might, I can't stop wondering what if, what if . . . And Phphillip – he nnever knew. It's like a ppunishment.

The piano's stopped.

FRANK. No, you mustn't think that. It's not. It was an accident, a dreadful accident, and you can't spend your life – you can't spend your life feeling guilty.

LAURA. I do ttry – to ccome to terms, to mmake my peace –

DENNIS (*from another part of the house*). Laura! . . . Laura! . . .

She opens the kitchen door.

LAURA (*calling*). Alright, Ddennis. It's alright.

She lights a cigarette and sits again at the French windows. The Bach resumes. She puts on her sunglasses. FRANK sits next to her.

FRANK. I'll write.

LAURA. Yes. Your pplay –

FRANK. No. To you, I mean.

She looks at him and smiles, then they gaze out at the garden. The sounds of the summer's day murmur on.

So I – I'd better be off.

We hear the final bars of the Aria as the lights fade to black.

End.